Contents

KU-495-347

<< BIG BEN
< LONDON EYE

INTRODUCTION TO
LONDON

London is a very big city. In fact, it's the largest capital in the European Union, stretching for more than thirty miles from east to west, and with a population of just over eight million. Ethnically and linguistically, it's also Europe's most diverse metropolis, offering cultural and culinary delights from right across the globe. The city dominates the national horizon, too: this is where most of the country's news and money are made, it's where central government resides and, as far as its inhabitants are concerned, provincial life begins beyond the circuit of the city's orbital motorway.

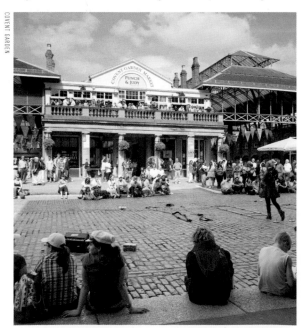

COVENT GARDEN

Best place for an alfresco drink

I f you're lucky enough to be in London when the weather's fine, there's nothing like an alfresco drink, whether in a leafy outdoor beer garden, or by the banks of the Thames. For a great riverside view of the Dome, head to *The Gun* in Docklands (see p.113), or if you're wandering along the south bank of the Thames, *The Anchor* in Bankside (see p.127) is hard to beat. After an invigorating stroll on nearby Hampstead Heath, *The Flask* in Highgate (see p.155) is the perfect place to sink a pint.

For the visitor, it's a thrilling destination. The biggest problem for newcomers is that the city can seem bewilderingly amorphous, with no single predominant focus of interest. Londoners tend to cope with all this by compartmentalizing their city, identifying strongly with the neighbourhoods in which they work or live, just making occasional forays into the West End, London's shopping and entertainment heartland. As a visitor, the key to enjoying London, then, is not to try and do everything in a single visit – concentrate on one or two areas and you'll get a lot more out of the place.

The capital's traditional sights – Big Ben, Westminster Abbey, Buckingham Palace, St Paul's Cathedral and the Tower of London – continue to draw in millions of tourists every year. Things change fast, though,

and the regular emergence of new attractions ensures that there's plenty to do even for those who've visited before. In the last decade or so, all of London's world-class museums, galleries and institutions have been reinvented, from the Royal Opera House to the British Museum, and the tourist and transport infrastructure had a major overhaul for the city's hugely successful 2012 Olympics games.

Monuments from the capital's glorious past are everywhere, from medieval banqueting halls and the great churches of Christopher Wren to the eclectic Victorian architecture of the triumphalist British Empire. There's also much enjoyment to be had from the city's quiet Georgian squares, the narrow alleyways of the City of London, the riverside walks, and the assorted quirks

5

When to visit

Despite the temperateness of the English climate, it's impossible to say with any degree of certainty that the weather will be pleasant in any given month. With average daily temperatures of around 22°C, English summers rarely get unbearably hot, while the winters (average daily temperature 6–10°C) don't get very cold – though they're often wet. However, whenever you come, be prepared for all eventualities: it has been known to snow at Easter and rain all day on August Bank Holiday weekend. As far as crowds go, tourists stream into London pretty much all year round, with peak season from Easter to October, and the biggest crush in July and August, when you'll need to book your accommodation well in advance.

of what is still identifiably a collection of villages. And urban London is offset by surprisingly large expanses of greenery: Hyde Park, Green Park and St James's Park are all within a few minutes' walk of the West End, while, further afield, you can enjoy the more expansive parklands of Hampstead Heath and Richmond Park.

You could spend days just shopping in London, too, mixing with the upper classes in the "tiara triangle" around Harrods, or sampling the offbeat weekend markets of Portobello Road, Camden and Spitalfields. The music, clubbing and gay/lesbian scenes are second to none, and mainstream arts are no less exciting, with regular opportunities to catch first-rate theatre companies, dance troupes, exhibitions and opera. The city's pubs have always had heaps of atmosphere, but food is a major attraction too, with over fifty Michelin-starred restaurants and the widest choice of cuisines on the planet.

TRAFALGAR SQUARE

LONDON AT A GLANCE

>>EATING

With thousands of cafés, pubs and restaurants, you're never far from a good place to fill your stomach. For the widest choice, make for **Soho** or nearby **Covent Garden**, where you'll find everything from triple-starred restaurants to cheap Chinese and hip diners. Head out of the centre, though, to sample the best of the city's diverse cuisines, whether Portuguese in **Ladbroke Grove** or Bangladeshi in **Tower Hamlets**. London's also a great place for snacking, with a vibrant street-food culture; **Borough Market, Maltby Street, Camden Market** and **Spitafields** are all good hunting grounds.

>>DRINKING

Found on just about every street corner, the pub remains one of the nation's most enduring social institutions and its popularity in London sees no sign of waning. **The City** has probably the best choice of long-established drinking holes – though with the average pint costing over £3, it's worth knowing that you can pay half that at Sam Smith's pubs. **Soho** and the **East End** attract a clubbier crowd, so you'll find a wide choice of bars and clubs alongside good-old fashioned pubs. For a riverside drink, head for the **South Bank** or **Docklands**, and for a lazy Sunday afternoon mosey on up to **Hampstead** or down to **Greenwich**.

>>SHOPPING

From the folie de grandeur of Harrods to the street markets of Camden and Spitalfields, London is a shopper's playground. In the West End, **Oxford Street** is Europe's busiest shopping street, followed closely by Regent Street – here you'll find pretty much every mainstream shop you could wish for. **Charing Cross Road** remains the centre of the city's book trade, while **Covent Garden** has become a fashion and designer wear hotspot. **St James's** equips the English gentleman; **Bond Street** deals with the ladies, but for haute couture – and Harrods – head for **Knightsbridge** and Sloane Street. For something more offbeat, or vintage, head out to **Camden Market** or **Spitalfields** and **Brick Lane**.

>>NIGHTLIFE

As well as two top-class **opera** houses, London has an enormous number of **theatres**, most of which are centrally located in the West End districts of Soho and Covent Garden, and boasts more **comedy venues** than any other city in the world. Although you'll find **clubs** and **live music venues** all across the capital, East London remains the epicentre of the city's clubland. London is also the **gay** capital of Europe, with Old Compton Street in Soho still, so to speak, the city's main drag.

OUR RECOMMENDATIONS FOR WHERE TO EAT, DRINK AND SHOP ARE LISTED AT THE END OF EACH PLACES CHAPTER.

Day One in London

1 Parliament Square > p.42. Gaze at two of the capital's most remarkable buildings: the Houses of Parliament and Westminster Abbey.

2 Whitehall > p.39. This wide avenue is lined with grandiose governmental ministries and dotted with statues recalling the days of the British Empire.

3 Churchill War Rooms > p.41. Explore the subterranean rooms used by Churchill and his War Cabinet during World War II.

4 St James's Park > p.46. One of London's smartest royal parks, with views across to Buckingham Palace, exotic ducks and even pelicans.

Lunch > p.51. Picnic in the park or tuck into some excellent British food on the lovely terrace at *Inn the Park*.

5 Trafalgar Square > p.36. London's finest set-piece square, overlooked by the National Gallery and famous for its fountains and pigeons.

6 Covent Garden Piazza > p.68. One of the city's few pedestrianized public spaces, Covent Garden's cobbled piazza is the place to see London's best buskers.

7 British Museum > p.78. One of the world's most amazing (and largest) museums, with everything from Egyptian mummies to Constructivist ceramics from the Russian Revolution.

Dinner > p.74. Experience the bustle of *Mr Kong* in the heart of Chinatown, before heading into the heart of Soho for a night of drinking and (maybe) dancing.

Day Two in London

1 Harrods > p.139. The queen of department stores, Harrods is a sight in itself, especially the Art Nouveau food hall and the Di and Dodi shrine.

2 Hyde Park > p.129. Stroll along the Serpentine, go for a dip (if you're feeling brave) and check out the Diana Memorial Fountain.

3 Serpentine Gallery > p.132. Sample some contemporary art for free and then have tea at the architecturally cutting-edge summer pavilion.

4 Albert Memorial > p.132. Stop by this incredible, over-the-top neo-Gothic memorial to Queen Victoria's husband.

🍴 **Lunch** > p.135. Housed in the museum's original refreshment rooms, the V&A café is a visual treat, and serves everything from sandwiches to grilled fish and meat.

5 V&A > p.135. South Kensington is home to a trio of fabulous museums, but the V&A's collection of applied arts is head and shoulders above the others.

6 Kensington Palace > p.132. Princess Diana's former residence houses a display of her glamorous frocks, as well as some finely frescoed rooms.

7 Portobello Road Market > p.137. Browse the antique shops or (if Saturday) the busy flea market.

🍴 **Dinner** > p.141 and p.142. Treat yourself to excellent English cuisine at *Hereford Road* or go for a drink and meal at *The Cow*.

9

Riverside London

London grew up around the Thames, and a stroll (or a boat ride) along its banks is one of the city's real treats.

1 London Eye > p.116. London's graceful millennial observation wheel has become one of the iconic symbols of the city despite its relative youth.

2 South Bank > p.114. The views along the river from the South Bank's car-free promenade are some of London's best.

3 Tate Modern > p.120. Feast your eyes on art from the last hundred years or so at the world's largest modern art gallery.

4 Millennium Bridge > p.120. London's only pedestrian-only river crossing offers great views of St Paul's Cathedral and the City.

(🍴) Lunch > p.126. Fill up at the food stalls in Borough Market (Wed–Sat) or Maltby Street (Sat & Sun), or enjoy a Spanish feast at *Pizarro*.

5 Boat to Greenwich > p.157. Catch a Thames Clipper from London Bridge pier, and check out the Tower of London, Tower Bridge and Docklands development en route to SE10.

6 Old Royal Naval College > p.156. This is the one building in London which exploits its riverside position to best effect, and harbours two fantastic eighteenth-century interiors to boot.

7 Somerset House > p.70. Take the boat back to Festival Pier and cross Waterloo Bridge to the sole survivor of the grandiose palaces that once lined the Strand.

(🍴) Dinner > p.74 and pp.97–99. Enjoy an authentic taste of France at *Green Man and French Horn* or, for something cheaper, head for one of Fleet Street's pubs.

The City

From the Romans to rogue traders, the City has more history than the rest of London combined.

1 Sir John Soane's Museum > p.88. The idiosyncratic home of the architect of the Bank of England is crammed with paintings and sculpture.

2 Temple Church > p.85. Fascinating medieval round church, famed for its effigy tombs and appearance in *The Da Vinci Code*.

3 St Paul's Cathedral > p.92. Climb up to the top of the dome of Wren's masterpiece for a fabulous view across the river.

Lunch > p.96 and p.97. Tuck into fresh, seasonal food at *The Café Below*, in the atmospheric crypt of St Mary-le-Bow, or pub grub at the wonderful Art Nouveau *Black Friar*.

4 Museum of London > p.91. From Roman mosaics to Wellington's boots, this museum encompasses the whole of London's history.

5 Bank of England > p.94. The Bank of England stands at the heart of the City, and forms part of a superb architectural set piece of Neoclassical edifices.

6 City skyscrapers > p.95. Stand outside Richard Rogers' Lloyds Building for a panoramic view of the City's latest generation of skyscrapers, including the iconic Gherkin.

7 Old Spitalfields Market > p.104. Though at its liveliest on Sundays, this old Victorian market hall has plenty of interest throughout the week.

Dinner > p.106. Have supper at *Tayyab's*, a smart Punjabi restaurant in Whitechapel, and then head up the road for a night in lively Shoreditch.

and let thy feet
millenniums hence
seet in midst of knowledge

Royal London

1 Hampton Court Palace This sprawling red-brick Tudor edifice is without a doubt the finest of London's royal palaces. **> p.168**

2 Buckingham Palace Unlike the rest of London's royal palaces, the Queen does actually live here (for some of the year, at least). > **p.48**

3 Tower of London England's most perfectly preserved medieval fortress and safe-deposit box for the Crown Jewels. > **p.108**

4 Westminster Abbey Venue for every coronation since William the Conqueror and resting place of countless kings and queens. > **p.42**

5 Changing of the Guard This daily royal ceremony is best viewed on Horse Guards Parade, where the Household Cavalry change shifts. > **p.40**

Outdoor London

1 St James's Park Probably London's smartest royal park, with a fine array of exotic ducks and pelicans in the lake and a great café. **> p.46**

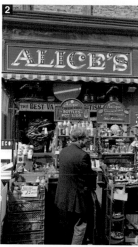

2 Portobello Market London's trendiest street market offers brilliant retro clothes, bric-à-brac, antiques, and fruit and veg. **> p.137**

3 Thames boat ride River services are now fast and frequent: hop on and off anywhere between Westminster and Greenwich. **> p.188**

4 Hampstead Heath North London's green lung and the city's most enjoyable public outdoor space. **> p.150**

5 South Bank Stroll along the riverbank's Thames Path from the London Eye to the Tate Modern and beyond. **> p.114**

London for kids

1 Double-decker bus Head upstairs on an old double-decker for a scenic tour of some of London's most famous sights. > **p.189**

2 Natural History Museum With animatronic dinosaurs and an earthquake simulator, the Natural History Museum is sure to prove a winner. > **p.134**

3 Diana Memorial Playground The city's most sophisticated, imaginative and popular outdoor playground, just a short walk from Diana's former home. > **p.132**

4 Pollock's Toy Museum Doll's house-like museum of paper theatres, dolls and games above a toyshop. > **p.68**

5 London Zoo Opened in 1828 as the world's first scientific zoo, and still a guaranteed hit with children of all ages. > **p.146**

Museums

1 British Museum The oldest and greatest public museum on the planet contains objects from every corner of the globe. **> p.78**

2 National Maritime Museum Imaginatively designed complex encompassing the old Royal Observatory as well as nautical exhibits. **> p.157**

3 V&A The world's greatest applied arts museum, with something for everyone, from Islamic art to Kylie Minogue's dressing room. **> p.135**

4 Imperial War Museum This military museum houses a huge art collection and gives a sober account of the horrors of war. **> p.117**

– every available piece of land must be cultivated

GROW YOUR OWN FOOD
supply your own cookhouse

5 Sir John Soane's Museum Part architectural set piece, part art gallery, the John Soane museum is small but perfectly formed. **> p.88**

Food

1 Afternoon tea The classic English afternoon tea – sandwiches, scones and cream cakes – is as popular as ever. **> p.56**

2 Dim Sum This bargain spread of dumplings and other little morsels is a Chinatown lunchtime ritual. **> p.74**

4 Street food A world of creative, unexpensive cuisine is served up at stalls and carts around London's liveliest markets. **> p.126**

3 Fish and chips The national dish – fish in batter with deep-fried potato chips – remains as popular and tasty as ever. **> p.61**

5 Curry London is the best place in Europe for curry, with cuisine from all over the Indian subcontinent well represented. **> p.106**

London art

1 Kenwood House Small but perfectly formed gallery of seventeenth- and eighteenth-century paintings, including works by Gainsborough, Rembrandt and Vermeer. > **p.150**

2 Tate Modern A wonderful hotchpotch of wild and wacky art, from video installations to gargantuan pieces that fill the vast turbine hall. > **p.120**

3 Courtauld Institute Quality, not quantity, is the hallmark of this gallery, best known for its superlative collection of Impressionist masterpieces. > **p.71**

4 Tate Britain The history of British painting from Holbein and Hogarth to Hockney and Hirst, plus pre-Raphaelites and Turners in abundance. > **p.44**

5 National Gallery A comprehensive overview of Western painting, from Renaissance classics in the airy Sainsbury Wing to fin-de-siècle Parisian works. > **p.38**

Pubs

1 Royal Oak Beautiful Victorian pub with a great range of real ales from the Harveys Brewery in Sussex. > **p.127**

2 Ye Olde Cheshire Cheese A dark, snug seventeenth-century tavern hidden down an alleyway off Fleet Street – look out for the sign. > **p.99**

3 Salisbury Flamboyant late-Victorian pub a stone's throw from Trafalgar Square, replete with bronze nymphs and etched glasswork. > **p.76**

5 The Lamb Classic, beautifully preserved nineteenth-century pub in a pretty street. > **p.83**

4 Dog & Duck Soho pub with genuine character that retains its original decor of tiles and mosaics. > **p.75**

Victorian London

1 Albert Memorial This bombastic monument to Queen Victoria's consort is a riot of semi-precious stones, marbles, bronze and gilding. **> p.132**

2 Westminster Cathedral
Still unfinished inside, London's neo-Byzantine Roman Catholic Cathedral represents the last gasp of the Victorian period. > **p.44**

3 St Pancras Station Revitalized Victorian railway station fronted by a gloriously over-the-top red-brick neo-Gothic hotel. > **p.81**

4 Houses of Parliament
A gargantuan, confident expression of nationhood, best known for its "Big Ben" clock-tower. > **p.43**

5 Leadenhall Market Cobblestones and graceful Victorian ironwork combine to create the City's most attractive market for luxury comestibles. > **p.94**

Nightlife

1 Live music Originally a train engine shed, the *Roundhouse* is one of London's most atmospheric music venues. > **p.149**

2 Theatre The country's top actors and directors ensure that high standards are maintained at the South Bank's National Theatre. **> p.119**

3 Jazz London's most famous jazz club, *Ronnie Scott's* is an intimate venue that nevertheless attracts big names. **> p.77**

4 Cabaret *Madame JoJo's* is a louche Soho institution that puts on variety, drag acts and comedy, but also disco, rock and funk. **> p.77**

5 Clubs *Fabric* in Clerkenwell is one of the city's finest clubs, with a devastating soundsystem and both DJs and live bands. **> p.99**

Modern London

1 **The Shard** Renzo Piano's bold spike is now the city's – and the country's – tallest building. **> p.124**

3 Canary Wharf Cesar Pelli's stainless steel skyscraper is the centrepiece of the Canary Wharf Docklands development. > **p.112**

2 The Gherkin This unusual cone-shaped affair is a distinctive, instantly recognizable feature of the City skyline. > **p.95**

4 Millennium Bridge This flashy millennial footbridge connects St Paul's Cathedral with the Tate Modern. > **p.120**

5 The Walkie Talkie This distinctive new addition to the City skyline has a public botanic "sky garden" on the top floor. > **p.95**

Whitehall and Westminster

Whitehall is synonymous with the faceless, pinstriped bureau-cracy who run the various governmental ministries located here, while Westminster remains home to the Houses of Parliament. Both are popular with visitors thanks to the Changing of the Guard, and familiar landmarks such as Nelson's Column, Big Ben, and Westminster Abbey, London's most historic church.

Political, religious and regal power has emanated from Whitehall and Westminster for almost a millennium. It was King Edward the Confessor who first established this spot as London's royal and ecclesiastical power base in the eleventh century. He built his palace and abbey some three miles upstream from the City of London, and it was in the abbey that the embryonic English parliament used to meet in the Middle Ages.

TRAFALGAR SQUARE

⊖ Charing Cross. MAP P.37, POCKET MAP G16

As one of the few large public squares in London, Trafalgar Square has been a focus for political demonstrations since it was laid out in the 1820s. Most days, however, it's scruffy urban pigeons that you're more likely to encounter, as

VIEW OF NELSON'S COLUMN, TRAFALGAR SQUARE

they wheel around the square hoping some unsuspecting visitor will feed them (though, it is, in fact, illegal to do so). Along with its fountains, the square's central focal point is the deeply patriotic **Nelson's Column**, which stands 170ft high and is topped by a 17ft statue of the one-eyed, one-armed admiral who defeated the French (and died) at the 1805 Battle of Trafalgar. Nelson himself is actually quite hard to see – not so the giant bronze lions at the base of the column, which provide a popular photo opportunity. Stranded on a nearby traffic island is an equestrian statue of Charles I, while in the square's northeastern corner is one of George IV, which he himself originally commissioned for the top of Marble Arch. The **fourth plinth**, in the northwest corner, was built for an eques-trian statue of William IV, but remained empty until 1999, since when it's been used to

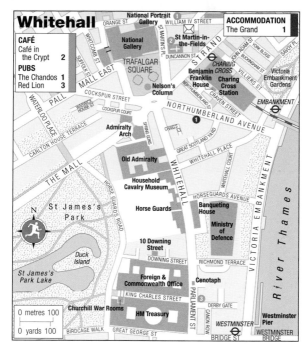

Whitehall

CAFÉ
Café in
the Crypt   2

PUBS
The Chandos   1
Red Lion   3

ACCOMMODATION
The Grand   1

0 metres 100
0 yards 100

display alternating works of modern sculpture (www.london.gov.uk/fourthplinth).

ST MARTIN-IN-THE-FIELDS

Duncannon St ⊖ Charing Cross ☎ 020 7766 1100, www.stmartin-in-the-fields.org. Mon, Tues, Thurs & Fri 8.30am–1pm & 2–6pm, Wed 8.30am–1.15pm & 2–5pm, Sat 9.30am–6pm, Sun 3.30–5pm. Free. MAP P.37, POCKET MAP G16

Something of a blueprint for eighteenth-century churches across the empire, St Martin-in-the-Fields is fronted by a magnificent Corinthian portico and topped by an elaborate tower and steeple. Designed by James Gibbs and completed in 1726, the barrel-vaulted interior features ornate, sparkling white Italian plasterwork and is best appreciated while listening to one of the church's free **lunchtime concerts** (Mon, Tues & Fri) or ticketed, candle-lit

evening performances. Down in the large **crypt** – accessible via an entrance north of the church – there's a licensed **café** (see p.45), shop, gallery and **brass-rubbing centre** (Mon–Wed 10am–6pm, Thurs–Sat 10am–8pm, Sun 11.30am–5pm).

ST MARTIN-IN-THE-FIELDS

UCCELLO'S BATTLE OF SAN ROMANO, NATIONAL GALLERY

NATIONAL GALLERY

Trafalgar Square ⊖ Charing Cross ☎ 020 7747 2885, ⓦ www.nationalgallery.org.uk. Daily 10am–6pm, Fri till 9pm. Free. MAP P.37, POCKET MAP G16

Despite housing more than 2300 paintings, the main virtue of the National Gallery is not so much the collection's size, but its range, depth and sheer quality. A quick tally of the **Italian** masterpieces, for example, includes works by Uccello, Botticelli, Mantegna, Piero della Francesca, Veronese, Titian, Raphael, Michelangelo and Caravaggio. From **Spain** there are dazzling pieces by El Greco, Velázquez and Goya; from the **Low Countries**, van Eyck, Memling and Rubens, and an array of Rembrandt paintings that features some of his most searching portraits. Poussin, Claude, Watteau and the only Jacques-Louis David paintings in the country are the early highlights of a **French** contingent, which also has a particularly strong showing of Cézanne and the Impressionists. **British** art is also well represented, with important works by Hogarth, Gainsborough, Stubbs and Turner, though for twentieth-century British art – and many more Turners – you'll need to move on to Tate Britain on Millbank (see p.44).

To view the collection chronologically, begin with the **Sainsbury Wing**, the softly-softly, postmodern 1980s adjunct which is linked to – and playfully imitates – the original Neoclassical building. However, with more than a thousand paintings on permanent display, you'll need stamina to see everything in one day, so if time is tight your best bet is to home in on your areas of special interest, having picked up a gallery plan at one of the information desks. Plans (£1) and audioguides (£4) are available – much better, though, are the gallery's **free guided tours** (daily 11.30am and 2.30pm), which set off from the Sainsbury Wing foyer, and focus on a representative sample of works.

NATIONAL PORTRAIT GALLERY

St Martin's Place ⊖ Charing Cross ☎ 020 7306 0055, ⓦ www.npg.org.uk. Daily 10am–6pm, Thurs & Fri till 9pm. Free. MAP P.37, POCKET MAP G16

Founded in 1856 to house uplifting depictions of the good and the great, the National Portrait Gallery has some fine individual works. However, many of the studies are of less interest than their subjects, and the overall impression is of an overstuffed shrine to famous Brits rather than a museum offering any insight into the history of portraiture. Nevertheless, it is fascinating to trace who has been deemed worthy of admiration at any moment: aristocrats and artists in previous centuries, warmongers and imperialists in the early decades of the twentieth century, writers and poets in the 1930s and 1940s, and latterly, sportsmen and women, politicians and film and pop stars. The NPG's audiovisual guide (£3) gives useful biographical background information and the gallery's **special exhibitions** (for which there's often an entrance charge) are well worth seeing – the photography shows, in particular, are usually excellent.

WHITEHALL

Westminster or Charing Cross. MAP P.37, POCKET MAP G17–G18

Whitehall, the unusually broad avenue connecting Trafalgar Square to Parliament Square, is synonymous with the faceless, pinstriped bureaucracy charged with the day-to-day running of the country. Yet during the sixteenth and seventeenth centuries it served as the chief residence of England's kings and queens. Having started out as the London seat of the Archbishop of York, **Whitehall Palace** was confiscated and

embellished by Henry VIII after a fire at Westminster made him homeless; it was here that he celebrated his marriage to Anne Boleyn in 1533, and where he died fourteen years later. Described by one contemporary chronicler as nothing but "a heap of houses erected at diverse times and of different models, made continuous", it boasted some two thousand rooms and stretched for half a mile along the Thames. Not much survived the fire of 1698, and subsequently, the royal residences shifted to St James's and Kensington. Since then, the key governmental ministries and offices have migrated here, rehousing themselves on an ever-increasing scale.

The statues dotted along Whitehall today recall the days when this street stood at the centre of an empire on which the sun never set, while just beyond the Downing Street gates, in the middle of the road, stands Edwin Lutyens' **Cenotaph**, commemorating the dead of both world wars. Eschewing any kind of Christian imagery, the plain monument is inscribed simply with the words "The Glorious Dead" and remains the focus of the country's Remembrance Sunday ceremony, held here in early November.

REMEMBRANCE SUNDAY AT THE CENOTAPH

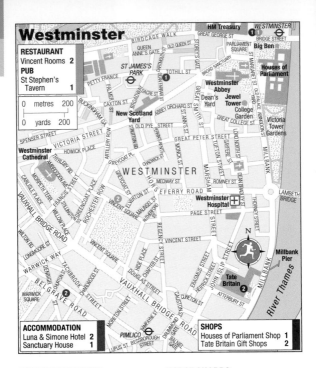

Westminster

RESTAURANT
Vincent Rooms 2
PUB
St Stephen's Tavern 1

ACCOMMODATION
Luna & Simone Hotel 2
Sanctuary House 1

SHOPS
Houses of Parliament Shop 1
Tate Britain Gift Shops 2

BANQUETING HOUSE

Whitehall ⊖ Westminster ☎ 020 3166 6000.
⊛ www.hrp.org.uk. Daily 10am–5pm. £5.
MAP P.37, POCKET MAP G18

One of the few sections of Whitehall Palace to escape the 1698 fire, the Banqueting House was one of the first Palladian buildings to be built in England. The one room open to the public has no original furnishings, but is well worth seeing for the superlative **Rubens ceiling paintings** commissioned by Charles I in the 1630s, depicting the union of England and Scotland, the peaceful reign of his father, James I, and finally his apotheosis (ask for an audioguide). Charles himself walked through the room for the last time in 1649, when he stepped onto the executioner's scaffold from one of its windows.

HORSE GUARDS

Whitehall ⊖ Charing Cross or Westminster.
MAP P.37, POCKET MAP G18

Outside this modest building, built in 1745 and once the old palace guard house, two mounted sentries of the **Queen's Household Cavalry** and two horseless colleagues, all in ceremonial uniform, are posted daily from 10am to 4pm. With nothing in particular to guard nowadays, the sentries are basically here for the tourists, though they are under orders not to smile. Try to coincide your visit with the **Changing of the Guard**, when a squad of mounted Household Cavalry in full livery arrives to relieve the guards (Mon–Sat 11am, Sun 10am) – if you miss it, turn up at 4pm for the elaborate **daily inspection** by the Officer of the Guard.

HOUSEHOLD CAVALRY MUSEUM

Whitehall ⬩ Westminster ☎ 020 7930 3070, ⓦ www.householdcavalrymuseum.co.uk. Daily: March–Sept 10am–6pm; Oct–Feb 10am–5pm. £6. MAP P.37, POCKET MAP G17

Round the back of Horse Guards, you'll find the Household Cavalry Museum, where you can try on a trooper's elaborate uniform, complete a horse quiz and learn about the regiments' history. With the stables immediately adjacent, it's a sweet-smelling place, and – horse-lovers will be pleased to know – you can see the beasts in their stalls through a glass screen. Don't miss the pocket Riot Act on display, which ends with the wise warning: "must read correctly: variance fatal".

10 DOWNING STREET

⬩ Westminster ⓦ www.number10.gov.uk. MAP P.37, POCKET MAP G18

Since the days of Margaret Thatcher, London's most famous address has been hidden behind wrought-iron security gates. A pretty plain, seventeenth-century terraced house, no. 10 has been home to every British **prime minister** since it was presented to Robert Walpole, Britain's first PM, by George II in 1732.

CHURCHILL WAR ROOMS

King Charles St ⬩ Westminster ☎ 020 7930 6961, ⓦ cwr.iwm.org.uk. Daily 9.30am–6pm. £17.50. MAP P.37, POCKET MAP G18

In 1938, in anticipation of Nazi air raids, the basement of the civil service buildings on the south side of King Charles Street was converted into the **Cabinet War Rooms**. It was here that Winston Churchill directed operations and held Cabinet meetings for the duration of World War II. The rooms have been left pretty much as they were when they were finally abandoned on VJ Day 1945, making for an atmospheric underground trot through wartime London. Also in the basement is the self-contained **Churchill Museum**, where you can hear snippets of Churchill's most famous speeches and check out his trademark bowler, spotted bow tie and half-chewed Havana, not to mention his wonderful burgundy zip-up "romper suit".

DAILY INSPECTION AT HORSE GUARDS

WESTMINSTER ABBEY

Parliament Square ⊖ Westminster ☏ 020 7222 5152, Ⓦ www.westminster-abbey.org. Mon–Fri 9.30am–4.30pm, Wed until 6pm, Sat 9.30am–2.30pm, though hours can vary. £18. MAP P.40, POCKET MAP G19

Venue for every coronation since William the Conqueror, and burial place of kings and queens, Westminster Abbey embodies much of England's history.

Entry is via the north transept, cluttered with monuments to politicians. From there you enter the nave itself, narrow, light and, at over 100ft in height, the tallest in the country. The choir leads through to the central sanctuary, site of the corona-tions, and the wonderful **Cosmati floor mosaic**, constructed in the thirteenth century by Italian craftsmen. At the east end lies the abbey's most dazzling architectural set piece, the **Lady Chapel**, added by Henry VII in 1503 as his future resting place. With its intricately carved vaulting and fan-shaped gilded pendants, the chapel represents the final

spectacular gasp of the English Perpendicular style. The public is no longer admitted to the **Shrine of Edward the Confessor**, the sacred heart of the building, except on a guided verger tour (£3). Nowadays, the abbey's royal tombs are upstaged by **Poets' Corner**, in the south transept. The first occupant, Geoffrey Chaucer, was buried here in 1400, not because he was a poet but because he lived nearby. By the eighteenth century, however, this zone had become an artistic pantheon, and since then has been filled with tributes to all shades of talent from William Blake to John Betjeman.

Doors in the south choir aisle lead to the **Great Cloisters** (daily 9am–6pm; free with Abbey ticket), rebuilt after a fire in 1298. At the eastern end of the cloisters lies the octagonal **Chapter House** (Mon–Sat 10am–4pm; free), where the House of Commons met from 1257. The thirteenth-century decorative paving tiles and apocalyptic wall-paintings have survived intact. Close by is the **Abbey Museum** (Mon–Sat 10.30am–4pm; free), filled with generations of bald royal death masks and wax effigies. From the cloisters you can make your way to the little-known **College Garden** (Tues–Thurs: April–Sept 10am–6pm; Oct–March 10am–4pm; free), a 900-year-old stretch of green which now provides a quiet retreat; brass band concerts take place in July and August between 12.30 and 2pm.

It's only after exploring the cloisters that you get to see Edward I's **Coronation Chair,** a decrepit oak throne from around 1300, and used at every coronation since. You exit via the west door.

WESTMINSTER ABBEY

HOUSES OF PARLIAMENT

Parliament Square ⊖ Westminster ☎ 020 7219 3000, ⓦ www.parliament.uk. MAP P.40, POCKET MAP H19

Also known as the **Palace of Westminster**, the Houses of Parliament are one of London's best-known monuments and the ultimate symbol of a nation once confident of its place at the centre of the world. The city's finest example of Victorian Gothic Revival, the complex is distinguished above all by the ornate, gilded clock-tower popularly known as **Big Ben**, after the thirteen-ton main bell that strikes the hour (and is broadcast across the airwaves by the BBC).

The original medieval palace burnt to the ground in 1834, but **Westminster Hall** survived, and its huge oak hammerbeam roof –and sheer scale – make it one of the most magnificent secular medieval halls in Europe; you get a glimpse of it en route to the public galleries. For centuries, the hall housed England's highest court of law and witnessed the trials of, among others, William Wallace, Guy Fawkes and Charles I.

To watch the proceedings in either the House of Commons or the Lords, simply join the queue for the **public galleries** (known as Strangers' Galleries) outside St Stephen's Gate. The public is let in slowly (from 4pm Mon & Tues, 1pm Wed, noon Thurs, 10am Fri); security checks are tight, and the whole procedure can take an hour or more. To avoid the queues, turn up an hour or more later, when the crowds have usually thinned; call ☎ 020 7219 4272 to check that the place is open.

To see **Question Time** (Mon 2.30pm, Tues–Thurs 11.30am),

BIG BEN

when the House is at its most raucous and entertaining, UK citizens must book a ticket several weeks in advance from their local MP.

Throughout the year there are weekly **guided tours** (every Sat) with daily ones in the summer (Easter & Aug Mon–Sat; £16.50; ☎ 0844 847 1672), in which visitors get to walk through the two chambers, see some of the state rooms and admire Westminter Hall. All year round UK residents are entitled to a free tour of the palace, as well as up Big Ben; both need to be organized through your local MP.

JEWEL TOWER

Abingdon St ⊖ Westminster ☎ 020 7222 2219. April–Oct daily 10am–5pm; Nov–March Sat – Sun 10am–4pm; £3.90. MAP P.40, POCKET MAP J9

The Jewel Tower is another remnant of the medieval palace. It once formed the corner of the original fortifications, and was constructed in around 1365 by Edward III as a giant strongbox for the crown jewels. These days, it houses an excellent exhibition on the history of parliament – worth checking out before you visit the Houses of Parliament.

WESTMINSTER CATHEDRAL

Victoria St ⊖ Victoria ☎ 020 7798 9055, ⓦ www.westminstercathedral.org.uk. Mon–Fri 7am–7pm, Sat 8am–7pm, Sun 8am–8pm. Free. MAP P.40, POCKET MAP G9

Begun in 1895, the stripy neo-Byzantine, Roman Catholic Westminster Cathedral is one of London's most surprising churches, as well as one of the last – and the wildest – monuments to the Victorian era. Brick-built, and decorated with hoops of Portland stone, it culminates in a magnificent 274-foot tapered **campanile**, served by a lift (Mon–Fri 9.30am–5pm, Sat & Sun 9.30am–6pm; £5). The interior is only half finished, so to get an idea of what the place should eventually look like, explore the side chapels whose rich, multicoloured decor uses over one hundred types of marble from around the world. Be sure, too, to check out the low-relief Stations of the Cross, sculpted by Eric Gill during World War I.

TATE BRITAIN

Millbank ⊖ Pimlico ☎ 020 7887 8888, ⓦ www.tate.org.uk. Daily 10am–6pm. Free. MAP P.40, POCKET MAP J10

A purpose-built gallery founded in 1897 with money from Henry Tate, inventor of the sugar cube, Tate Britain is devoted almost exclusively to British art from 1500 to the present day. In addition, the gallery showcases contemporary British artists and sponsors the Turner Prize, the country's most prestigious modern-art award.

The pictures are rehung more or less annually, but always include a fair selection of works by British artists such as Hogarth, Constable, Gainsborough, Reynolds and Blake, plus foreign artists like van Dyck who spent much of their career over here. The ever-popular **Pre-Raphaelites** are well represented, as are established twentieth-century greats including Stanley Spencer, Francis Bacon and Lucian Freud and living artists such as David Hockney. Lastly, don't miss the Tate's outstanding **Turner collection**, displayed in the Clore Gallery.

WESTMINSTER CATHEDRAL

Shops

HOUSES OF PARLIAMENT SHOP

12 Bridge St ⊖ Westminster. Mon–Thurs
9.30am–5.30pm, Fri 9am–4pm. MAP P.40.
POCKET MAP G19

Pick up copies of *Hansard*
(the word-for-word account of
parliament), the government's
white and green papers and
plenty of political literature.

TATE BRITAIN GIFT SHOPS

Millbank ⊖ Pimlico. Daily 10am–5.50pm.
MAP P.40, POCKET MAP J10

Lots of art posters, from
Constable to Turner Prize
nonsense, plus books –
covering history and culture,
as well as art – and funky,
arty accessories.

Cafés and restaurants

CAFÉ IN THE CRYPT

St Martin-in-the-Fields, Duncannon St
⊖ Charing Cross. Mon & Tues 8am–8pm,
Wed 8am–10.30pm, Thurs–Sat 8am–9pm,
Sun 11am–6pm. MAP P.37, POCKET MAP G16

The tasty comfort food,
veggie dishes, and handy
(and atmospheric) location
– below the church in the
crypt – make this an ideal
spot to fill up. Jazz nights Wed
from 6.30pm.

VINCENT ROOMS

76 Vincent Square ⊖ Victoria or St
James's Park ☎ 020 7802 8391. Mon–Fri
noon–2pm, plus Wed & Thurs 6.30–9pm;
closed Easter, summer and Xmas. MAP P.40,
POCKET MAP H9

Elegant brasserie serving
up dishes cooked by the
student chefs of Westminster
Kingsway College, where
Jamie Oliver learnt his trade.
A real bargain.

ST STEPHEN'S TAVERN

Pubs

THE CHANDOS

29 St Martin's Lane ⊖ Charing Cross.
Mon–Sat 11am–11pm, Sun noon–10.30pm.
MAP P.37, POCKET MAP G16

If you can get one of the booths
downstairs, or the leather sofas
upstairs in the more relaxed
Opera Room Bar, then you'll
find it difficult to leave this
Sam Smith's pub.

RED LION

48 Parliament St ⊖ Westminster. Mon–Fri
10am–11pm, Sat 10am–9pm, Sun noon–9pm.
MAP P.37, POCKET MAP G18

Classic old pub with good pies,
convenient for Westminster
Abbey and Parliament. You
may spot an MP or two
enjoying a quiet pint.

ST STEPHEN'S TAVERN

10 Bridge St ⊖ Westminster. Mon–Thurs &
Sat 10am–11.30pm, Sun 10am–10.30pm.
MAP P.40, POCKET MAP H19

A beautifully restored and
opulent Victorian pub, built in
1867, wall to wall with civil
servants and MPs. Good real
ales (including unusual
seasonal brews) and food; they
even offer breakfast.

St James's

An exclusive little enclave sandwiched between St James's Park and Piccadilly, St James's was laid out in the 1670s close to the royal seat of St James's Palace. Regal and aristocratic residences overlook nearby Green Park and the stately avenue of The Mall, while gentlemen's clubs cluster along Pall Mall and St James's Street, and jacket-and-tie restaurants and expense-account gentlemen's outfitters line Jermyn Street. Hardly surprising, then, that most Londoners rarely stray into this area. Plenty of folk, however, frequent St James's Park, with large numbers heading for the Queen's chief residence, Buckingham Palace, and the adjacent Queen's Gallery and Royal Mews.

THE MALL

⊖Charing Cross. MAP P.47, POCKET MAP G17–E18

The tree-lined sweep of The Mall was laid out in the early twentieth century as a memorial to Queen Victoria. The bombastic **Admiralty Arch** was erected to mark the eastern entrance to The Mall, from Trafalgar Square, while at the other end, in front of Buckingham Palace, stands the ludicrously overblown **Victoria Memorial**, Edward VII's tribute to his mother. The Mall is best visited on a Sunday, when it's closed to traffic.

ST JAMES'S PARK

⊖St James's Park ⓦwww.royalparks .gov.uk. MAP P.47, POCKET MAP F18

St James's Park is the oldest of London's royal parks, having been enclosed for hunting purposes by Henry VIII and later opened to the public by Charles II. It was landscaped by Nash in the 1820s, and today its tree-lined lake is a favourite picnic spot for Whitehall's civil servants. Pelicans chill out at the eastern end, and there are exotic ducks, swans and geese aplenty. From the bridge across the lake there's also a fine view

ST JAMES'S PARK

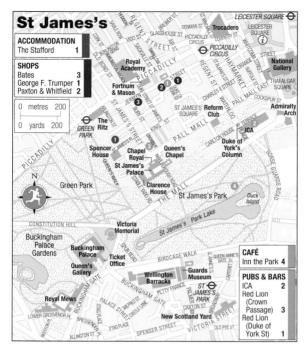

St James's

ACCOMMODATION	
The Stafford	1

SHOPS	
Bates	3
George F. Trumper	1
Paxton & Whitfield	2

| 0 metres | 200 |
| 0 yards | 200 |

CAFÉ	
Inn the Park	4

PUBS & BARS	
ICA	2
Red Lion (Crown Passage)	3
Red Lion (Duke of York St)	1

over to Westminster and the jumble of domes and pinnacles along Whitehall, with the London Eye peeking over it all – even dull Buckingham Palace looks majestic from here.

GUARDS MUSEUM

Birdcage Walk ⊖ St James's Park ☏ 020 7414 3271, ⓦ www.theguardsmuseum.com. Daily 10am–4pm. £5. MAP P.47, POCKET MAP E19

The Neoclassical facade of the **Wellington Barracks**, built in 1833 and fronted by a parade ground, runs along the south side of St James's Park. In a bunker opposite the barracks' modern chapel, the Guards Museum endeavours to explain the complicated evolution of the Queen's Household Regiments, and provides a potted military history since the Civil War. Among the exhibits are the guards' glorious scarlet and

blue uniforms, a lock of Wellington's hair and a whole load of war booty, from Dervish prayer mats plundered from Sudan in 1898 to items taken from an Iraqi POW during the 1990 Gulf War.

ADMIRALTY ARCH

BUCKINGHAM PALACE

Buckingham Gate ⊖ Green Park
Ⓦ royalcollection.org.uk. Aug daily
9.30am–7pm; Sept daily 9.30am–6pm.
Advance booking on ☎ 020 7766 7300.
£19.75. MAP P.47, POCKET MAP D19

The graceless colossus of Buckingham Palace, popularly known as "Buck House", has served as the monarch's permanent London residence only since Queen Victoria's reign. Bought by George III in 1762, the building was overhauled in the late 1820s, and again in time for George V's coronation in 1913, producing a Neoclassical monolith that's about as bland as it's possible to be.

For two months of the year, the hallowed portals are grudgingly nudged open to the public; timed tickets are sold from the box office on the south side of the palace. The interior, however, is a bit of an anticlimax: of the palace's 775 rooms, you're permitted to see around twenty, and there's little sign of life as the Queen decamps to Scotland every summer. If the decor is disappointing, at least the art on display is top-notch, with several van Dycks, two Rembrandts, two Canalettos, a Poussin, a de Hooch and a wonderful Vermeer hanging in the Picture Gallery.

For the other ten months of the year, the palace is closed to visitors – not that this deters the crowds who mill around the railings and gather in some force to watch the Foot Guards' **Changing of the Guard** ceremony (April–July daily 11.30am; Sept–March alternate days; no ceremony if it rains). If the Queen is at home, the Royal Standard flies from the roof of the palace and four guards patrol; if not, the Union flag flutters aloft and just two guards stand out front.

QUEEN'S GALLERY

Buckingham Gate ⊖ Victoria ☎ 020 7766
7300. Ⓦ royalcollection.org.uk. Daily
10am–5.30pm. £9.50. MAP P.47, POCKET MAP D19

The changing exhibitions here are drawn from the **Royal Collection**, the vast array of artworks snapped up by the royal family over the centuries, which is three times larger than that at the National Gallery. Among the thousands of works the curators have to choose from are some incredible masterpieces by Michelangelo, Reynolds, Gainsborough, Vermeer, van Dyck, Rubens, Rembrandt and Canaletto, as well as numerous Fabergé eggs and heaps of Sèvres porcelain.

BUCKINGHAM PALACE

ROYAL MEWS

Buckingham Gate ⊖ Victoria
ⓦ royalcollection.org.uk. April–Oct daily
10am–5pm; Nov, Feb & March Mon–Sat
10am–4pm. £8.75. MAP P.47, POCKET MAP D19

At the Nash-built Royal Mews, you can view the **Queen's horses** – or at least their backsides – in their luxury stables, along with an exhibition of equine accoutrements, but it's the royal carriages, lined up under a glass canopy in the courtyard, that are the main attraction. The most ornate is the **Gold State Coach**, made for George III in 1762, smothered in 22-carat gilding, panel paintings by Cipriani, and weighing four tons, its axles supporting four life-size Tritons blowing conches. Eight horses are needed to pull it and the whole experience apparently made Queen Victoria feel quite sick; since then it has only been used for coronations and jubilees. The mews also house the Royal Family's fleet of five Rolls-Royce Phantoms and three Daimlers, none of which is obliged to carry numberplates.

ST JAMES'S PALACE

Marlborough Rd ⊖ Green Park ⓦ www.royal
.gov.uk. MAP P.47, POCKET MAP E18

Originally built by Henry VIII for Anne Boleyn, St James's Palace became the principal royal residence after Whitehall Palace burnt to the ground in 1698, until the court moved down the road to Buckingham Palace under Queen Victoria. The imposing red-brick gate-tower that forms the main entrance, and the **Chapel Royal**, are all that remain of the original Tudor palace. The rambling complex is off-limits to the public, though you can attend services at the Chapel Royal (Oct to Good Friday 8.30am and 11.15am), venue for numerous royal weddings, and at the Neoclassical **Queen's Chapel** (Easter Sun to July Sun 8.30am and 11.15am).

ST JAMES'S PALACE

The gentlemen's clubs

The **gentlemen's clubs** of St James's remain the final bastions of the male chauvinism and public-school snobbery for which England is famous. Their origins lie in the coffee- and chocolate-houses of the eighteenth century, though the majority were founded in the post-Napoleonic peace of the early nineteenth century by those who yearned for the officers' mess; drinking, whoring and gambling were the major features of early club life. The oldest clubs – like White's, Brooks's and Boodle's – still boast a list of members that includes royals, politicians and the military top brass. The Reform Club, on Pall Mall, from which Phileas Fogg set off in Jules Verne's *Around the World in Eighty Days*, is one of the more "progressive" – it was one of the first to admit women as members.

CLARENCE HOUSE

Stable Yard Rd ⊖ Green Park ☎ 020 7766 7303, ⓦ royalcollection.org.uk. Aug Mon–Fri 10am–4pm, Sat & Sun 10am–5.30pm. £9.50. MAP P.47, POCKET MAP E18

Built in the 1820s by John Nash for the future William IV, and used as his principal residence, Clarence House was home to the **Queen Mother**, widow of George VI, until 2002, and is now the official London home of Charles and Camilla. A handful of rooms can be visited over the summer when the royals are in Scotland. Visits must be booked in advance and are by guided tour only, and the rooms are pretty unremarkable, so apart from a peek behind the scenes in a working royal palace, and a few mementoes of the Queen Mum, the main draw is the twentieth-century British paintings on display by the likes of Walter Sickert and Augustus John.

SPENCER HOUSE

St James's Place ⊖ Green Park ☎ 020 7514 1958, ⓦ www.spencerhouse.co.uk. Feb–July & Sept–Dec Sun 10.30am–5.45pm. No under 10s. £12. MAP P.47, POCKET MAP E18

Most of St James's palatial residences are closed to the public, with the exception of this superb Palladian mansion, built between 1756 and 1766. Ancestral home of the late Diana, Princess of Wales, it was last lived in by the family in 1926. Inside, guides take you on an hour-long tour through eight of the state rooms.

The Great Room features a stunning coved and coffered ceiling in green, white and gold, while the **Painted Room** is a feast of Neoclassicism, decorated with murals in the "Pompeian manner". The most outrageous decor, though, is in **Lord Spencer's Room**, with its gilded palm-tree columns.

GREEN PARK

⊖ Green Park ⓦ www.royalparks.gov.uk. MAP P.47, POCKET MAP D18

Laid out on the burial ground of the old lepers' hospital by Henry VIII, Green Park was left more or less flowerless – hence its name (officially "The Green Park") – and, apart from the springtime swaths of daffodils and crocuses, it remains mostly meadow, shaded by graceful London plane trees. In its time, however, it was a popular place for duels (banned from neighbouring St James's Park), ballooning and fireworks displays. One such display was immortalized by Handel's *Music for the Royal Fireworks*, performed here on April 27, 1749 to celebrate the Peace of Aix-la-Chapelle, which ended the eight-year War of the Austrian Succession – over ten thousand fireworks were let off, setting fire to the custom-built Temple of Peace and causing three fatalities. The music was a great success, however. Along the east side of the park runs the wide path of **Queen's Walk**, laid out for Queen Caroline, wife of George II, who had a little pavilion built nearby.

LORD SPENCER'S ROOM, SPENCER HOUSE

Shops

BATES

73 Jermyn St ⊖ Green Park. Daily
9.30am–6pm. MAP P.47, POCKET MAP E17

A venerable "gentleman's
hatter", hidden within Hilditch
& Key the shirtmakers, selling
everything from boaters and
panamas to tweed caps and felt
hats – look out for Binks, the
stuffed cat, who first entered
the shop in 1921.

GEORGE F. TRUMPER

1 Duke of York St ⊖ Piccadilly Circus.
Mon–Fri 9am–5.30pm, Sat 9am–5pm.
MAP P.47, POCKET MAP E16

Founded in 1875, this
impeccably discreet
"gentlemen's perfumer" is
the barber of choice, with a
shaving school that will
teach you how to execute the
perfect wet shave.

PAXTON & WHITFIELD

93 Jermyn St ⊖ Piccadilly Circus. Mon–Sat
9.30am–6pm, Sun 11am–5pm. MAP P.47,
POCKET MAP E16

Quintessentially English, this
200-year-old cheese shop
offers a very traditional
selection of British and
European varieties, plus a good
range of wine and port.

Cafés

INN THE PARK

St James's Park ⊖ Westminster or
St James's Park. Mon–Fri 8–11am &
noon–4pm, Sat & Sun 9–11am & noon–4pm.
MAP P.47, POCKET MAP F18

The panoramic windows
of this curving wooden
building look onto the park's
lake. The restaurant serves
delicious but pricey British
food, and there's a classy
takeaway section.

INN THE PARK

Pubs and bars

ICA

94 The Mall ⊖ Charing Cross. Tues–Sun
11am–11pm. MAP P.47, POCKET MAP F17

Cool drinking venue, with a
noir dress code observed by
the arty crowd and staff.
Buy-one-get-one-free cocktails
on Tuesdays (6–7.30pm).

RED LION

23 Crown Passage ⊖ Green Park. Mon–Sat
11.30am–11pm. MAP P.47, POCKET MAP E17

Hidden away in a passageway
off Pall Mall, this is a genuinely
warm and cosy local, with
super friendly bar staff,
well-kept Adnams beer and
good sandwiches.

RED LION

2 Duke of York St ⊖ Piccadilly Circus.
Mon–Sat 11.30am–11pm. MAP P.47,
POCKET MAP E16

Glorious old Victorian gin
palace with elegant etched
mirrors and lots of polished
wood. Offers a commendable
range of ales, with seasonal
selections that change every
few weeks.

Mayfair and Marylebone

A whiff of exclusivity still pervades the streets of Mayfair, particularly Bond Street and its tributaries, where designer clothes emporia jostle for space with jewellers, bespoke tailors and fine art dealers. Most Londoners, however, stick to the more prosaic pleasures of Regent and Oxford streets, home to the flagship branches of the country's most popular chain stores. It's here that Londoners are referring to when they talk of the West End. Marylebone, to the north of Oxford Street, may not have quite the pedigree and snob value of Mayfair, but it's still a wealthy and aspirational area, and its mesh of smart Georgian streets and squares are a pleasure to wander, especially the chi-chi, village-like quarter around the High Street.

PICCADILLY CIRCUS

⊖ Piccadilly Circus. MAP P.53, POCKET MAP F16

Characterless and congested it may be, but for many Londoners, Piccadilly Circus is the nearest their city comes to having a centre.

EROS, PICCADILLY CIRCUS

Originally laid out in 1812 and now a major traffic bottleneck, it's by no means a picturesque place, and is probably best seen at night when the spread of vast illuminated signs (a feature since the Edwardian era) provide a touch of Las Vegas dazzle, and when the human traffic is at its most frenetic. Somewhat inexplicably, Piccadilly Circus attracts a steady flow of tourists, who come here to sit on the steps of the central fountain, which is topped by an aluminium statue popularly known as **Eros**, designed by Alfred Gilbert and first unveiled in 1893. Despite the bow and arrow, it depicts not the god of love but Anteros, the lesser-known god of requited love, and was erected to commemorate the Earl of Shaftesbury, a Bible-thumping social reformer who campaigned against child labour.

RIPLEY'S BELIEVE IT OR NOT!

1 Piccadilly Circus ⊖ Piccadilly Circus
☏ 020 3238 0022, ⓦ www.ripleyslondon.com.

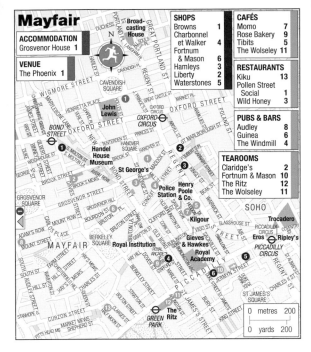

Mayfair

ACCOMMODATION
Grosvenor House 1

VENUE
The Phoenix 1

SHOPS
Browns	1
Charbonnel et Walker	4
Fortnum & Mason	6
Hamleys	3
Liberty	2
Waterstones	5

CAFÉS
Momo	7
Rose Bakery	9
Tibits	5
The Wolseley	11

RESTAURANTS
Kiku	13
Pollen Street Social	1
Wild Honey	3

PUBS & BARS
Audley	8
Guinea	6
The Windmill	4

TEAROOMS
Claridge's	2
Fortnum & Mason	10
The Ritz	12
The Wolseley	11

Daily 10am–midnight. £27. MAP P.53, POCKET MAP F16

Housed in what was once the London Pavilion music hall, right on Piccadilly Circus next to the Trocadero centre, you'll find the world's largest branch of Ripley's Believe It or Not!, which bills itself as an odditorium. It's half waxworks, half old-fashioned Victorian freak show, with a mirror maze thrown in for good measure.

Delights on display include shrunken heads and dinosaur eggs, a chewing gum sculpture of the Fab Four, and Tower Bridge rendered in 264,345 matchsticks.

Booking online will save you a few pounds off the stratospheric admission charge.

TAXI IN PICCADILLY CIRCUS

REGENT STREET

⊖ Piccadilly Circus or Oxford Circus.
MAP P.53, POCKET MAP D14–E16

Drawn up by John Nash in 1812 as both a luxury shopping street and a new, wide triumphal approach to Regent's Park, Regent Street was the city's first real attempt at dealing with traffic congestion. At the same time, it helped clear away a large area of slums, and create a tangible borderline to shore up fashionable Mayfair against the chaotic maze of Soho. Even today, it's still possible to admire the stately intentions of Nash's plan, particularly evident in the **Quadrant**, the street's partially arcaded section which curves westwards from Piccadilly Circus. During the course of the nineteenth century, however, the increased purchasing power of the city's middle classes brought the tone of the street "down", and heavyweight stores catering for the masses now predominate.

PICCADILLY

⊖ Piccadilly Circus or Green Park. MAP P.53,
POCKET MAP F16–C18

Piccadilly apparently got its name from the ruffs or "pickadills" worn by the dandies who promenaded along this wide boulevard in the late seventeenth century. Despite its fashionable pedigree, and the presence of **The Ritz** halfway along, it's no place for promenading in its current state, with traffic careering down it nose to tail day and night. Infinitely more pleasant places to window-shop are the various **nineteenth-century arcades** leading off the street, originally built to protect shoppers from the mud and horse-dung on the streets, but now equally useful for escaping exhaust fumes.

BURLINGTON ARCADE

Piccadilly ⊖ Green Park. Mon–Sat 9am–8pm, Sun 11am–6pm. MAP P.53,
POCKET MAP D16–E16

Awash with mahogany-fronted jewellers and gentlemen's outfitters, the Burlington Arcade is Piccadilly's longest and most expensive nineteenth-century arcade. It was built in 1819 for Lord Cavendish, then owner of neighbouring Burlington House, to prevent commoners throwing rubbish into his garden. Upholding Regency decorum, it is still illegal to whistle, sing, hum,

REGENT STREET ARCADES

hurry, carry large packages or open umbrellas on this small stretch – the arcade's beadles (known as Burlington Berties), in their Edwardian frock-coats and gold-braided top hats, take the prevention of such criminality very seriously.

ROYAL ACADEMY

Burlington House, Piccadilly ⊖ Green Park
☏ 020 7300 8000, ⊛ www.royalacademy
.org.uk. Daily 10am–6pm, Fri till 10pm.
Tickets £10–15. MAP P.53, POCKET MAP E16

The Royal Academy of Arts (RA) occupies the enormous Burlington House, one of the few survivors of the aristocratic mansions that once lined Piccadilly. The country's first-ever formal art school, the Academy was founded in 1768 by a group of English painters including Thomas Gainsborough and Joshua Reynolds, the first president, whose statue now stands in the main courtyard, palette in hand.

The Academy usually has two or three art exhibitions on at any one time, but is best known for its **Summer Exhibition**, which opens in June and runs until mid-August. Anyone can enter paintings in any style, and the lucky winners' works get exhibited and sold. In addition, RA "Academicians" are allowed to display six of their own works – no matter how awful. The result is a bewildering display, which gets annually panned by the critics. As well as hosting exhibitions, the RA has a small selection of works from its own collection on **permanent display** in the newly restored white and gold John Madejski Fine Rooms (guided tours Tues 1pm, Wed–Fri 1 & 3pm, Sat 11.30am; free). Highlights include a Rembrandtesque self-portrait by Reynolds,

BURLINGTON ARCADE

as well as works by the likes of John Constable, Stanley Spencer and David Hockney.

ROYAL INSTITUTION

21 Albemarle St ⊖ Green Park ☏ 020 7409
2992, ⊛ www.rigb.org. Mon–Fri 9am–6pm.
Free. MAP P.53, POCKET MAP D16

Founded in 1799 "for teaching by courses of philosophical lectures and experiments the application of science to the common purposes of life", the Royal Institution is best known for its six Christmas Lectures, begun by **Michael Faraday** and designed to popularize science among schoolchildren. In the basement, there's an enjoyable interactive **museum** aimed at both kids and adults, where you can learn about the ten elements that have been discovered at the RI, and the famous experiments that have taken place here: Tyndall's blue sky tube, Humphry Davy's early lamps and Faraday's explorations into electricity and electromagneticism – there's even a reconstruction of Faraday's lab from the 1850s.

BOND STREET AND AROUND

Bond Street or Green Park. MAP P.53, POCKET MAP C15–D16

While Oxford Street, Regent Street and Piccadilly have all gone downmarket, Bond Street has carefully maintained its exclusivity. It is, in fact, two streets rolled into one: the southern half, laid out in the 1680s, is known as Old Bond Street; its northern extension, which followed less than fifty years later, is New Bond Street. Both are pretty unassuming architecturally, but the shops that line them – and those of neighbouring Conduit Street and South Molton Street – are among the flashiest in London, dominated by **perfumeries**, **jewellers** and **designer clothing** emporia such as Versace, Gucci and Yves Saint-Laurent.

In addition to fashion, Bond Street is also renowned for its auction houses, the oldest of which is **Sotheby's**, at no. 34–35.

The viewing galleries (free) are open to the public, as are the auctions themselves. Bond Street's **art galleries** are another favourite place for the wealthy to offload their heirlooms; for contemporary art, head for neighbouring Cork Street. Both locations' galleries have somewhat intimidating staff, but if you're interested, walk in and look around. They're only shops, after all.

SAVILE ROW

Green Park. MAP P.53, POCKET MAP D15–E16

A classic address in sartorial matters, Savile Row has been *the* place to go for bespoke tailoring since the early nineteenth century. **Gieves & Hawkes**, at no. 1, were the first tailors to establish themselves here, back in 1785, with Nelson and Wellington among their first customers, while modernist **Kilgour**, at no. 8, famously made Fred Astaire's

Afternoon tea

The classic English **afternoon tea** – assorted sandwiches, scones and cream, cakes and tarts, and, of course, lashings of tea – is available all over London. The best venues are the capital's top hotels and most fashionable department stores; a selection of the best is given below. Expect to spend at least £40 a head, and leave your jeans and trainers at home – most hotels will expect "smart casual attire", though only *The Ritz* insists on jacket and tie. It's essential to book ahead.

Claridge's 49 Brook St ⊖ Bond Street ☎ 020 7107 8886. Daily 3pm, 3.30pm, 5pm & 5.30pm. MAP P.53, POCKET MAP C15

Fortnum & Mason 181 Piccadilly ⊖ Green Park or Piccadilly Circus ☎ 0845 602 5694. Mon–Sat noon–9pm, Sun noon–8pm. MAP P.53, POCKET MAP E16

The Ritz Palm Court, 150 Piccadilly ⊖ Green Park ☎ 020 7493 8181. Daily 11.30am, 1.30pm, 3.30pm, 5.30pm and 7.30pm. MAP P.53, POCKET MAP D17

The Wolseley 160 Piccadilly ⊖ Green Park ☎ 020 7409 6996. Mon–Fri 3–6.30pm, Sat 3.30–5.30pm, Sun 3.30–6.30pm. MAP P.53, POCKET MAP D13

morning coat for *Top Hat*, helping to popularize Savile Row tailoring in the US. **Henry Poole & Co**, who moved to no. 15 in 1846, has cut suits for the likes of Napoleon III, Dickens, Churchill and de Gaulle, and invented the short smoking jacket (originally designed for the future Edward VII), later popularized as the tuxedo.

HANDEL HOUSE MUSEUM

25 Brook St ⊖ Bond Street ☎ 020 7495 1685, 🌐 www.handelhouse.org. Tues-Sat 10am-6pm, Thurs till 8pm, Sun noon-6pm. £6. MAP P.53, POCKET MAP C15

The German-born composer **George Frideric Handel** (1685–1759) spent the best part of his life in London, producing all his best-known works at what's now the Handel House Museum. The composer used the ground floor of the building as a sort of shop where subscribers could buy scores, while the first floor was employed as a rehearsal room. Although containing few original artefacts, the house has been painstakingly restored, and its atmosphere is enhanced by music students who come to practise on the harpsichords. For information on more formal recitals that regularly take place, see the website. Access to the house is via the chic cobbled yard at the back.

ST GEORGE'S CHURCH

Hanover Square ⊖ Oxford Circus ☎ 020 7629 0874, 🌐 www.stgeorgeshanoversquare.org. Mon, Tues, Thurs, Fri 8am-4pm, Wed 8am-6pm, Sun 8am-noon. MAP P.53, POCKET MAP D15

The much-copied Corinthian portico of St George's Church was the first of its kind in London when built in the 1720s. The church has long been Mayfair's most fashionable wedding venue, and those who tied the knot here have

SELFRIDGES, OXFORD STREET

included the Shelleys, Benjamin Disraeli, George Eliot and Teddy Roosevelt. Handel, a confirmed bachelor, was a church warden for many years and even had his own pew.

OXFORD STREET

⊖ Marble Arch, Bond Street, Oxford Circus or Tottenham Court Road. MAP PP.53 & 59, POCKET MAP F14-15, E6-H6

The old Roman road to Oxford has been London's main **shopping** mecca for the last century. Today, despite successive recessions and sky-high rents, this aesthetically unremarkable two-mile hotchpotch of shops is still one of the world's busiest streets. East of Oxford Circus, it forms the northern border of Soho; to the west, the one great landmark is **Selfridges**, a huge Edwardian pile fronted by giant Ionic columns, with the Queen of Time riding the ship of commerce and supporting an Art Deco clock above the main entrance. The store was opened in 1909 by Chicago millionaire Gordon Selfridge, who flaunted its 130 departments under the slogan, "Why not spend a day at Selfridges?"; he was later pensioned off after an altercation with the Inland Revenue.

MAYFAIR AND MARYLEBONE

WALLACE COLLECTION

Hertford House, Manchester Square
⊖ Bond Street ☎ 020 7563 9500, Ⓦ www
.wallacecollection.org. Daily 10am–5pm. Free.
MAP P.59, POCKET MAP B14

Housed in a miniature eighteenth-century French-style chateau, the Wallace Collection is an old-fashioned place, with exhibits piled high in glass cabinets, paintings covering every inch of wall space and a bloody great armoury. The collection is best known for its eighteenth-century French furniture and paintings (especially Watteau); look out, too, for Franz Hals' *Laughing Cavalier*, Titian's *Perseus and Andromeda*, Velázquez's *Lady with a Fan* and Rembrandt's affectionate portrait of his teenage son, Titus. Labelling can be pretty terse and paintings occasionally move about, so you might consider renting an audioguide.

RIBA

66 Portland Place ⊖ Regent's Park ☎ 020
7580 5533, Ⓦ www.architecture.com. Mon,
Wed & Thurs 8am–7pm, Tues 8am–9pm,
Fri 8am–6pm, Sat 9am–5pm. Free. MAP P.59,
POCKET MAP C12

With its sleek 1930s Portland-stone facade, the headquarters of the **Royal Institute of British Architects** is easily the finest building on Portland Place. Inside, the main staircase remains a wonderful period piece, with etched glass balustrades, walnut veneer and two large columns of black marble rising up on either side. You can view the interior en route to the institute's often thought-provoking first-floor architectural exhibitions (free) and to its café. The excellent ground-floor bookshop is also worth a browse.

MADAME TUSSAUDS

Marylebone Rd ⊖ Baker Street ☎ 0871 894
3000, Ⓦ www.madametussauds.com. Mon–Fri
9.30am–5.30pm, Sat & Sun 9am–6pm. Online
tickets from £22.50. MAP P.59, POCKET MAP A12

Madame Tussaud's waxworks have been pulling in the crowds ever since the good lady arrived in London from France in 1802 bearing the sculpted heads of guillotined aristocrats. The entrance fee is extortionate, the likenesses occasionally dubious and the automated dummies inept, but you can still rely on finding London's biggest queues

WALLACE COLLECTION

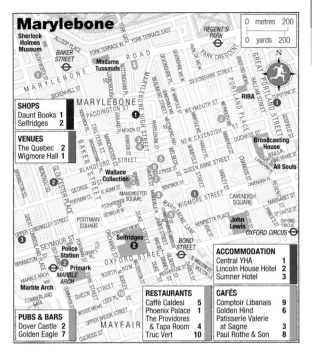

Marylebone

Sherlock
Holmes
Museum

BAKER STREET

Madame Tussauds

REGENT'S PARK

0	metres 200
0	yards 200

N

SHOPS
Daunt Books 1
Selfridges 2

VENUES
The Quebec 2
Wigmore Hall 1

Wallace Collection

RIBA

Broadcasting House

All Souls

John Lewis

OXFORD CIRCUS

Police Station

Primark

Selfridges 2

BOND STREET

ACCOMMODATION
Central YHA 1
Lincoln House Hotel 2
Sumner Hotel 3

Marble Arch

PUBS & BARS
Dover Castle 2
Golden Eagle 7

MAYFAIR

RESTAURANTS
Caffè Caldesi 5
Phoenix Palace 1
The Providores
& Tapa Room 4
Truc Vert 10

CAFÉS
Comptoir Libanais 9
Golden Hind 6
Patisserie Valerie
at Sagne 3
Paul Rothe & Son 8

here – to avoid joining them, book your ticket online. There are photo opportunities galore throughout the first few sections, which are peppered with contemporary **celebrities** from the BBC to Bollywood. Keep your eyes out for the elderly and diminutive Madame Tussaud herself, and the oldest wax model, Madame du Barry, Louis XV's mistress, who gently respires as Sleeping Beauty – in reality she was beheaded in the French Revolution, as was Madame Tussaud's uncle. The **Chamber of Horrors**, the most popular section of all, is irredeemably tasteless, and now features live, costumed actors who jump out at you in the dark (you can opt out of this). The Tussauds finale is a manic five-minute "ride" through the history of London in a miniaturized taxi cab,

followed by a thirty-minute high-tech presentation, usually on a celebrity/Hollywood-inspired theme, projected onto the dome of the adjoining Auditorium (formerly the Planetarium).

SHERLOCK HOLMES MUSEUM

239 Baker St ⊖ Baker Street ☎ 020 7224 3688, ⓦ www.sherlock-holmes.co.uk. Daily 9.30am–6pm. £8. MAP P.59. POCKET MAP A12
Sherlock Holmes's fictional address was 221b Baker Street, hence the number on the door of the museum. Unashamedly touristy, the place is stuffed full of Victoriana and life-size models of characters from the books. It's an atmospheric and very competent exercise in period reconstruction – you can even don a deerstalker to have your picture taken by the fireside, looking like the great detective himself.

Shops

BROWNS

23–27 South Molton St ⊖ Bond Street.
Mon–Sat 10am–6.30pm, Thurs till 7pm.
MAP P.53, POCKET MAP C15

London's largest range of designer wear, with big international names under the same roof as the more cutting-edge, up-and-coming designers, with clothing for women and men.

CHARBONNEL ET WALKER

1 Royal Arcade, 28 Old Bond St ⊖ Green
Park. Mon–Sat 10am–6pm, Sun noon–5pm.
MAP P.53, POCKET MAP D16

Established in 1875, this is where Her Majesty stocks up on chocolate, which is presented in the most exquisite wrapping.

DAUNT BOOKS

83 Marylebone High St ⊖ Baker Street.
Mon–Sat 9am–7.30pm, Sun 11am–6pm.
MAP P.59, POCKET MAP B13

Wide and inspirational range of travel literature and guidebooks, plus fiction and non-fiction, presented by expert staff in the beautiful, galleried interior of this famous shop.

LIBERTY

FORTNUM & MASON

181 Piccadilly ⊖ Green Park or Piccadilly
Circus. Mon–Sat 10am–9pm, Sun noon–6pm.
MAP P.53, POCKET MAP E16

Beautiful and eccentric 300-year-old store with heavenly murals, cherubs, chandeliers and fountains as a backdrop to its perfectly English offerings. Justly famous for its fabulous, pricey food, it also specializes in upmarket designer clothes, furniture, luggage and stationery.

HAMLEYS

188–196 Regent St ⊖ Oxford Circus.
Mon–Wed 10am–8pm, Thurs & Fri 10am–9pm,
Sat 9.30am–9pm, Sun noon–6pm. MAP P.53,
POCKET MAP D15

Possibly the world's largest toy shop, and certainly a feast for the eyes of most small children, with lots of gadget demonstrations going on throughout its six floors of mayhem.

LIBERTY

210–220 Regent St ⊖ Oxford Circus.
Mon–Sat 10am–8pm, Sun noon–6pm. MAP P.53,
POCKET MAP D15

A fabulous, partly mock-Tudor emporium of luxury. Best known for its fabrics, though it is, in fact, a full-blown department store.

SELFRIDGES

400 Oxford St ⊖ Bond Street. Hours vary;
usually Mon–Sat 9.30am–9pm, Sun
noon–6pm. MAP P.59, POCKET MAP B14

London's first great department store, and still one of its best: a huge, airy mecca of clothes, food and furnishings.

WATERSTONES

203–206 Piccadilly ⊖ Piccadilly Circus.
Mon–Sat 9am–10pm, Sun 11.30am–6pm.
MAP P.53, POCKET MAP E16

This flagship bookstore – Europe's largest – boasts a café, bar, gallery and events rooms as well as six floors of books.

Cafés

COMPTOIR LIBANAIS

65 Wigmore St ⊖ Bond Street. Mon–Sat 8am–11.30pm, Sun 9am–10.30pm. MAP P.59, POCKET MAP B14

Bursting with atmosphere, this is a colourful, stylish Middle Eastern deli and diner; food is simple and honest. Try the home-made lemonade.

GOLDEN HIND

73 Marylebone Lane ⊖ Bond Street. Mon–Fri noon–3pm & 6–10pm, Sat 6–10pm. MAP P.59, POCKET MAP B2

Marylebone's heritage fish-and-chip restaurant, founded in 1914, serves classic cod and chips from around £6, as well as slightly fancier food.

MOMO

25 Heddon St ⊖ Piccadilly Circus. Mon–Fri 8am–1am, Sat 10am–1am, Sun noon–1am. MAP P.53, POCKET MAP E16

Serving reasonably priced, tasty snacks in a wonderful Arabic tearoom, with a greenery-entangled terrace screened off from the restaurant-packed alleyway.

PATISSERIE VALERIE AT SAGNE

105 Marylebone High St ⊖ Bond Street. Mon–Fri 7am–8pm, Sat 8am–8pm, Sun 8.30am–7pm. MAP P.59, POCKET MAP B14

Founded as Swiss-run *Maison Sagne* in 1926, and preserving its wonderful ambience from those days, the café is now a branch of the *Valerie* chain, with the usual array of sumptuous patisserie.

PAUL ROTHE & SON

35 Marylebone Lane ⊖ Bond Street. Mon–Fri 8am–6pm, Sat 11.30am–5.30pm. MAP P.59, POCKET MAP B3

Old-fashioned deli established in 1900, selling "English & Foreign Provisions", offering breakfasts, plus toasties and

PATISSERIE VALERIE AT SAGNE

sandwiches made to order. Take away or sit at one of the formica tables inside the shop.

ROSE BAKERY

17–18 Dover St ⊖ Green Park. Mon–Sat 11am–5pm, Sun noon–4pm. MAP P.53, POCKET MAP D16

An offshoot of Paris's favourite English tearoom, serving simple home-made lunches and fabulous cakes in the high-fashion Dover Street Market designer store.

TIBITS

12–14 Heddon St ⊖ Piccadilly Circus. Mon–Wed 9am–10.30pm, Thurs–Sat 9am–midnight, Sun 11.30am–10.30pm. MAP P.53, POCKET MAP E16

Spacious, rather glam veggie café serving more than forty salads and hot dishes from across the globe. Pay by weight.

THE WOLSELEY

160 Piccadilly ⊖ Green Park ☎ 020 7409 6996. Mon–Fri 7am–midnight, Sat 8am–midnight, Sun 8am–11pm. MAP P.53, POCKET MAP D17

The European brasserie food is good if rather pricey, but the big draw is the lofty and stylish 1920s interior (built as the showroom for Wolseley cars). It's a great place for breakfast or a cream tea (see box, p.56) and very popular so book ahead.

Restaurants

CAFFE CALDESI

118 Marylebone Lane ⊖ Bond Street
☎ 020 7487 0753. Mon–Fri 9.30am–11pm,
Sat 10.30am–11pm, Sun 10.30am–10pm.
MAP P.59, POCKET MAP B13

Eat in the downstairs bar rather
than the formal dining room
upstairs and enjoy wonderfully
executed Tuscan staples. Set
lunches for around £15.

KIKU

17 Half Moon St ⊖ Green Park ☎ 020 7499
4208. Mon–Sat noon–2.30pm & 6–10.15pm,
Sun 5.30–9.45pm. MAP P.53, POCKET MAP C17

"Kiku" translates as pricey, but
at least this place serves up
top-quality sushi and sashimi
(£3–30). Take a seat at the
traditional sushi bar and
wonder at the dexterity of the
knife man. Set lunch £22.

POLLEN STREET SOCIAL

8/10 Pollen St ⊖ Oxford Circus ☎ 020 7290
7600. Mon–Sat noon–2.30pm & 6–10.30pm.
MAP P.53, POCKET MAP D15

Innovative restaurant from
wunderkind chef Jason
Atherton, who produces

delicate cuisine with wit – the
"English breakfast" starter, for
example – and flair. Mains
from £30; set lunches from £26.

PHOENIX PALACE

5 Glentworth St ⊖ Baker Street ☎ 020 7486
3515. Mon–Sat noon–11.30pm, Sun
11am–10.30pm. MAP P.59, POCKET MAP A12

There's plenty to choose from
in this huge, popular restaurant
with dishes from all over
China. Good dim sum, too,
served till 5pm. Mains £10–25.

THE PROVIDORES & TAPA ROOM

109 Marylebone High St ⊖ Baker Street or
Bond Street ☎ 020 7935 6175. Mon–Fri
9am–10.30pm, Sat 9am–3pm & 4–10.30pm,
Sun 9am–3pm & 4–10pm. MAP P.59,
POCKET MAP B13

Outstanding fusion restaurant
split into two: the *Tapa Room*
café downstairs and an elegant
restaurant upstairs. The food in
both is inventive and beautiful.
Mains £12.50–25; tapas from
£5; menus £33–63.

TRUC VERT

42 North Audley St ⊖ Bond Street
☎ 020 7491 9988. Mon–Fri 7am–10pm,
Sat 9am–10pm, Sun 9am–6pm. MAP P.59,
POCKET MAP B15

An upmarket but friendly
restaurant, offering robust
brasserie food. The menu
changes daily and begins early
with breakfast (£5–11); also has
a small deli section. Mains
from £17; quiche £8.50.

WILD HONEY

12 St George St ⊖ Oxford Circus or
Bond Street ☎ 020 7758 9160. Mon–Sat
noon–2.30pm & 6–11pm. MAP P.53,
POCKET MAP D15

Very popular, high end
wood-panelled brasserie,
serving up a daily-changing
menu of slow-cooked,
UK-sourced haute cuisine.
Mains from £25; lunch
menus £29.

TRUC VERT

Pubs and bars

AUDLEY

41 Mount St ⊖ Bond Street or Green Park.
Mon–Sat 11am–11pm, Sun noon–10.30pm.
MAP P.53, POCKET MAP B16

A grand Mayfair pub, with its original Victorian lincrusta ceiling, chandeliers and clocks.

DOVER CASTLE

43 Weymouth Mews ⊖ Regent's Park or Great Portland Street. Mon–Sat 11.30am–11pm. MAP P.59, POCKET MAP C13

A quiet, traditional boozer hidden away down a picturesque mews. The dark wood and strapwork ceiling add to the atmosphere. Cheap Sam Smith's bitter too.

GOLDEN EAGLE

59 Marylebone Lane ⊖ Bond Street.
Mon–Sat 11am–11pm, Sun noon–7pm.
MAP P.59, POCKET MAP B13

Proper old neighbourhood pub, made up of one single room – they even have regular singalongs on the old "Joanna" (Tues, Thurs & Fri).

GUINEA

30 Bruton Place ⊖ Bond Street or Oxford Circus. Mon–Fri 11am–11pm, Sat 6–11pm.
MAP P.53, POCKET MAP C16

Pretty, old-fashioned, flower-strewn back-lane pub, serving good Young's bitter and top-notch pub grub at lunch. There's a traditional steak restaurant (*The Guinea Grill*) attached.

THE WINDMILL

6–8 Mill St ⊖ Oxford Circus. Mon–Fri 11am–11pm, Sat noon–5pm. MAP P.53, POCKET MAP D15

Convivial, well-regarded pub just off Regent Street, and a perfect retreat for exhausted shoppers. The Young's beers are top-notch, as are the award-winning pies.

DOVER CASTLE

Venues

THE PHOENIX

37 Cavendish Square ⊖ Oxford Circus
☎ 020 7493 8003, ⓦ www.phoenixcavendish square.co.uk. MAP P.53, POCKET MAP D14

Friendly pub/club with a roster of enjoyable basement club nights from indie via disco to soul, plus good comedy nights.

THE QUEBEC

12 Old Quebec St ⊖ Marble Arch
☎ 020 7629 6159. Mon–Thurs noon–2am, Fri & Sat noon–3am, Sun noon–1am.
MAP P.59, POCKET MAP A15

Long-established and busy gay venue with a downstairs disco and late licence. Especially popular with the older crowd, and believed to be the oldest gay pub in London.

WIGMORE HALL

36 Wigmore St ⊖ Bond Street ☎ 020 7935 2141, ⓦ www.wigmore-hall.org.uk. MAP P.59, POCKET MAP C14

With its near-perfect acoustics, this intimate classical and chamber music venue – originally a piano showroom – is a favourite with artists and audiences alike. Book ahead.

Soho and Covent Garden

Soho is very much the heart of the West End, home to more theatres and cinemas than any other single area in London. As the city's premier red-light district for centuries, it retains an unorthodox and slightly raffish air that's unique in central London. Conventional sights are few and far between, yet it's a great area to wander through – whatever the hour there's always something going on. Soho is also a very upfront gay quarter, focused around Old Compton Street. More sanitized and brazenly commercial, Covent Garden is one of London's chief tourist attractions, thanks to its buskers, pedestrianized piazza and old Victorian market hall. Some three centuries ago the piazza was the great playground of eighteenth-century London. Nowadays, while the market is pretty, but touristy, the streets to the north boast some very fashionable boutiques.

LEICESTER SQUARE

⊖ Leicester Square. MAP PP.66–67.
POCKET MAP G16

By night, when the big cinemas and nightclubs are doing brisk business and the buskers are entertaining passers-by,

ODEON, LEICESTER SQUARE

Leicester Square is one of the most crowded places in London; on a Friday or Saturday night, it can seem as if half the youth of the city's suburbs have congregated here to get drunk, supplemented by a vast number of tourists. As a result, most Londoners avoid the place unless they're heading for one of the cinemas. It wasn't until the mid-nineteenth century that the square began to emerge as an entertainment zone, with accommodation houses (for prostitutes and their clients) and music halls. These included the grandiose **Empire**, now a cinema that's a favourite for big red-carpet premieres, and a couple of blocks east the **Hippodrome** – designed by Frank Matcham in 1900 – which is now the UK's biggest casino. Purpose-built movie houses moved in during the 1930s – a golden age evoked by the sleek black lines of the **Odeon** on the east side – and maintain their grip on the area.

CHINATOWN

Leicester Square. MAP PP.66–67, POCKET MAP F15–G15

A self-contained jumble of shops, cafés and restaurants, Chinatown is one of London's most distinct and popular ethnic enclaves. Centred around **Gerrard Street**, it's a tiny area of no more than three or four blocks, thick with the aromas of Chinese cooking and peppered with ersatz touches. Few of London's 60,000 Chinese actually live in Chinatown, but it nonetheless remains a focus for the community: a place to do business or the weekly shopping, celebrate a wedding, or just meet up for meals – particularly on Sundays, when the restaurants overflow with Chinese families tucking into dim sum. Most Londoners come to Chinatown simply to eat – easy and inexpensive enough to do. Cantonese cuisine predominates, and you're unlikely to be disappointed wherever you go.

CHARING CROSS ROAD

Leicester Square. MAP PP.66–67, POCKET MAP F14–G16

Charing Cross Road, which marks Soho's eastern border, boasts the highest concentration of bookshops anywhere in London. One of the first to open here, in 1906, was **Foyles** at no. 119 – Éamon de Valera, George Bernard Shaw, Walt Disney and Arthur Conan Doyle were all once regular customers. You'll find more of Charing Cross Road's original character at the string of specialist and secondhand bookshops south of Cambridge Circus. One of the nicest places for specialist and antiquarian book-browsing is **Cecil Court**, the southernmost pedestrianized alleyway between

CHINATOWN

Charing Cross Road and St Martin's Lane. These short, civilized, paved alleys boast specialist bookshops, plus various antiquarian dealers selling modern first editions, old theatre posters, coins and notes, cigarette cards, maps and children's books.

OLD COMPTON STREET

Leicester Square. MAP PP.66–67, POCKET MAP F15–G15

If Soho has a main drag, it has to be Old Compton Street, which runs parallel to Shaftesbury Avenue. The corner shops, peep shows, boutiques and trendy cafés here are typical of the area and a good barometer of the latest Soho fads. The liberal atmosphere of Soho has also made it a permanent fixture on the **gay scene** since the last century, though nowadays it's not just gay bars, clubs and cafés jostling for position on Old Compton Street: there's a gay-run houseshare agency, a financial advice outfit and even a gay taxi service.

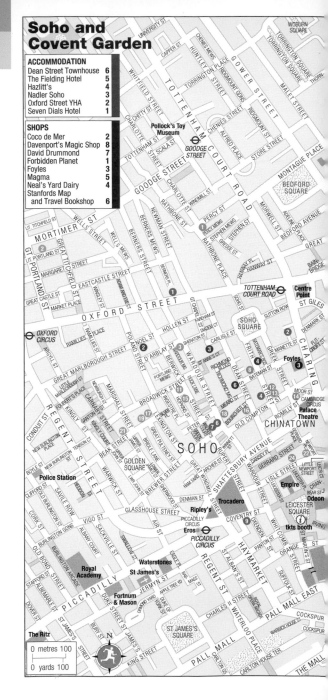

Soho and Covent Garden

SOHO AND COVENT GARDEN

ACCOMMODATION

Dean Street Townhouse	6
The Fielding Hotel	5
Hazlitt's	4
Nadler Soho	3
Oxford Street YHA	2
Seven Dials Hotel	1

SHOPS

Coco de Mer	2
Davenport's Magic Shop	8
David Drummond	7
Forbidden Planet	1
Foyles	3
Magma	5
Neal's Yard Dairy	4
Stanfords Map and Travel Bookshop	6

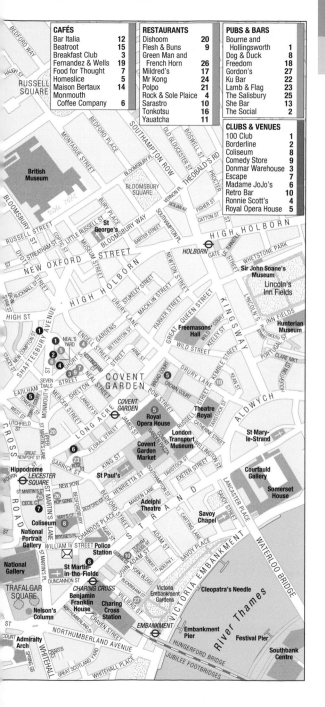

CAFÉS	
Bar Italia	12
Beatroot	15
Breakfast Club	3
Fernandez & Wells	19
Food for Thought	7
Homeslice	5
Maison Bertaux	14
Monmouth Coffee Company	6

RESTAURANTS	
Dishoom	20
Flesh & Buns	9
Green Man and French Horn	26
Mildred's	17
Mr Kong	24
Polpo	21
Rock & Sole Plaice	4
Sarastro	10
Tonkotsu	16
Yauatcha	11

PUBS & BARS	
Bourne and Hollingsworth	1
Dog & Duck	8
Freedom	18
Gordon's	27
Ku Bar	22
Lamb & Flag	23
The Salisbury	25
She Bar	13
The Social	2

CLUBS & VENUES	
100 Club	1
Borderline	2
Coliseum	8
Comedy Store	9
Donmar Warehouse	3
Escape	7
Madame JoJo's	6
Retro Bar	10
Ronnie Scott's	4
Royal Opera House	5

CARNABY STREET

⊖ Oxford Circus. MAP PP.66–67, POCKET MAP E15

Carnaby Street was famous as the fashion epicentre of London's Swinging Sixties. A victim of its own hype, it quickly declined into an avenue of overpriced tack, and so it remained for several decades. Nowadays, it's pedestrianized and smart again, but dominated by chains – for any sign of contemporary London fashion, you have to go round the corner to **Foubert's Place** and **Newburgh Street**.

POLLOCK'S TOY MUSEUM

1 Scala St ⊖ Goodge Street ☏ 020 7636 3452. ⓦ www.pollockstoymuseum.com. Mon–Sat 10am–5pm. £6. MAP PP.66–67, POCKET MAP E12

This highly atmospheric, doll's house-like toy museum is housed above a wonderful toy shop. Its collections include a fine example of the Victorian paper theatres popularized by Benjamin Pollock, who sold them under the slogan "a penny plain, two pence coloured". The other exhibits range from vintage teddy bears to Sooty and Sweep, and from Red Army soldiers to wax dolls, filling every nook and cranny of the museum's six tiny, rickety rooms and the stairs – be sure to look out for the dalmatian, Dismal Desmond.

COVENT GARDEN PIAZZA

⊖ Covent Garden. MAP PP.66–67, POCKET MAP H15

London's oldest planned square, laid out in the 1630s by Inigo Jones, Covent Garden Piazza was initially a great success – its novelty value alone ensured a rich and aristocratic clientele for the surrounding properties. Over the next century, though, the tone of the place fell as the fruit and vegetable **market** expanded, and theatres and coffee houses began to move in. Eventually, a large covered market was constructed in the middle of the square, but when the market closed in 1974, it was very nearly demolished to make way for an office development. Instead, the elegant Victorian market hall and its largely pedestrianized, cobbled piazza were restored to house shops, restaurants and craft stalls. The piazza is now one of London's major tourist attractions, its success prompting a wholesale gentrification of the streets all around.

COVENT GARDEN MARKET HALL

BALLET AT THE ROYAL OPERA HOUSE

ST PAUL'S CHURCH

Bedford St ⊖ Covent Garden ☎ 020 7836 5221, ⓦ www.actorschurch.org. Mon–Sat 8.30am–5pm, Sun 9am–1pm. Free. MAP PP.66–67, POCKET MAP H15

The proximity of so many theatres has earned this church the nickname of the "**Actors' Church**", and it's filled with memorials to international thespians from Boris Karloff to Gracie Fields. The space in front of the church's Tuscan portico – where Eliza Doolittle was discovered selling violets by Henry Higgins in George Bernard Shaw's *Pygmalion* – is now a legalized venue for the piazza's buskers and street performers, who must audition for a slot months in advance. Round the back, the **churchyard** provides a tranquil respite from the activity outside.

LONDON TRANSPORT MUSEUM

Covent Garden Piazza ⊖ Covent Garden ☎ 020 7379 6344, ⓦ www.ltmuseum.co.uk. Daily 10am–6pm, Fri 11am–6pm. £15. MAP PP.66–67, POCKET MAP H15

Housed in the piazza's former flower market, the ever-popular London Transport Museum is a surefire hit for families with kids under ten. To follow the story of London's transport

chronologically, head for Level 2, where you'll find a reconstructed 1829 Shillibeer's Horse Omnibus, which provided the city's first regular horse-bus service. Level 1 tells the story of the world's first underground system and contains a lovely 1920s Metropolitan line carriage, fitted out in burgundy and green with pretty, drooping lamps. Down on the ground floor, you can peep inside the first tube train, from the 1890s, whose lack of windows earned it the nickname "the padded cell". Most of the interactive stuff is aimed at kids, but visitors of all ages should check out the tube driver simulator. The artistically inclined can buy reproductions of the Tube's stylish maps and posters, many commissioned from well-known artists, at the shop on the way out.

ROYAL OPERA HOUSE

Bow St ⊖ Covent Garden ☎ 020 7304 4000, ⓦ www.roh.org.uk. MAP PP.66–67, POCKET MAP H15

The arcading in the northeast corner of the piazza was rebuilt as part of the multi-million pound refurbishment of the Royal Opera House. whose Neoclassical facade, dating from 1811, opens onto Bow Street (which you can reach via a passageway in the corner of the arcading). The market's spectacular wrought-iron **Floral Hall** (daily 10am–3pm) now serves as the opera house's impressive first-floor foyer; both this and the glorious terrace overlooking the piazza, beyond the *Amphitheatre* bar/restaurant, are open to the public. **Backstage tours** (Mon–Fri 10.30am, 12.30 and 2.30pm; Sat hourly 10.30am–2.30pm; £12) of the opera house are also available.

FREEMASONS' HALL

60 Great Queen St ⊖ Covent Garden
☎ 020 7395 9257, Ⓦ www.freemasonry
.london.museum. Mon–Fri 10am–5pm. Free.
MAP PP.66–67, POCKET MAP H14

It's difficult to miss the austere, Pharaonic mass of the Freemasons' Hall, built as a memorial to all the masons who died in World War I. The interior is worth a peek for the **Grand Temple** alone, whose pompous, bombastic decor is laden with heavy symbolism. To see it, you must sign up for one of the free guided tours (Mon–Fri 11am, noon, 2, 3 & 4pm) and bring ID. Take a look at the shop, too, which sells masonic merchandise – aprons, wands, rings and books about alchemy and the cabbala – as do several other shops on Great Queen Street.

BENJAMIN FRANKLIN HOUSE

36 Craven St ⊖ Charing Cross ☎ 020 7925 1405, Ⓦ www.benjaminfranklinhouse.org. Mon & Wed–Sun noon–5pm. £7. MAP PP.66–67, POCKET MAP H16

From 1757 to 1775, **Benjamin Franklin** (1706–90) lived in London espousing the cause of the British colonies (of which the US was then one), before returning to America to help draft the Declaration of Independence and the US Constitution. Wisely, the curators have left Franklin's house pretty much empty, eschewing any attempt to install period furniture. Instead, aided by a costumed guide and a series of impressionistic audiovisuals, visitors are transported back to the time of Franklin, who lived here with his "housekeeper" in cosy domesticity while his wife and daughter languished in Philadelphia. Note that visits are by guided tour only and should be booked in advance.

VICTORIA EMBANKMENT

⊖ Temple or Embankment. MAP PP.66–67, POCKET MAP J16–H19

Built between 1868 and 1874, the Victoria Embankment was the inspiration of civil engineer **Joseph Bazalgette**, whose project simultaneously relieved congestion along the Strand, provided an extension to the underground railway and sewage systems, and created a new stretch of parkland, now dotted with statues and memorials, and a riverside walk – no longer much fun due to the volume of traffic that barrels along it, though it does afford some good views over the river.

SOMERSET HOUSE

Victoria Embankment ⊖ Temple ☎ 020 7845 4600, Ⓦ www.somersethouse.org.uk. Courtyard & terrace daily 8am–11pm, interior daily 10am–6pm. Free. MAP PP.66–67, POCKET MAP J16

Sole survivor of the grand edifices which once lined this stretch of the riverfront, Somerset House's four wings enclose an elegant and surprisingly large courtyard. From March to October,

EMBANKMENT GARDENS

Cleopatra's Needle

London's oldest monument, **Cleopatra's Needle** MAP PP.66–67, POCKET MAP J16 languishes little-noticed on the busy Victoria Embankment, guarded by two Victorian sphinxes (facing the wrong way). The 60-foot-high, 180-ton stick of granite actually has nothing to do with Cleopatra – it's one of a pair erected in Heliopolis in 1475 BC (the other one is in New York's Central Park) and taken to Alexandria by Emperor Augustus fifteen years after Cleopatra's suicide. This obelisk was presented to Britain in 1819 by the Turkish viceroy of Egypt, but nearly sixty years passed before it finally made its way to London. It was erected in 1878, above a time capsule containing, among other things, the day's newspapers, a box of hairpins, a railway timetable and pictures of the country's twelve prettiest women.

a wonderful 55-jet fountain spouts straight from the courtyard's cobbles; in winter, an ice rink is set up in its place. The monumental Palladian building itself was begun in 1776 by William Chambers as a purpose-built governmental office development, but now houses a series of exhibition spaces, and puts on events throughout the year.

In the house's north wing is the **Courtauld Gallery** (daily 10am–6pm; £6, £3 all day Mon; Ⓦwww.courtauld.ac.uk), chiefly known for their dazzling permanent collection of Impressionist and Post-Impressionist paintings. Among the most celebrated works are a small-scale version of Manet's nostalgic *Bar at the Folies-Bergère,* Renoir's *La Loge,* and Degas' *Two Dancers,* plus a whole heap of Cézanne's canvases, including one of his series of *Card Players.* The Courtauld also boasts a fine selection of works by the likes of Bellini, Brueghel, Rubens, van Dyck, Tiepolo and Cranach the Elder, as well as twentieth-century paintings and sculptures by, among others, Kandinksy, Matisse, Dufy, Derain, Rodin, Roger Fry and Henry Moore.

ICE SKATING AT SOMERSET HOUSE

Shops

COCO DE MER

23 Monmouth St ⊖ Covent Garden.
Mon–Sat 11am–7pm, Thurs until 8pm, Sun
noon–6pm. MAP PP.66–67, POCKET MAP G14

Upmarket and stylish, this sex
shop for women has an inviting
boudoir feel. The lingerie
ranges from floaty to filthy, but
is always in the best possible
taste. Pick up a feather tickler
while you're here.

DAVENPORT'S MAGIC SHOP

7 Charing Cross Tube Arcade, Strand
⊖ Charing Cross. Mon–Fri 9.30am–5.30pm,
Sat 10.30am–4.30pm. MAP PP.66–67,
POCKET MAP H16

The world's oldest family-run
magic business, stocking a
huge array of marvellous
tricks for amateurs and
professionals.

DAVID DRUMMOND

11 Cecil Court ⊖ Leicester Square. Tues,
Wed & Sat noon–6pm, Thurs & Fri 11am–6pm.
MAP PP.66–67, POCKET MAP G15

Treasure trove for second-hand
books, including vintage
showbiz titles and curiosities,
rare finds, posters, prints and
old postcards.

NEAL'S YARD DAIRY

FORBIDDEN PLANET

179 Shaftesbury Ave ⊖ Tottenham Court
Road. Mon & Tues 10am–7pm, Wed, Fri & Sat
10am–7.30pm, Thurs 10am–8pm, Sun
noon–6pm. MAP PP.66–67, POCKET MAP G14

Two jam-packed floors of all
things science fiction- and
fantasy-related, ranging from
comics and graphic novels to
books, games and ephemera.

FOYLES

107 Charing Cross Rd ⊖ Tottenham Court
Road. Mon–Sat 9.30am–9pm, Sun noon–6pm.
MAP PP.66–67, POCKET MAP G14

A new location for this
long-established, famous and
huge London bookshop with
an excellent selection of titles
old and new, plus jazz on vinyl,
a café and a gallery.

MAGMA

16 Earlham St ⊖ Covent Garden. Mon–Sat
11am–7pm, Sun noon–6pm. MAP PP.66–67,
POCKET MAP G15

It's difficult to leave this sleek
store empty-handed, filled as it
is with beautifully designed,
whimsical and affordable gifts,
toys, homeware, stationery
and gizmos.

NEAL'S YARD DAIRY

17 Shorts Gardens ⊖ Covent Garden. Mon–Sat
10am–7pm. MAP PP.66–67, POCKET MAP G14

London's finest cheese shop,
with a huge selection of quality
cheeses from around the
British Isles, as well as a few
exceptionally good ones from
further afield. They're happy for
you to taste before you buy.

STANFORDS MAP AND
TRAVEL BOOKSHOP

12–14 Long Acre ⊖ Covent Garden. Mon–Fri
9am–8pm, Sat 10am–8pm, Sun noon–6pm.
MAP PP.66–67, POCKET MAP G15

The world's largest specialist
travel bookshop, stocking
pretty much any map of
anywhere, plus a huge range of
guides and travel literature.

Cafés

BAR ITALIA

22 Frith St ⊖ Tottenham Court Road. Daily
7am–5am. MAP PP.66–67, POCKET MAP F15

This tiny café is a Soho
institution, serving espressos,
croissants and sandwiches
more or less around the clock
– as it has been since 1949.

BEATROOT

92 Berwick St ⊖ Piccadilly Circus. Mon–Fri
9am–9pm, Sat 11am–9pm. MAP PP.66–67,
POCKET MAP F15

Great little veggie café by the
market, doling out hot
savoury bakes, stews and
salads (plus delicious cakes) in
boxes of varying sizes from
around £5.

BREAKFAST CLUB

33 D'Arblay St ⊖ Oxford Circus. Mon–Sat
8am–10pm, Sun 8am–7pm. MAP PP.66–67,
POCKET MAP F14

A laid-back Aussie-style
place, with battered leather
couches, offering all-day
breakfasts, brunches, burritos,
burgers, coffees and juices.
Free wi-fi.

FERNANDEZ & WELLS

73 Beak St ⊖ Piccadilly Circus. Mon–Fri
7.30am–6pm, Sat & Sun 9am–6pm.
MAP PP.66–67, POCKET MAP E15

Superlative, freshly prepared
sandwiches for around £5, great
coffee and amazing cakes for
around £2 – most folk take
away but there are one or two
tables inside.

FOOD FOR THOUGHT

31 Neal St ⊖ Covent Garden. Mon–Sat
noon–8.30pm, Sun noon–5.30pm. MAP PP.66–67,
POCKET MAP G14

Long-established but minuscule
bargain veggie café – the tasty
and filling menu changes twice
daily, and includes vegan and
wheat-free options. Be

BAR ITALIA

prepared to queue, and don't
expect to linger at peak times.

HOMESLICE

13 Neal's Yard ⊖ Covent Garden. Mon–Sat
noon–11pm, Sun noon–6pm. MAP PP.66–67,
POCKET MAP G14

Funky place offering
wood-fired thin-crust
gourmet pizzas plus Prosecco
on tap; £4 per slice, £20 for
a 20 inch pizza.

MAISON BERTAUX

28 Greek St ⊖ Leicester Square or
Tottenham Court Road. Mon–Sat
9.30am–10pm, Sun 9.30am–8pm. MAP PP.66–67,
POCKET MAP G15

Long-standing, old-fashioned
and wonderfully French
patisserie with two floors
inside and charming
street-side tables. Fabulous
cakes, tarts and croissants in a
buzzing, pretty setting.

MONMOUTH COFFEE COMPANY

27 Monmouth St ⊖ Covent Garden.
Mon–Sat 8am–6.30pm. MAP PP.66–67,
POCKET MAP G14

The marvellous aroma hits you
when you walk in. Pick and
mix your coffee from a fine
selection, then settle into one of
the cramped wooden booths
and savour.

Restaurants

DISHOOM

12 Upper St Martin's Lane ⊖ Leicester Square ☎ 020 7420 9320. Mon–Thurs 8am–11pm, Fri 8am–midnight, Sat 9am–midnight, Sun 9am–11pm. MAP PP.66–67, POCKET MAP G15

Re-creating the atmosphere of the Persian cafés of Old Bombay, this is a buzzy, witty place which serves delicious Indian food; the breakfasts are a hit too. Arrive early to get a table for dinner.

FLESH & BUNS

41 Earlham St ⊖ Covent Garden ☎ 020 7632 9500. Mon & Tues noon–3pm & 5–10.30pm, Wed–Fri noon–3pm & 5–11.30pm, Sat noon–11.30pm, Sun noon–9.30pm. MAP PP.66–67, POCKET MAP H15

Enjoy delicious rice buns with meat or fish, washed down with sake, at this loud, friendly, rock'n'roll *izakaya*-style basement restaurant.

GREEN MAN AND FRENCH HORN

54 St Martins Lane ⊖ Leicester Square ☎ 020 7836 2645. Mon–Sat noon–3pm & 5.30–11pm. MAP PP.66–67, POCKET MAP G16

Seasonal, simple and gutsy French food from the Loire, plus superb organic and biodynamic wines. Mains from £11, menus from £12.50.

MILDRED'S

45 Lexington St ⊖ Oxford Circus ☎ 020 7494 1634. Mon–Sat noon–11pm. MAP PP.66–67, POCKET MAP E15

Fresher and more stylish than many veggie restaurants, serving wholesome, delicious and inexpensive stir-fries, pasta dishes and burgers, as well as wicked but wonderful puddings. Mains £8–11.

MR KONG

21 Lisle St ⊖ Leicester Square ☎ 020 7437 7341. Mon–Sat noon–2.45am, Sun noon–1.45am. MAP PP.66–67, POCKET MAP G15

One of Chinatown's finest places to eat, with a huge choice of Cantonese dishes and friendly service. There's always something intriguing among the specials – jellyfish, anyone? Mains £7–25.

POLPO

41 Beak St ⊖ Piccadilly Circus ☎ 020 7734 4479. Mon–Sat noon–11pm, Sun noon–4pm. MAP PP.66–67, POCKET MAP E15

Warm restaurant modelled on a Venetian *bacaro*. Small plates from £3 – try grilled fennel with white anchovy, *pizzette* or any of the *polpette* (meatballs). Reservations for lunch only.

ROCK & SOLE PLAICE

47 Endell St ⊖ Covent Garden ☎ 020 7836 3785. Daily noon–10.30pm. MAP PP.66–67, POCKET MAP H14

No-nonsense fish-and-chip shop, where they do all the staples just right; you eat in or at one of the pavement tables.

SARASTRO

126 Drury Lane ⊖ Covent Garden ☎ 020 7836 0101. Mon–Fri 12.30–10.30pm, Sat 12.30–11pm, Sun 12.30–4pm & 6–10pm. MAP PP.66–67, POCKET MAP J15

Theatrically over-the-top, gloriously kitsch restaurant that's also a great place to hear young opera stars perform live (Mon & Sun), while enjoying food from the eastern Med. Mains £10–27; set menus from £28.95.

TONKOTSU

63 Dean St ⊖ Tottenham Court Road ☎ 020 7437 0071. Mon–Fri noon–3pm & 5–10.30pm, Sat noon–10.30pm, Sun noon–10pm. MAP PP.66–67, POCKET MAP F15

Slurpable, silky home-made ramen noodles in rich, savoury stocks, with pork belly, smoked haddock or veggie options. Prices from £9

YAUATCHA

15 Broadwick St ⊖ Piccadilly Circus ☎ 020 7494 8888. Mon–Sat noon–11.30pm, Sun noon–10.30pm. MAP PP.66–67, POCKET MAP E15

Very popular, minimalist Chinese teahouse-restaurant serving up dim sum (£4.50–12) all day long.

Pubs and bars

BOURNE AND HOLLINGSWORTH

28 Rathbone Place ⊖ Goodge Street. Mon & Tues 5pm–1am, Wed–Sat 5pm–1.30am. MAP PP.66–67, POCKET MAP F13

Prohibiton-style vintage cocktail bar, offering creative gin concoctions and punches served in jars, tin mugs and tea cups.

DOG & DUCK

18 Bateman St ⊖ Tottenham Court Road. Daily 10am–11pm. MAP PP.66–67, POCKET MAP F15

Tiny Soho pub that retains much of its old character, with beautiful Victorian tiling and mosaics, plus a good range of real ales.

FREEDOM

66 Wardour St ⊖ Piccadilly Square. Mon–Thurs 4pm–3am, Fri & Sat 2pm–3am, Sun 2–10.30pm. MAP PP.66–67, POCKET MAP F15

Established gay bar, popular with a straight/gay Soho crowd. The basement, with pink banquettes and glitter balls, plays host to various cabaret and club nights

GORDON'S

47 Villiers St ⊖ Embankment. Mon–Sat 11am–11pm, Sun noon–10pm. MAP PP.66–67, POCKET MAP H17

Cavernous, shabby, atmospheric wine bar specializing in ports and sherries. The excellent and varied wine list, decent buffet food and genial atmosphere make this a favourite with local office workers, who spill outdoors in the summer.

KU BAR

30 Lisle St ⊖ Leicester Square. Mon–Sat noon–3am, Sun noon–midnight MAP PP.66–67, POCKET MAP F15

The Lisle Street original, with a downstairs club open late, is one of Soho's largest and best-loved gay bars, serving a scene-conscious yet low-on-attitude clientele. It's joined by a stylish sibling bar on Frith Street.

BOURNE AND HOLLINGSWORTH

LAMB & FLAG

33 Rose St ⊖ Leicester Square or Covent Garden. Mon–Sat 11am–11.30pm, Sun noon–10.30pm. MAP PP.66–67, POCKET MAP H15

Tiny and highly atmospheric old pub, hidden away down an alley between Garrick Street and Floral Street. The Poet Laureate, John Dryden, was beaten up here in 1679 by a group of thugs, hired most probably by his rival poet, the Earl of Rochester.

THE SALISBURY

90 St Martin's Lane ⊖ Leicester Square. Mon–Thurs 11am–11pm, Fri 11am–midnight, Sat noon–midnight, Sun noon–10.30pm. MAP PP.66–67, POCKET MAP G16

Superbly preserved Victorian pub with cut, etched and engraved windows, bronze lampstands, red-leather seating and a fine lincrusta ceiling, plus a wide range of ales.

SHE BAR

23 Old Compton St ⊖ Leicester Square. Mon–Thurs 4–11.30pm, Fri & Sat 4pm–12.30am, Sun 4–10.30pm. MAP PP.66–67, POCKET MAP F15

Rather swish lesbian bar in the heart of Soho, with occasional DJ nights.

THE SALISBURY

THE SOCIAL

5 Little Portland St ⊖ Oxford Circus Ⓦ www.thesocial.com. Mon–Wed noon–midnight, Thurs & Fri 9am–1am, Sat 6pm–1am. MAP PP.66–67, POCKET MAP D13

Retro club-bar and diner with great DJs playing everything from afro to electronica to a truly hedonistic, hard-drinking crowd.

Clubs and venues

100 CLUB

100 Oxford St ⊖ Tottenham Court Road ☎ 020 7636 0933, Ⓦ www.the100club.co.uk. MAP PP.66–67, POCKET MAP E14

Fun venue whose history stretches back to 1942 and takes in Louis Armstrong, Glenn Miller and the Sex Pistols. Now hosts a mix of jazz, rock and R&B, with weekend club nights.

BORDERLINE

Orange Yard, off Manette St ⊖ Tottenham Court Road ☎ 0844 847 2465, Ⓦ www.mamacolive.com. MAP PP.66–67, POCKET MAP G14

Hosts consistently good, eclectic live music with an indie edge, ranging from nu-folk to punk, plus lively club nights.

COLISEUM

St Martin's Lane ⊖ Leicester Square ☎ 020 7845 9300, Ⓦ www.eno.org. MAP PP.66–67, POCKET MAP G16

Home to the English National Opera, which differs from its Royal Opera House counterpart in that all its operas are sung in English, productions tend to be more experimental, and tickets cost a lot less.

COMEDY STORE

1a Oxendon St ⊖ Piccadilly Circus ☎ 0844 871 7699, Ⓦ www.thecomedystore.co.uk. MAP PP.66–67, POCKET MAP F16

Birthplace of alternative comedy, with impro by in-house comics and a regular stand-up bill. Weekends are busiest, with two shows – book ahead.

DONMAR WAREHOUSE

41 Earlham St ⊖ Covent Garden ☎ 0844 871 7624, ⓦ www.donmarwarehouse.com. MAP PP.66–67, POCKET MAP H15

Theatre noted for its new plays, top-quality reappraisals of the classics and star-studded casts.

ESCAPE

10 Brewer St ⊖ Piccadilly Circus ☎ 020 7734 3040, ⓦ www.escapesoho.com. MAP PP.66–67, POCKET MAP F15

Trendy DJ bar in the heart of Soho, attracting a young, mixed gay crowd for lively club nights and trannyoke.

MADAME JOJO'S

8–10 Brewer St ⊖ Tottenham Court Road ☎ 020 7734 3040, ⓦ www.madamejojos.com. MAP PP.66–67, POCKET MAP F15

Louche, enjoyable Soho institution, known for its wickedly diverse range of entertainment – alongside variety, drag and comedy, you'll find electronica, disco, rock and funk.

RETRO BAR

2 George Court, off Strand ⊖ Charing Cross ☎ 020 7839 8760, ⓦ retrobarlondon.co.uk. MAP PP.66–67, POCKET MAP H16

Indie/retro gay-bar tucked down a quiet alleyway, playing 1970s and 80s rock, pop, rockabilly and alternative sounds, and featuring regular DJ nights.

RONNIE SCOTT'S

47 Frith St ⊖ Tottenham Court Road ☎ 020 7439 0747, ⓦ www.ronniescotts.co.uk. MAP PP.66–67, POCKET MAP F15

The most famous jazz club in London, this small and atmospheric place has smartened up its decor, upped its prices, and stretched its remit, but still hosts the best jazz acts in town.

ROYAL OPERA HOUSE

Bow St ⊖ Covent Garden ☎ 020 7304 4000, ⓦ www.roh.org.uk. MAP PP.66–67, POCKET MAP H15

The ROH still has a reputation for elitism, and certainly its lavish operas are expensive. Tickets are hard to come by, so make sure that you get in line early if you want to buy one of the 67 day seats that are put on sale from 10am on the day of a performance.

Half-price theatre tickets

The Society of London Theatre (ⓦ www.tkts.co.uk) runs the **tkts booth** in Leicester Square (Mon–Sat 10am–7pm, Sun 11am–4.30pm), which sells on-the-day tickets for all the West End shows, with discounts of up to fifty percent. On average, you're looking at £20–40 (including a service charge of £3 per ticket) with tickets limited to four per person.

Bloomsbury

Bloomsbury was built in grid-plan style from the 1660s onwards, and the formal, bourgeois Georgian squares laid out then remain the area's main distinguishing feature. In the twentieth century, Bloomsbury acquired a reputation as the city's most learned quarter, dominated by the dual institutions of the British Museum and London University, and home to many of London's chief book publishers, but perhaps best known for its literary inhabitants, among them T.S. Eliot and Virginia Woolf. Only in its northern fringes does the character of the area change dramatically, as you near the busy main-line train stations of Euston, St Pancras and King's Cross.

BRITISH MUSEUM

Great Russell St ⊖ Tottenham Court Road
☎ 020 7323 8299, ⊕ www.britishmuseum.org.
Daily 10am–5.30pm, Fri until 8.30pm. Free.
MAP P.80, POCKET MAP G13

One of the great museums of the world, the BM contains an incredible collection of antiquities, prints, drawings and books. Begun in 1823, the building itself is the grandest of London's Greek Revival edifices, with its central **Great Court** (daily 9am–6pm, Fri until 8.30pm) featuring a remarkable curving glass-and-steel roof designed by Norman Foster. At the Court's centre stands the copper-domed former **Round Reading Room** of the British Library, where Karl Marx penned *Das Kapital*.

The BM's collection of **Roman and Greek antiquities** is unparalleled, and is most famous for the Parthenon sculptures, better known as the **Elgin Marbles** after the British aristocrat who walked off with the reliefs in 1801. Elsewhere, the **Egyptian collection** is easily the most

GREAT COURT, BRITISH MUSEUM

PARTHENON SCULPTURES, BRITISH MUSEUM

The **King's Library**, in the east wing, displays some of the museum's earliest acquisitions, brought back from the far reaches of the British Empire: everything from Javanese puppets to a model gamelan orchestra, collected by Stamford Raffles. Don't miss the museum's expanding **ethnographic collection**, including the superb African galleries in the basement. And in the north wing of the museum, closest to the back entrance on Montague Place, there are also fabulous **Asian** treasures including ancient Chinese porcelain, ornate snuffboxes, miniature landscapes and a bewildering array of Buddhist and Hindu gods.

significant outside Egypt, ranging from monumental sculptures to the ever-popular mummies and their ornate outer caskets. Also on display is the **Rosetta Stone**, which enabled French professor Champollion to finally unlock the secret of Egyptian hieroglyphs. Other highlights include a splendid series of **Assyrian reliefs** from Nineveh, and several extraordinary artefacts from **Mesopotamia** such as the enigmatic Ram in the Thicket (a goat statuette in lapis lazuli and shell) and the remarkable hoard of goldwork known as the Oxus Treasure.

The leathery half-corpse of the 2000-year-old **Lindow Man**, discovered in a Cheshire bog, and the Anglo-Saxon treasure from the **Sutton Hoo** ship burial, by far the richest single archeological find made in Britain, are among the highlights of the **Europe** collection, which ranges from the twelfth-century Lewis chessmen carved from walrus ivory to avant-garde Russian ceramics celebrating the 1917 revolution.

FOUNDLING MUSEUM

40 Brunswick Square ⊖ Russell Square ☎ 020/7841 3600, ⓦ www.foundlingmuseum .org.uk. Tues–Sat 10am–5pm, Sun 11am–5pm. £7.50. MAP P.80, POCKET MAP J4

This museum tells the fascinating story of the **Foundling Hospital**, London's first home for abandoned children founded in 1756 by retired sea captain Thomas Coram. As soon as it was opened, it was besieged, and soon forced to reduce its admissions drastically and introduce a ballot system. Among the most tragic exhibits are the tokens left by the mothers in order to identify the children should they ever be in a position to reclaim them: these range from a heart-rending poem to a simple enamel pot label reading "ale". The museum also boasts an impressive **art collection** including works by Hogarth, Gainsborough and Reynolds, now hung in carefully preserved eighteenth-century interiors of the original hospital.

79

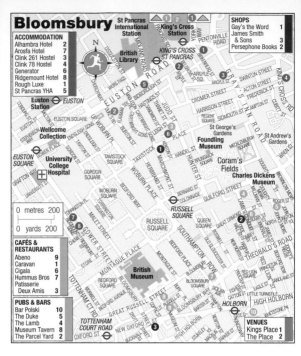

Bloomsbury

ACCOMMODATION
Alhambra Hotel	2
Arosfa Hotel	7
Clink 261 Hostel	3
Clink 78 Hostel	4
Generator	6
Ridgemount Hotel	8
Rough Luxe	1
St Pancras YHA	5

SHOPS
Gay's the Word	1
James Smith	
& Sons	3
Persephone Books	2

CAFÉS & RESTAURANTS
Abeno	9
Caravan	1
Cigala	6
Hummus Bros	7
Patisserie	
Deux Amis	3

PUBS & BARS
Bar Polski	10
The Duke	5
The Lamb	4
Museum Tavern	8
The Parcel Yard	2

VENUES
Kings Place	1
The Place	3

CHARLES DICKENS MUSEUM

48 Doughty St ⊖ Russell Square ☎ 020 7405 2127, ⓦ www.dickensmuseum.com. Daily 10am–5pm. £8. MAP P.80, POCKET MAP K4

Dickens moved to this house, now a museum, in 1837 shortly after his marriage to Catherine Hogarth, and they lived here for two years, during which time he wrote *Nicholas Nickleby* and *Oliver Twist*. Catherine gave birth to two of their children in the bedroom here, and her youngest sister, who lived with them after their marriage, died tragically in Dickens's arms aged only seventeen. Much of the house's furniture belonged to Dickens, at one time or another, and there's an early portrait miniature painted by his aunt in 1830. The museum puts on special exhibitions in the adjacent

house, no. 49, where you'll also find a café.

WELLCOME COLLECTION

183 Euston Rd ⊖ Euston or Euston Square ☎ 020 7611 2222, ⓦ www.wellcomecollection .org. Mon–Sat 10am–6pm, Thurs until 10pm, Sun 11am–6pm. Free. MAP P.80, POCKET MAP H4

Excellent temporary exhibitions on topical scientific issues are staged in the ground-floor gallery of the Wellcome Collection, originally founded by American-born pharmaceutical magnate Henry Wellcome (1853–1936). Also worth a look is the permanent collection, on the first floor, beginning with **Medicine Now**, which focuses on contemporary medical questions such as the body, genomes, obesity and malaria. Next door, **Medicine Man** showcases the weird and wonderful collection of historical and scientific artefacts amassed by Wellcome himself. These range from Florence Nightingale's moccasins to a sign for a Chinese doctor's hung with human teeth, and from erotic figurines and phallic amulets to Inuit snow goggles and a leper clapper – in other words, this section is an absolute must.

BRITISH LIBRARY

96 Euston Rd ⊖ King's Cross St Pancras ☎ 0843 208 1144, ⓦ www.bl.uk. Mon & Wed–Fri 9.30am–6pm, Tues 9.30am–8pm, Sat 9.30am–5pm, Sun 11am–5pm. Free. MAP P.80, POCKET MAP H3

The red-brick brutalism of the British Library may be horribly out of fashion, but the public exhibition galleries inside are superb. The first place to head for is the dimly lit **John Ritblat Gallery**, where a superlative selection of ancient manuscripts, maps, documents and precious books, including the Magna Carta and the richly illustrated Lindisfarne Gospels, are displayed. You can also see the Gutenberg Bible, the first to be printed

using moveable type (and therefore capable of being mass-produced). The special exhibitions, for which there is sometimes an admission charge, are always excellent.

ST PANCRAS AND KING'S CROSS STATIONS

Euston Rd. MAP P.80, POCKET MAP J3

Completed in 1876, the former Midland Grand Hotel's majestic sweep of Neo-Gothic lancets, dormers and chimney-pots forms the facade of **St Pancras Station**, where Eurostar trains now arrive. The adjacent **King's Cross Station**, opened in 1850, is a mere shed in comparison, albeit one with a spectacular new, semi-circular, glass-roofed concourse on the side. King's Cross is more famous as the station from which **Harry Potter** and his wizarding chums leave for school on the *Hogwarts Express* from platform 9¾. The scenes from the films were shot between platforms 4 and 5, and a station trolley is now embedded in the new concourse wall, providing a perfect photo opportunity for passing Potter fans.

ST PANCRAS INTERNATIONAL STATION

Shops

GAY'S THE WORD

66 Marchmont St ⊖ Russell Square.
Mon–Sat 10am–6.30pm, Sun 2–6pm. MAP P.80,
POCKET MAP J4

An extensive collection of
lesbian and gay classics,
contemporary fiction and
non-fiction, plus cards,
calendars and weekly lesbian
discussion groups and readings.

JAMES SMITH & SONS

53 New Oxford St ⊖ Tottenham Court Road.
Mon & Wed–Fri 10am–5.45pm, Tues
11am–5.45pm, Sat 10am–5.15pm. MAP P.80,
POCKET MAP G14

A survivor from an earlier time
(it was established in 1830),
this beautiful and venerable
shop purveys hip-flasks,
portable seats and canes, but its
main trade is in umbrellas.

PERSEPHONE BOOKS

59 Lamb's Conduit St ⊖ Russell Square.
Mon–Fri 10am–6pm, Sat noon–5pm. MAP P.80,
POCKET MAP J12

Lovely bookshop offspring of
a publishing house that
specializes in neglected early

and mid-twentieth-century
writing, mostly by women.

Cafés and restaurants

ABENO

47 Museum St ⊖ Tottenham Court Road
☎ 020 7405 3211. Daily noon–10pm. MAP P.80,
POCKET MAP H13

Japanese place that specializes in
okonomiyaki (£9–20), a stuffed
cabbage, egg and ginger pancake
prepared before your eyes.
Noodles and set menus, too.

CARAVAN

1 Granary Square ⊖ King's Cross St Pancras
☎ 0207 101 7661. Mon & Tues 8am–10.30pm,
Wed & Thurs 8am–11pm, Fri 8am–midnight,
Sat 10am–midnight, Sun 10am–4pm. MAP P.80,
POCKET MAP J2

A trailblazer on the hip new
King's Cross scene, this buzzy
spot, occupying an old grain
store, serves fabulous Modern
European food and coffee to
a lively, in-the-know crowd.
Small plates from £5.

CIGALA

54 Lamb's Conduit St ⊖ Russell Square
☎ 020 7405 1717. Mon–Fri noon–10.45pm,
Sat 12.30–10.45pm, Sun 12.30–9.45pm.
MAP P.80, POCKET MAP J12

You get robust dishes, strong,
simple flavours and fresh
ingredients at this smart Iberian
restaurant. The menu changes
daily. Mains £12–20; tapas
£4–9; set lunch from £17.50.

HUMMUS BROS

37–63 Southampton Row ⊖ Holborn.
Mon–Fri 11am–9pm. MAP P.80, POCKET MAP H13

Tiny "hummus bar", with a
couple of benches and formica
tables, offering hummus with
warm pitta (from £4) plus
toppings from guacamole to
chunky beef, salads and falafel.

JAMES SMITH & SONS

PATISSERIE DEUX AMIS

63 Judd St ⊖ King's Cross St Pancras.
Mon–Sat 9am–5.30pm, Sun 9.30am–2pm.
MAP P.80, POCKET MAP J4

Small, sweetly old-fashioned
French tea shop specializing
in pastries, filled baguettes
and coffee.

Pubs and bars

BAR POLSKI

11 Little Turnstile ⊖ Holborn. Mon 4–11pm,
Tues–Thurs 12.30–11pm, Fri 12.30–11.30pm,
Sat 6–11pm. MAP P.80, POCKET MAP J13

Great Polish bar hidden in an
alleyway near Holborn tube,
with a wicked selection of
flavoured vodkas and beers,
and good, cheap Polish food.

THE DUKE

7 Roger St ⊖ Russell Square or Holborn.
Mon–Sat noon–11pm. MAP P.80, POCKET MAP J12

Lovely little neighbourhood
gastropub, without the
pretensions often associated
with the breed, and an unfussy
Art Deco bent to the decor.

THE LAMB

94 Lamb's Conduit St ⊖ Russell Square.
Mon–Wed noon–11pm, Thurs & Fri noon–
midnight, Sat 11am–midnight, Sun
noon–10.30pm. MAP P.80, POCKET MAP J12

Marvellously well-preserved
Victorian pub of mirrors,
polished wood and "snob"
screens, plus intriguing old
photos. The excellent Young's
ales round things off splendidly.

MUSEUM TAVERN

49 Great Russell St ⊖ Tottenham Court
Road. Mon–Thurs 11am–11.30pm, Fri & Sat
11am–midnight, Sun 10am–10pm. MAP P.80,
POCKET MAP G13

Large and characterful old pub,
right opposite the main
entrance to the British
Museum, and the erstwhile
drinking hole of Karl Marx.
Choice range of ales.

THE LAMB

THE PARCEL YARD

King's Cross station ⊖ King's Cross St
Pancras. Mon–Sat 8am–11pm, Sun
9am–10.30pm. MAP P.80, POCKET MAP J3

Welcoming Fuller's pub in
King's Cross station, using
original Victorian parcel office
features to create a comfy, retro
space, and offering craft cider,
real ales and good coffee – plus
posh pub grub and great
platform views.

Venues

KINGS PLACE

90 York Way ⊖ King's Cross St Pancras
☎ 0207 520 1490, ⓦ www.kingsplace.co.uk.
MAP P.80, POCKET MAP J2

Eclectic purpose-built venue
for acoustic and classical
music of all stripes, plus
spoken word performances
and comedy.

THE PLACE

17 Duke's Rd ⊖ Euston ☎ 020 7121 1100,
ⓦ www.theplace.org.uk. MAP P.80, POCKET MAP H4

Small dance theatre presenting
the work of new choreo-
graphers and student
performers, and hosting some
of the finest small-scale
contemporary dance from
across the globe.

The City

The City is where London began, and its boundaries today are only slightly larger than those marked by the Roman walls and their medieval successors. However, you'll find few visible leftovers of London's early days, since four-fifths of it burned down in the Great Fire of 1666. The majority of Londoners lived and worked in or around the City up until the eighteenth century – nowadays, it's primarily one of the world's main financial centres and although 300,000 commuters work here fewer than 10,000 actually live here. The City is only really busy Monday to Friday during the day, so if you're looking for nightlife, you're best off heading for Clerkenwell, which lies on the City's northwest fringe.

TEMPLE

⊖ Temple. MAP PP.86–87, POCKET MAP K15

Temple is the largest and most complex of the **Inns of Court**, where, since medieval times, every aspiring barrister in England and Wales has had to study in order to qualify for the bar. Despite the fact that only a few very old buildings survive here, the overall atmosphere is like that of an Oxbridge college and the maze of courtyards and passageways is fun to explore – especially after dark, when Temple is gas-lit.

Medieval students ate, attended lectures and slept in the **Middle Temple Hall** (Mon–Fri 10–11.30am and 3–4pm; free), still the Inn's main dining room. Constructed in the 1560s, the hall provided the setting for many great Elizabethan masques and plays – probably including Shakespeare's *Twelfth Night*, which is believed to have been premiered here in 1602. The hall is worth a visit for its fine hammerbeam roof, wooden panelling and decorative Elizabethan screen.

TEMPLE CHURCH

The complex's oldest building, **Temple Church** (Mon, Tues, Thurs & Fri 11am–4pm, Wed 2–4pm; £4; ⓦ www.temple church.com) was built in 1185 by the Knights Templar, the military monks who protected pilgrims heading for the Holy Land. Despite wartime damage, the original round church – modelled on the Holy Sepulchre in Jerusalem – still stands, with its striking Purbeck-marble piers, recumbent marble effigies of knights, and tortured grotesques grimacing in the spandrels of the blind arcading. The church features in both the book and the film of *The Da Vinci Code* by Dan Brown.

ST BRIDE'S CHURCH

FLEET STREET

⊖ Temple. MAP PP.86–87, POCKET MAP K6–L6

In the nineteenth century, all the major national and provincial dailies had their offices and **printing presses** in and around Fleet Street. Computer technology rendered the presses here obsolete in the 1980s, however, and within a decade or so all the newspaper headquarters had gone, leaving just a couple of landmarks to testify to five hundred years of printing history. The most remarkable is the city's first glass curtain-wall construction, the former **Daily Express** building at no. 127, with its sleek black Vitrolite facade.

ST DUNSTAN-IN-THE-WEST

186a Fleet St ⊖ Temple ⓦ www .stdunstaninthewest.org. Mon–Fri 9.30am–5pm. Free. MAP PP.86–87, POCKET MAP K6

With its distinctive neo-Gothic tower and lantern from the 1830s, St Dunstan dominates the top of Fleet Street. To the side is a clock temple from 1671, erected in thanks for escaping the Great Fire which stopped just short of the church and featuring the legendary giants Gog and Magog. The statues of Elizabeth I and King Lud and his sons used to adorn the City gateway that once stood on Ludgate Hill.

ST BRIDE'S

Fleet St ⊖ Blackfriars or Temple ⓦ www.stbrides.com. Mon–Fri 9am–6pm, Sat 11am–3pm, Sun 10am–6.30pm. Free. MAP PP.86–87, POCKET MAP L6

To get a sense of Fleet Street in the days when the press dominated the area, head for the "journalists' and printers' cathedral", St Bride's Church, which boasts Wren's tallest and most exquisite spire (said to be the inspiration for the tiered wedding cake). The crypt contains a little museum of Fleet Street's newspaper history, with information on the *Daily Courant* and the *Universal Daily Register,* which later became *The Times*, claiming to be "the faithful recorder of every species of intelligence … circulated for a particular set of readers only".

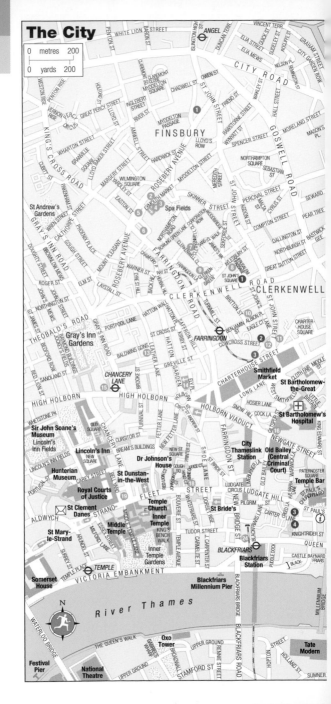

The City

0	metres 200
0	yards 200

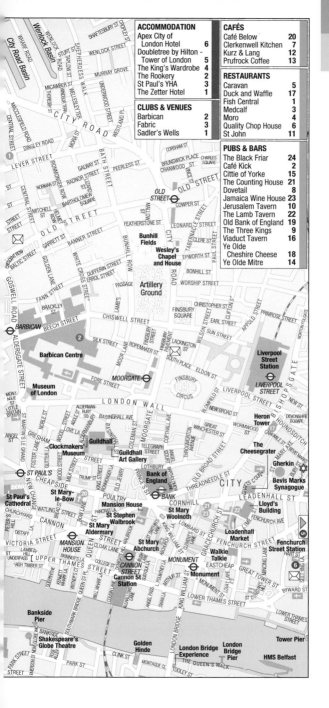

ACCOMMODATION	
Apex City of London Hotel	6
Doubletree by Hilton - Tower of London	5
The King's Wardrobe	4
The Rookery	2
St Paul's YHA	3
The Zetter Hotel	1

CLUBS & VENUES	
Barbican	2
Fabric	3
Sadler's Wells	1

CAFÉS	
Café Below	20
Clerkenwell Kitchen	7
Kurz & Lang	12
Prufrock Coffee	13

RESTAURANTS	
Caravan	5
Duck and Waffle	17
Fish Central	1
Medcalf	3
Moro	4
Quality Chop House	6
St John	11

PUBS & BARS	
The Black Friar	24
Café Kick	2
Cittie of Yorke	15
The Counting House	21
Dovetail	8
Jamaica Wine House	23
Jerusalem Tavern	10
The Lamb Tavern	22
Old Bank of England	19
The Three Kings	9
Viaduct Tavern	16
Ye Olde Cheshire Cheese	18
Ye Olde Mitre	14

LINCOLN'S INN

Lincoln's Inn Fields ⊖ Chancery Lane
☎ 020 7405 1393, ⓦ www.lincolnsinn.org.uk.
Mon–Fri 7am–7pm. Free. MAP PP.86–87,
POCKET MAP K14

Lincoln's Inn, on the east side of Lincoln's Inn Fields, was the first of the Inns of Court, and in many ways is the prettiest, having miraculously escaped the ravages of the Blitz. Famous alumni include Thomas More, Oliver Cromwell and Margaret Thatcher. The main entrance is the diamond-patterned, red-brick Tudor gateway on Chancery Lane, adjacent to which is the early seventeenth-century **chapel** (Mon–Fri noon–2.30pm), with its unusual fan-vaulted open undercroft and, on the first floor, a late Gothic nave, hit by a zeppelin in World War I and much restored since. The Inn's oldest building, the fifteenth-century **Old Hall** (appointment only), where the lawyers used to live and where Dickens set the case Jarndyce and Jarndyce in *Bleak House*, features a fine timber roof, linenfold panelling and an elaborate, early Jacobean screen.

SIR JOHN SOANE'S MUSEUM

13 Lincoln's Inn Fields ⊖ Holborn ☎ 020 7405 2107, ⓦ www.soane.org. Tues–Sat 10am–5pm. Free. MAP PP.86–87, POCKET MAP J14

The chief architect of the Bank of England, **John Soane** (1753–1837) designed this house not only as a home and office but also as a place to stash his large collection of art and antiquities. Arranged much as it was in his lifetime, the ingeniously planned house has an informal, treasure-hunt atmosphere, with countless surprises. The star exhibits are **Hogarth**'s satirical *Election* series and his merciless morality tale *The Rake's Progress,* as well as the alabaster Egyptian sarcophagus of Seti I rejected by the British Museum. Note that the museum is extremely popular, particularly on Saturdays, when there's a fascinating hour-long **guided tour** (£5) at 11am, and on the **candlelit evenings** on the first Tuesday of the month (6–9pm).

HUNTERIAN MUSEUM

Royal College of Surgeons, Lincoln's Inn Fields ⊖ Holborn or Temple ☎ 020 7869 6560, ⓦ www.rcseng.ac.uk. Tues–Sat 10am–5pm. Free. MAP PP.86–87, POCKET MAP J14

SIR JOHN SOANE'S MUSEUM

Containing the unique specimen collection of the surgeon-scientist John Hunter (1728–93), the Hunterian Museum first opened in 1813. Since most of the exhibits are jars of pickled skeletons and body pieces, it's certainly not a museum for the squeamish. Among the prize exhibits are the skeletons of the Irish giant, Charles Byrne (1761–83), who was seven feet ten inches tall, and the Sicilian dwarf Caroline Crachami (d.1824), who was just one foot ten and a half inches when she died at the age of nine.

DR JOHNSON'S HOUSE

17 Gough Square ⊖ Blackfriars or Temple ☎ 020 7353 3745, ⓦ www.drjohnsonshouse.org. May–Sept Mon–Sat 11am–5.30pm; Oct–April Mon–Sat 11am–5pm. £4.50. MAP PP.86–87, POCKET MAP L6

Despite appearances, Dr Johnson's House is the only authentic eighteenth-century building on Gough Square. It was here the great savant, writer and lexicographer lived from 1747 to 1759 whilst compiling the 41,000 entries for the first dictionary of the English language. The grey-panelled rooms of the house are peppered with period furniture and lined with portraits and etchings, including one of Johnson's servant Francis Barber. Two first-edition copies of the great *Dictionary* are on display, while the open-plan attic, in which Johnson and his six helpers put the tome together, is now lined with explanatory panels on lexicography.

OLD BAILEY

Newgate St ⊖ St Paul's ☎ 020 7248 3277, ⓦ www.cityoflondon.gov.uk. Mon–Fri 10am–1pm & 2–5pm. Free. MAP PP.86–87, POCKET MAP L6

DR JOHNSON'S HOUSE

The **Central Criminal Court** is more popularly known as the Old Bailey after the street on which it stands, which used to form the outer walls of the medieval city. It was built on the site of the notoriously harsh Newgate Prison, where folk used to come to watch public hangings. The current, rather pompous Edwardian building is distinguished by its green dome, surmounted by a gilded statue of Justice, unusually depicted without blindfold, holding her sword and scales. The country's most serious criminal court cases take place here, and have included, in the past, the trials of Lord Haw-Haw, the Kray twins, and the Guildford Four and Birmingham Six "IRA bombers". You can watch the proceedings from the visitors' gallery, but bags, cameras, mobiles, personal stereos and food and drink are not allowed in, and there is no cloakroom.

SMITHFIELD

Farringdon. MAP PP.86–87, POCKET MAP L5

For more than three centuries Smithfield was a popular venue for **public executions**: the Scottish hero, William Wallace, was hanged, disembowelled and beheaded here in 1305, and the Bishop of Rochester's cook was boiled alive in 1531, but the local speciality was burnings, which reached a peak in the mid-sixteenth century during the reign of "Bloody" Mary, when hundreds of Protestants were burned at the stake for their beliefs. These days, Smithfield is dominated by its historic **meat market**, housed in a colourful and ornate Victorian market hall on Charterhouse Street; if you want to see it in action, get here early – the activity starts around 4am and is all over by 9am or 10am.

ST BARTHOLOMEW-THE-GREAT

Cloth Fair Barbican 020 7606 5171, www.greatstbarts.com. Mon–Fri 8.30am–5pm, Sat 10.30am–4pm, Sun

8.30am–8pm; mid-Nov to mid-Feb Tues–Fri closes 4pm. £4. MAP PP.86–87, POCKET MAP L5

Begun in 1123, St Bartholomew-the-Great is London's oldest and most atmospheric parish church. Its half-timbered Tudor gatehouse on Little Britain incorporates a thirteenth-century arch that once formed the entrance to the nave; above, a wooden statue of St Bartholomew stands holding the knife with which he was flayed. One side of the medieval cloisters survives to the south, immediately to the right as you enter the church. The rest is a confusion of elements, including portions of the transepts and, most impressively, the chancel, where stout Norman pillars separate the main body of the church from the ambulatory. There are various pre-Fire monuments to admire, the most prominent being the tomb of Rahere, court jester to Henry I, which shelters under a fifteenth-century canopy north of the main altar.

ST BARTHOLOMEW'S HOSPITAL MUSEUM

West Smithfield Barbican. Tues–Fri 10am–4pm. Free. MAP PP.86–87, POCKET MAP L5

Among the medical artefacts, this hospital museum boasts some fearsome amputation instruments, a pair of leather "lunatic restrainers", some great jars with labels such as "poison – for external use only", and a cricket bat autographed by W.G. Grace, who was a student at Bart's in the 1870s. To see the magnificent **Great Hall** you must go on one of the fascinating guided tours (Fri 2pm; £5; 020 7837 0546), which take in Smithfield and the surrounding area as well; the meeting point is the Henry VIII gate.

SMITHFIELD MARKET

ST BARTHOLOMEW-THE-GREAT

MUSEUM OF LONDON

London Wall ⊖ Barbican ☎ 020 7001 9844, ⓦ www.museumoflondon.org.uk. Daily 10am–6pm. Free. MAP PP.86–87, POCKET MAP M5

Despite London's long pedigree, very few of its ancient structures are still standing. However, numerous Roman, Saxon and Elizabethan remains have been discovered and are now displayed at the Museum of London. The permanent exhibition provides an imaginative and educational trot through London's past from prehistory to the present day. Specific exhibits to look out for include the Bucklersbury Roman mosaic; a model of Old St Paul's; and the Lord Mayor's heavily gilded coach (still used for state occasions). The real strength of the museum, though, lies in the excellent temporary exhibitions, lectures, walks and films it organizes throughout the year.

GUILDHALL

Gresham St ⊖ Bank or Mansion House ☎ 020 7606 3030, ⓦ www.cityoflondon .gov.uk. May–Sept daily 10am–5pm; Oct–April Mon–Sat 10am–5pm. Free. MAP PP.86–87, POCKET MAP M6

Situated at the geographical centre of the City, Guildhall has been the area's administrative seat for over eight hundred years. It remains the headquarters of the **City of London Corporation**, the City's governing body, and is used for grand civic occasions. Architecturally, however, it's not quite the beauty it once was, having been badly damaged in both the Great Fire and the Blitz, and somewhat scarred by the addition of a grotesque 1970s concrete cloister and wing.

Nonetheless, the **Great Hall**, basically a postwar reconstruction on the fifteenth-century walls, is worth a look if there isn't an event going on. In 1553 the venue for the high-treason trials of Lady Jane Grey and her husband, Lord Dudley, the hall is home to a handful of vainglorious late eighteenth- and early nineteenth-century monuments, replete with lions, cherubs and ludicrous allegorical figures. You might also pop into the **Clockmakers' Museum** (Mon–Fri 9.30am–4.45pm; free), a collection of over six hundred timepieces, including one of the clocks that won John Harrison the Longitude prize.

Also worth a visit is the purpose-built **Guildhall Art Gallery** (Mon–Sat 10am–5pm, Sun noon–4pm; free), which contains one or two exceptional works, such as Rossetti's *La Ghirlandata* and Holman Hunt's *The Eve of St Agnes*, plus a massive painting depicting the 1782 Siege of Gibraltar, commissioned by the Corporation. In the basement, you can view the remains of a **Roman amphitheatre**, dating from around 120 AD, which was discovered during the gallery's construction.

ST PAUL'S CATHEDRAL

⊖ St Paul's ☎ 020 7246 8348, ⓦ www
.stpauls.co.uk. Mon–Sat 8.30am–4.30pm.
From £14.50 online. MAP 86–87, POCKET MAP M6

Designed by **Christopher
Wren** and completed in 1710,
St Paul's remains a dominating
presence in the City despite
the encroaching tower blocks.
It's topped by an enormous
lead-covered dome that's
second in size only to St Peter's
in Rome, and its showpiece
west facade is particularly
magnificent. However,
compared to its great rival,
Westminster Abbey, St Paul's
is a soulless but perfectly
calculated architectural set
piece, a burial place for
captains rather than kings.

The best place to appreciate
the building's glory is from
beneath the **dome**, adorned
(against Wren's wishes) by

ST PAUL'S CATHEDRAL

trompe l'oeil frescoes. The most
richly decorated section of the
cathedral is the **chancel**, where
the late Victorian mosaics of
birds, fish, animals and
greenery are particularly
spectacular. The intricately
carved oak and lime-wood
choir stalls, and the imposing
organ case, are the work of
Wren's master carver,
Grinling Gibbons.

Beginning in the south aisle,
a series of stairs leads to the
dome's three galleries, the first
of which is the internal
Whispering Gallery, so called
because of its acoustic
properties – words whispered
to the wall on one side are
distinctly audible over one
hundred feet away on the other,
though you often can't hear
much above the hubbub. Of
the two exterior galleries, the
best views are from the tiny
Golden Gallery, below the
golden ball and cross which top
the cathedral.

Although the nave is
crammed full of overblown
monuments to military types,
burials in St Paul's are confined
to the **crypt**, reputedly the
largest in Europe. The
whitewashed walls and bright
lighting make this one of
London's least atmospheric
mausoleums, but **Artists'
Corner** here does boast as
many painters and architects as
Westminster Abbey has poets,
including Christopher Wren
himself. The star tombs,
though, are those of Nelson
and Wellington, both
occupying centre stage and
both with more fanciful
monuments upstairs.

It's well worth attending one of
the cathedral's **services**, if only
to hear the ethereal choir, who
perform during most evensongs
(Mon–Sat 5pm), and on
Sundays at 10.15am and 3.15pm.

City churches

The City is crowded with churches (www.visitthecity.co.uk) – well over forty at the last count, the majority of them built or rebuilt by Wren after the Great Fire. Those particularly worth seeking out include **St Mary Abchurch** (Mon–Fri 11am–3pm; Cannon Street; MAP PP.86–87, POCKET MAP N6) on Abchurch Lane, dominated by an unusual and vast dome fresco painted by a local parishioner and lit by oval lunettes; the superlative lime-wood reredos is by Gibbons. On Lombard Street, **St Mary Woolnoth** (Mon–Fri 7.15am–5.15pm; Bank; MAP PP.86–87, POCKET MAP N6) is a typically idiosyncratic creation of Nicholas Hawksmoor, one of Wren's pupils, featuring an ingenious lantern lit by semicircular clerestory windows and a striking altar canopy held up by barley-sugar columns. **St Mary Aldermary** on Queen Victoria Street (Mon–Fri 9am–4.30pm; Mansion House; MAP PP.86–87, POCKET MAP M6) is Wren's most successful stab at Gothic, with fan vaulting in the aisles and a panelled ceiling in the nave; there's also a café. Finally on Walbrook is Wren's most spectacular church interior after St Paul's, **St Stephen Walbrook** (Mon–Fri 10am–4pm; Bank; MAP PP.86–87, POCKET MAP M6), where sixteen Corinthian columns are arranged in clusters around a central coffered dome, and the exquisite dark-wood furnishings are again by Grinling Gibbons.

PATERNOSTER SQUARE

St Paul's. MAP PP.86–87, POCKET MAP L6

The Blitz destroyed the area immediately to the north of St Paul's, incinerating all the booksellers' shops and around six million books. In their place a modernist pedestrianized piazza was built, only to be torn down in the 1980s and replaced with post-classical office blocks in Portland stone and a Corinthian column topped by a gilded urn. One happy consequence of the square's redevelopment is that **Temple Bar**, the gateway which used to stand at the top of Fleet Street, has found its way back to London after over a hundred years of exile in a park in Hertfordshire. Designed by Wren himself, the triumphal arch, looking weathered but clean, now forms the entrance to Paternoster Square, with the Stuart monarchs, James I and Charles II, and their consorts occupying the niches.

PATERNOSTER SQUARE

BANK OF ENGLAND

Threadneedle St ⊖ Bank ☎ 020 7601 5545, ⓦ www.bankofengland.co.uk. Mon–Fri 10am–5pm. Free. MAP PP.86–87, POCKET MAP M6

Established in 1694 by William III to raise funds for the war against France, the Bank of England stores the official gold reserves of many of the world's central banks. All that remains of the original building, on which John Soane spent the best part of his career (from 1788 onwards), is the windowless outer curtain wall, which wraps itself round the 3.5-acre island site. However, you can view a reconstruction of Soane's Bank Stock Office, with its characteristic domed skylight, in the **museum** (free), which has its entrance on Bartholomew Lane. The permanent exhibition here includes a scaled-down model of Soane's bank and a Victorian-style diorama of the night in 1780 when the bank was attacked by rioters. Sadly most of the gold bars are fakes, but there are specimens of every note issued by the Bank over the centuries.

BANK OF ENGLAND

MANSION HOUSE

Mansion House Place ⊖ Bank ☎ 020 7397 9306. Tues 2pm. £7. MAP PP.86–87, POCKET MAP M6

The Lord Mayor's sumptuous Neoclassical lodgings are now open to the public by guided tour. Designed in 1753, the building's grandest room is the columned **Egyptian Hall** with its barrel-vaulted, coffered ceiling. Also impressive is the vast collection of gold and silver tableware, the mayor's 36-pound gold mace and the pearl sword given by Elizabeth I. Scattered about the rooms are an impressive array of Dutch and Flemish paintings.

LEADENHALL MARKET

Leadenhall St ⊖ Monument. Mon–Fri 11am–4pm. MAP PP.86–87, POCKET MAP N6

Leadenhall Market's picturesque cobbles and graceful Victorian cast-ironwork date from 1881. Inside, the traders cater mostly for the lunchtime City crowd, their barrows laden with exotic food and wines.

BEVIS MARKS SYNAGOGUE

Bevis Marks ⊖ Aldgate ☎ 020 7626 1274, ⓦ www.bevismarks.org.uk. Mon, Wed & Thurs 10.30am–2pm, Tues & Fri 10.30am–1pm, Sun 10.30am–12.30pm. Guided tours Wed & Fri noon, Sun 11am. £5. MAP PP.86–87, POCKET MAP N6

Hidden behind a modern red-brick office block, the Bevis Marks Synagogue was built in 1701 by Sephardic Jews who had fled the Inquisition in Spain and Portugal. It's the country's oldest surviving synagogue, and the roomy, rich interior gives an idea of just how wealthy the worshippers were at the time. The Sephardic community has now dispersed across London and the congregation has dwindled, but the magnificent array of chandeliers ensure that it's a popular venue for candle-lit Jewish weddings.

MONUMENT

Monument St ⊖ Monument ☎ 020 7626 2717,
ⓦ www.themonument.info. Daily: April–Sept
9.30am–6pm; Oct–March 9.30am–5 30pm. £3.
MAP PP.86–87, POCKET MAP N6

The Monument was designed by Wren to commemorate the **Great Fire of London**, which raged for five days in early September 1666 and destroyed four-fifths of the City. A plain Doric column crowned with spiky gilded flames, it stands 202ft high, making it the tallest isolated stone column in the world; if it were laid out flat it would touch the site of the bakery where the Fire started, east of the Monument. The bas-relief on the base depicts Charles II and the Duke of York in Roman garb conducting the emergency relief operation. The 311 steps to the viewing gallery once guaranteed an incredible view; nowadays it is somewhat dwarfed by the buildings surrounding it.

City skyscrapers

Throughout the 1990s, most people's favourite modern building in the City was Richard Rogers' glitzy **Lloyd's Building** – a vertical version of Rogers' own Pompidou Centre in Paris – a startling array of glass and blue steel pipes. Lloyd's was eclipsed in the mid-2000s by its near neighbour, Norman Foster's 590ft-high, glass diamond-clad **Gherkin**, which has endeared itself to Londoners thanks to its cheeky shape.

Despite the economic recession, the City skyline continues to sprout yet more skyscrapers, with **The Cheesegrater**, Richard Rogers' 737ft wedge-shaped office block, opposite the Lloyd's Building, leading the charge. Still to rise, close by, is the **Scalpel**, a 620ft twisted angular shard of glass due for completion in 2017. More controversial has been Rafael Viñoly's 525ft **Walkie Talkie**, on Fenchurch Street, which features a public "sky garden" on the top floor. Meanwhile, on the other side of the river, of course, is the tallest of the lot, Renzo Piano's 1016ft **Shard**, by London Bridge (see p.124).

Cafés

CAFÉ BELOW

St Mary-le-Bow, Cheapside ⊖ St Paul's or
Mansion House. Mon–Fri 7.30am–2.30pm.
MAP PP.86–87, POCKET MAP M6

A rare City gem: a café, set
in a wonderful Norman
church crypt, serving
excellent, good-value
bistro-style dishes plus
delicious breakfast pastries.

CLERKENWELL KITCHEN

27–31 Clerkenwell Close ⊖ Farringdon.
Mon–Fri 8am–5pm, plus Thurs 6.30–10.30pm.
MAP PP.86–87, POCKET MAP L4

Bright, modern airy place
decked in light wood and brick,
with an open-plan kitchen that
serves up everything from
breakfast through to afternoon
tea. The menu is short and
admirably seasonal.

KURZ & LANG

1 St John St ⊖ Farringdon. Mon–Wed
11am–11.30pm, Thurs 11am–1am, Fri
11am–4am, Sat noon–2.30am, Sun
noon–5pm. MAP PP.86–87, POCKET MAP L5

An *echt* German *Bratwurst* café
in a prominent corner site off
Smithfield. Choose from a
variety of sausages, and help
them down with bread,
mustard and sauerkraut.

PRUFROCK COFFEE

23–25 Leather Lane ⊖ Chancery Lane or
Farringdon. Mon–Fri 8am–6pm, Sat & Sun
10am–5pm. MAP PP.86–87, POCKET MAP K5

Super-hip shrine to the
coffee bean, spearheaded by
world barista champion
Gwilym Davies.

Restaurants

CARAVAN

11–13 Exmouth Market ⊖ Farringdon
☎ 020 7833 8115. Mon–Fri 8am–10.30pm, Sat
10am–10.30pm, Sun 10am–4pm. MAP PP.86–87,
POCKET MAP K4

Creative brunches, modern
fusion food and home-roasted
coffee are on offer at this
relaxed, cool all-day place.
Small and large plates £5–18.

DUCK AND WAFFLE

Heron Tower, 110 Bishopsgate ⊖ Aldgate
☎ 020 3640 7310. Daily 24hr. MAP PP.86–87,
POCKET MAP N5

Forty floors up, this smart place
offers amazing City views and
hipster comfort food with
creative flair. The signature dish
features waffles, duck confit,
fried duck egg and mustard
maple syrup (£17), while 2am
offerings include spicy ox cheek
doughnuts (£10).

FISH CENTRAL

149–155 Central St ⊖ Old Street
☎ 020 7253 4970. Mon–Thurs noon–2.30pm
& 5–10.30pm, Fri & Sat noon–10.30pm.
MAP PP.86–87, POCKET MAP M4

Sitting on the edge of the
Barbican/City and Clerkenwell's
council estates, this is both a
reliable chippy and a smart
fish restaurant.

CAFÉ BELOW

MEDCALF

40 Exmouth Market ⊖ Angel or Farringdon
☎ 020 7833 3533. Mon–Fri noon–3pm &
5.30–10.30pm, Sat 9.30am–3pm &
5.30–10.30pm, Sun 9.30am–5pm. MAP PP.86–87,
POCKET MAP K4

A converted hundred-year-old
butcher's shop, fashionably
unchic, serving pricey Modern
British cuisine with fresh
ingredients and excellent puds.

MORO

34–36 Exmouth Market ⊖ Angel or Farringdon
☎ 020 7833 8336. Mon–Sat noon–2.30pm &
6–10.30pm, Sun 12.30–2.45pm. MAP PP.86–87,
POCKET MAP K4

This attractive restaurant is a
place of pilgrimage for
disciples of the restaurant's
Moorish cookbooks. Food is
excellent and you have to
book well in advance. Tapas
(around £4) served all day.
Mains £16–21.

QUALITY CHOP HOUSE

88–94 Farringdon Rd ⊖ Farringdon
☎ 020 7278 1452. Mon–Sat noon–3pm &
6–10.30pm, Sun noon–4pm; wine bar
Mon–Sat noon–midnight. MAP PP.86–87,
POCKET MAP K4

Beautiful old dining room,
butchers and wine bar with
a daily changing menu
focusing on the best cuts of
British meat and freshest
produce. Weekday lunch
mains from £13; set menus at
dinner (£35) and Sunday
lunch (£28).

ST JOHN

26 St John St ⊖ Farringdon
☎ 020 7251 0848. Mon–Fri noon–3pm &
6–11pm, Sat 6–11pm, Sun 1–3pm.
MAP PP.86–87, POCKET MAP L5

Pared-down former smoke-
house close to Smithfield meat
market that's become famous
for serving outstanding British
dishes, often involving
unfashionable animal parts.
Mains £17–30.

THE BLACK FRIAR

Pubs and bars

THE BLACK FRIAR

174 Queen Victoria St ⊖ Blackfriars.
Mon–Sat 10am–11pm, Sun noon–10.30pm.
MAP PP.86–87, POCKET MAP L6

A gorgeous pub, with Art
Nouveau marble friezes of
boozy monks and a highly
decorated alcove – all original,
dating from 1905. A lovely
fireplace and an unhurried
atmosphere make this a
relaxing place to drink.

CAFÉ KICK

43 Exmouth Market ⊖ Farringdon or
Angel. Mon–Thurs 11am–11pm, Fri & Sat
11am–midnight, Sun noon–10.30pm.
MAP PP.86–87, POCKET MAP K4

This ramshackle, memorabilia-
packed French-style café/bar is
great fun, the friendly
atmosphere enlivened by its
busy table-football games. A
daytime menu of hearty soups
and veggie dishes gives way in
the evening to tapas and
sharing boards.

CITTIE OF YORKE

22 High Holborn ⊖ Chancery Lane.
Mon–Sat 11am–11pm. MAP PP.86–87.
POCKET MAP K13

A venerable London lawyers'
pub now run by Sam Smith's.
Head for the vaulted cellar bar
or the grand quasi-medieval
wine hall at the back with its
rows of cosy cubicles.

THE COUNTING HOUSE

50 Cornhill ⊖ Bank. Mon–Fri 11am–11pm.
MAP PP.86–87, POCKET MAP N6

An inspired Fuller's bank
conversion, the magnificent
interior featuring high
ceilings, marble pillars, mosaic
flooring and a large, oval
island bar, plus an enormous
glass dome.

DOVETAIL

9 Jerusalem Passage ⊖ Farringdon.
Mon–Sat noon–11pm. MAP PP.86–87.
POCKET MAP L4

Marvellous, understated
Belgian bar offering 101
varieties of beer (including a
dozen or so on tap). The

unfussy decor comprises
pew-style seating, green-tiled
tables and ceramic wall tiling.
First-rate Belgian food, too.

JAMAICA WINE HOUSE

St Michael's Alley ⊖ Bank. Mon–Fri
11am–11pm. MAP PP.86–87, POCKET MAP N6

Located down a narrow
alleyway, on the site of
London's first coffee house
(1652), this old City
institution is known locally as
the "Jam Pot". Despite the
name, it is really just a pub,
divided into four large "snugs"
by original high wooden-
panelled partitions.

JERUSALEM TAVERN

55 Britton St ⊖ Farringdon. Mon–Fri
11am–11pm. MAP PP.86–87, POCKET MAP L5

Converted Georgian coffee
house – the frontage dates from
1810 – that has retained much
of its original character. Better
still, the excellent draught beers
are from St Peter's Brewery in
Suffolk. Something of a gem in
these parts.

THE LAMB TAVERN

10–12 Leadenhall Market ⊖ Monument or
Bank. Mon–Fri 11am–11pm. MAP PP.86–87.
POCKET MAP N6

It's almost exclusively standing
room only (both inside and
out) at this super Young's pub
situated in the middle of
beautiful Leadenhall Market.
The tilted *Tom's Bar*
downstairs offers good cheese/
sausage platters.

OLD BANK OF ENGLAND

194 Fleet St ⊖ Temple or Chancery Lane.
Mon–Fri 11am–11pm. MAP PP.86–87.
POCKET MAP K14

Not the actual Bank of
England, but the former Law
Courts' branch, this imposing
High Victorian banking hall is
now a magnificently opulent
Fuller's ale-and-pie pub.

VIADUCT TAVERN

THE THREE KINGS

7 Clerkenwell Close ⊖ Farringdon.
Mon–Fri noon–11pm, Sat 5.30–11pm.
MAP PP.86–87, POCKET MAP L4

Tucked away north of
Clerkenwell Green, this
atmospheric pub has a
delightfully eclectic interior
and two small rooms upstairs
perfect for long occupation.

VIADUCT TAVERN

126 Newgate St ⊖ St Paul's. Mon–Fri
8.30am–11pm. MAP PP.86–87, POCKET MAP L5

Fuller's pub situated across
from the Old Bailey, with a
glorious Victorian interior
including a red ceiling and
walls adorned with oils of
faded ladies representing
Commerce, Agriculture and
the Arts.

YE OLDE CHESHIRE CHEESE

Wine Office Court, 145 Fleet St ⊖ Temple.
Mon–Fri 11.30am–11pm, Sat noon–11pm
MAP PP.86–87, POCKET MAP L6

A seventeenth-century
watering hole – famous chiefly
because of patrons such as
Dickens and Dr Johnson –
with several snug, dark-
panelled rooms and real fires.
Popular with tourists, but by
no means exclusively so.

YE OLDE MITRE

1 Ely Court, off Hatton Garden ⊖ Farringdon.
Mon–Fri 11am–11pm. MAP PP.86–87, POCKET MAP L5

Hidden down a tiny alleyway
off Ely Place or Hatton Garden,
this wonderfully atmospheric
Fuller's pub dates back to 1546,
although it was actually rebuilt
in the eighteenth century. The
real ales are excellent.

Clubs and venues

BARBICAN

Silk St ⊖ Barbican ☎ 020 7638 8891,
🖥 www.barbican.org.uk. MAP PP.86–87,
POCKET MAP M5

With the outstanding resident
London Symphony Orchestra,
and top foreign orchestras and
big-name soloists in regular
attendance, the Barbican is one
of the city's best venues for
classical music, opera, theatre,
dance and film.

FABRIC

77a Charterhouse St ⊖ Farringdon
☎ 020 7336 8898, 🖥 www.fabriclondon.com.
MAP PP.86–87, POCKET MAP L5

Despite big queues (book
online) and a confusing layout,
this 1600-capacity club remains
one of the world's finest. Live
bands and lengthy DJ line-ups
mean you can hear a huge
variety of acts – usually
underground, and almost
always of high quality.

SADLER'S WELLS

Rosebery Ave ⊖ Angel ☎ 0844 412 4300,
🖥 www.sadlerswells.com. MAP PP.86–87,
POCKET MAP L3

Home to Britain's best
contemporary dance companies,
and host to the finest international outfits, Sadler's Wells
also puts on theatre pieces and
children's shows.

The East End

Despite the area's lack of obvious aesthetic charm, over the last decade, the East End has become one of the city's most vibrant artistic enclaves, peppered with art galleries and a whole host of cutting-edge bars and clubs. Spitalfields –and in particular Brick Lane – lies at the heart of the old East End, once the first port of call for thousands of immigrants over the centuries, and best known today for Sunday markets and cheap curries. The scene has now spread north to Shoreditch and Dalston, and east to the edges of the Olympic Park, former home of the 2012 Olympic Games.

DALSTON

⊖ Dalston Kingsland or Dalston Junction Overground. MAP P.102, POCKET MAP D1

Dalston has undergone a seismic transformation, and has now overtaken Shoreditch as London's hippest, grittiest new quartier. Among the early pioneers was the excellent *Vortex Jazz Club* on the frankly sleazy Gillett Square. It was followed by the Arcola Theatre, one of the city's most dynamic fringe venues, now in a paint factory on Ashwin Street, next door to avant-garde music venue *Café OTO*. This trio has been accompanied by bars and clubs along the high street, all helped by the fact that the area's transport links have vastly improved with the expansion of the Overground.

GEFFRYE MUSEUM

Kingsland Rd ⊖ Hoxton Overground ☏ 020 7739 9893, ⊛ www.geffrye-museum .org.uk. Tues–Sun 10am–5pm. Free. MAP P.102, POCKET MAP D3

Hoxton's chief attraction is the Geffrye Museum, housed in a grandiose enclave of eighteenth-century iron-mongers' almshouses. In 1911, at a time

GEFFRYE MUSEUM

COLUMBIA ROAD FLOWER MARKET

when the East End furniture trade was concentrated in the area, the almshouses were converted into a museum for the "education of craftsmen". The Geffrye remains, essentially, a furniture museum, with the almshouses rigged out as period living rooms of the urban middle class, ranging from the oak-panelled decor of the seventeenth century, through refined Georgian to cluttered Victorian style. Beyond lies the museum's modern extension, home to a pleasant café/restaurant and the excellent twentieth-century section. One of the **almshouses** has been restored to its original condition and can be visited (second and fourth Tues of the month, first Sat and first and third Wed; £2.50).

COLUMBIA ROAD FLOWER MARKET

Shoreditch High Street Overground or Hoxton Overground. Sun 8am–3pm. MAP P.102, POCKET MAP O3

Columbia Road is the city's most popular market for flowers and plants; it's also the liveliest, with the loud and upfront stallholders catering to an increasingly moneyed clientele. As well as seeds, bulbs, potted plants and cut flowers from the stalls, you'll also find every kind of gardening accessory from the chi-chi shops that line the street, and you can keep yourself sustained with bagels, cakes and coffee from the local cafés.

WESLEY'S CHAPEL & HOUSE

49 City Rd Old Street 020 7253 2262, www.wesleyschapel.org.uk. Mon–Sat 10am–4pm, Sun 12.30–1.45pm. Free. MAP P.102, POCKET MAP N4

A place of pilgrimage for Methodists from all over the world, Wesley's Chapel was built in 1777, and heralded the coming of age of the faith founded by **John Wesley** (1703–91). The interior is uncharacteristically ornate, with powder-pink columns of French jasper and a superb, Adam-style gilded plasterwork ceiling. Predictably enough, the **Museum of Methodism** in the basement has only a passing reference to the insanely jealous 40-year-old widow Wesley married, and who eventually left him. Wesley himself spent his last two years in Wesley's House, a delightful Georgian place to the right of the main gates. On display inside are his deathbed and an early shock-therapy machine he was particularly keen on.

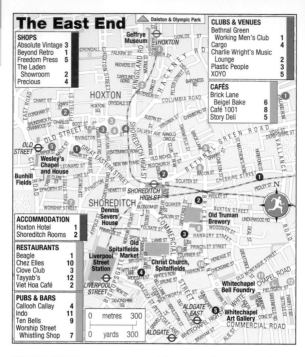

The East End

△ Dalston & Olympic Park

SHOPS
Absolute Vintage 3
Beyond Retro 1
Freedom Press 5
The Laden
  Showroom
Precious 4

CLUBS & VENUES
Bethnal Green
  Working Men's Club 1
Cargo 4
Charlie Wright's Music
  Lounge 2
Plastic People 3
XOYO 5

CAFÉS
Brick Lane
  Beigel Bake 6
Café 1001 8
Story Deli 5

ACCOMMODATION
Hoxton Hotel 1
Shoreditch Rooms 2

RESTAURANTS
Beagle 1
Chez Elles 10
Clove Club 3
Tayyab's 12
Viet Hoa Café 2

PUBS & BARS
Calloh Callay 4
Indo 11
Ten Bells 9
Worship Street
  Whistling Shop 7

0   metres   300
0   yards   300

BUNHILL FIELDS

City Rd ⊖ Old Street. April–Sept Mon–Fri
7.30am–7pm, Sat & Sun 9.30am–7pm;
Oct–March closes 4pm. MAP P.102, POCKET MAP M4

The main burial ground for
Dissenters or Nonconformists
(practising Christians who
were not members of the
Church of England), Bunhill
Fields contains three famous
graves in the central paved
area: the simple tombstone of
poet and artist **William Blake**
stands next to a replica of
writer **Daniel Defoe**'s, while
opposite lies the recumbent
statue of **John Bunyan**,
seventeenth-century author of
The Pilgrim's Progress.

WHITECHAPEL ART GALLERY

80–82 Whitechapel High St ⊖ Aldgate East
☎ 020 7522 7888, ⓦ www.whitechapelgallery
.org. Tues–Sun 11am–6pm (Thurs until 9pm).
Free. MAP P.102, POCKET MAP O5

The East End institution that
draws in more outsiders than
any other is the Whitechapel
Art Gallery, housed in a
beautiful crenellated 1899 Arts
and Crafts building, embellished with gilded leaves by
sculptor Rachel Whiteread.
The gallery puts on some of
London's most innovative
exhibitions of contemporary art
The complex also has a pleasant
café overlooking Angel Alley,
where there's a stainless steel
anarchist portrait gallery
courtesy of the Freedom Press
bookshop (see p.105).

WHITECHAPEL BELL FOUNDRY

32–34 Whitechapel Rd ⊖ Aldgate East ☎ 020
7247 2599, ⓦ www.whitechapelbellfoundry
.co.uk. Mon–Fri 9am–5pm; free. Guided tours
Sat 10am, 1.30pm & 4pm; £12. MAP P.102

Big Ben, the Liberty Bell, the
Bow Bells and numerous
English church bells (including

those of Westminster Abbey) all hail from this foundry, established in 1570. There's a small exhibition on site.

BRICK LANE

⊖ Aldgate East or Shoreditch High Street Overground. MAP P.102, POCKET MAP 04–05

Brick Lane lies at the heart of London's Bengali community, whose inexpensive curry houses dominate the southern end of the street. The red-brick chimney half-way up Brick Lane heralds the **Old Truman Brewery**, founded in 1666 and the largest in the world at the end of the nineteenth century. It ceased operations in 1989 and is now at the centre of a whole series of indoor markets – the Backyard Market and the Sunday Upmarket – all of which are buzzing on Sundays, with stalls selling clothes, accessories, crafts and food. The streets north of the brewery and the railway arches are the venue for Brick Lane's **Sunday market** (Sun 8am–2pm). There are virtually no stalls in Brick Lane itself. Instead, the market extends along Sclater Street and Cheshire Street, with stalls selling everything from household tat to antique furniture – all going for a song.

CHRIST CHURCH, SPITALFIELDS

Commercial St ⊖ Liverpool Street ☎ 020 7377 2400, ⊕ www.ccspitalfields.org. Mon–Fri 10am–4pm. Free. MAP P.102, POCKET MAP 05

Built between 1714 and 1729 by **Nicholas Hawksmoor**, Christ Church features a huge 225ft-high broach spire and giant Tuscan portico. Inside, there's a forest of columned bays, with a lion and a unicorn playing peekaboo on the top of the chancel beam and London's largest Georgian organ.

OLD SPITALFIELDS MARKET

Commercial St ⊖ Liverpool Street. Mon–Wed 10am–5pm, Thurs & Sun 9am–5pm, Fri 10am–4pm, Sat 11am–5pm. MAP P.102, POCKET MAP 05

Spitalfields Market was the capital's premier wholesale fruit and vegetable market until 1991. The western 1920s half of the market was replaced by a Norman Foster office development, although part of the original facade survives on the north side of Brushfield Street. The market now hosts a large, eclectic and fairly sophisticated selection of shops and stalls selling crafts, clothes and food in the original red-brick and green-gabled 1893 building, to the east.

OLD SPITALFIELDS MARKET

DENNIS SEVERS' HOUSE

DENNIS SEVERS' HOUSE

18 Folgate St ⊖ Liverpool Street ☎ 020
7247 4013, Ⓦ www.dennissevershouse.co.uk.
MAP P.102, POCKET MAP D5

Visiting the former home of the American eccentric Dennis Severs (1948–1999) is a bizarre and uncanny theatrical experience, which Severs once described as "passing through a frame into a painting". The house is entirely candle-lit and log-fired, and decked out as it would have been over two hundred years ago. Visitors are free to explore the ten rooms unhindered, and are left with the distinct impression that someone has literally just popped out – Severs called it a "still-life drama". The house cat prowls, there's the smell of gravy bubbling, and the sound of horses' hooves on the cobbled street outside. Daytime visits take place on Sundays (noon–4pm; £10), and selected Mondays (noon–2pm; £7); for the "Silent Night" you must book ahead (Mon & Wed 6–9pm; £14).

The Olympic Park

The focus of the 2012 Olympics was the **Olympic Park** (Ⓦ www .queenelizabetholympicpark.co.uk) laid out over a series of islands formed by the River Lee and its various tributaries and canals. Since the Olympics, the whole area has been replanted with swathes of grass, trees and flowers, and peppered with cafés, making it a great new park in which to hang out on a sunny day. The centerpiece of the park is the **Olympic Stadium**, set to become home to West Ham United football club in 2015. Standing close to the stadium is the **Orbit Tower** (daily: April–Sept 11am–6pm; Oct–March 11am–5pm; £15), a 377ft-high continuous loop of red recycled steel designed by Anish Kapoor. But the most eye-catching venue is Zaha Hadid's wave-like **London Aquatics Centre** (Mon–Fri 6am–9.30pm, Sat & Sun 9am–5pm), four times over budget, but looking very cool and costing under £5 for a swim. Other venues to look out for are the curvy **Velodrome** with its banked, Siberian pine track and adjacent BMX circuit – part of the **Lee Valley VeloPark** (Mon–Sun 9am–10pm; from £15) – and the **Copper Box Arena**, used for handball during the Olympics and now a multi-sports centre (Mon–Sun 7am–10pm; from £5 for non-members). The nearest tube is Stratford, near the Olympic Village (now renamed East Village) and the Westfield shopping centre.

Shops

ABSOLUTE VINTAGE

15 Hanbury St ⊖ Liverpool Street or Shoreditch High Street Overground. Daily 11am–7pm. MAP P.102, POCKET MAP O5

A Spitalfields treasure-trove of Twenties to Eighties clobber, with one of the biggest collections of vintage shoes in the UK.

BEYOND RETRO

110–112 Cheshire St ⊖ Shoreditch High Street Overground. Mon–Wed, Fri & Sat 10am–7pm, Thurs 10am–8pm, Sun 11.30am–6pm. MAP P.102.

Cavernous warehouse of twentieth-century classics, with thousands of goodies including vintage jeans, 1950s frocks, battered cowboy boots, punk gear and disco dolly trinkets.

FREEDOM PRESS

Angel Alley, 84b Whitechapel High St ⊖ Aldgate East. Mon–Sat noon–6pm, Sun noon–4pm. MAP P.102, POCKET MAP O5

Upholding a long East End tradition of radical politics, this small anarchist bookshop is packed with everything from Bakhunin to Chomsky.

THE LADEN SHOWROOM

103 Brick Lane ⊖ Shoreditch High Street Overground. Mon–Fri 11am–6.30pm, Sat 11am–7pm, Sun 10.30am–6.30pm. MAP P.102, POCKET MAP O4

This hip women's clothing store showcases loads of independent designers, and is great for exuberant dressers on a budget.

PRECIOUS

16 Artillery Passage ⊖ Liverpool Street. Mon–Fri 11am–6.30pm, Sat 11am–5pm. MAP P.102, POCKET MAP O5

An elegant little store tucked away in a narrow street near Spitalfields. Cool designer gear with a dressed-up feel, including accessories.

BEYOND RETRO

Cafés

BRICK LANE BEIGEL BAKE

159 Brick Lane ⊖ Shoreditch High Street Overground. Daily 24hr. MAP P.102, POCKET MAP O4

Classic no-frills bagel shop in the heart of the East End – unbelievably cheap, even for fillings such as smoked salmon with cream cheese. Stand at the counter and munch, or take away.

CAFÉ 1001

1 Dray Walk, 91 Brick Lane ⊖ Shoreditch High Street Overground Ⓦ www.cafe1001.co.uk. Daily 6am–midnight. MAP P.102, POCKET MAP O5

Just off Brick Lane, this café has a beaten-up student look, with lots of sofas to crash on upstairs and banks of seating outside, plus simple snacks and delicious cakes to sample. DJ sets nightly (except Mon) and comedy, too

STORY DELI

123 Bethnal Green Rd ⊖ Shoreditch High Street. Daily noon–10.30pm. MAP P.102, POCKET MAP O4

Light-bathed ex-scout hut serving wafer-thin flatbread pizzas (£17, enough for two), topped with gourmet organic goodies. Cards not accepted.

Restaurants

BEAGLE

397–400 Geffrye St ⊖ Hoxton ☎ 020 7613
2967. Mon 6–10.30pm, Tues 6–10.30pm,
Wed–Fri noon–3pm & 6–10.30pm, Sat
11am–3pm & 6–10.30pm, Sun 11am–5pm.
MAP P.102, POCKET MAP 03

Occupying three railway
arches, this Hoxton stalwart
buzzes with a young crowd
enjoying robust Modern British
food and tempting cocktails.
Mains from £10.

CHEZ ELLES

45 Brick Lane ⊖ Aldgate East ☎ 020 7247
9699. Tues noon–3pm, Wed–Sat noon–3pm &
6.30–10.30pm, Sun 11am–5pm. MAP P.102,
POCKET MAP 05

Incongruously set on
curry-house-lined Brick Lane,
this pretty, very French bistro
offers rustic Gallic classics –
onion soup, duck confit, *moules*
– served with charm. Mains
£12.50–17.50.

CLOVE CLUB

Shoreditch Town Hall, 380 Old St
⊖ Old Street ☎ 020 7729 6496. Mon
6–10pm, Tues–Sat noon–2.30pm & 6–10pm.
MAP P.102, POCKET MAP N4

At the vanguard of
Shoreditch's foodie scene,
offering multi-course tasting
menus (£55) and sharing
plates at the bar. Delicious,
inventive cooking.

TAYYAB'S

83–89 Fieldgate St ⊖ Whitechapel ☎ 020
7247 9543. Daily noon–11.30pm. MAP P.102

This smart place has been
serving good, freshly cooked,
straightforward Punjabi food
for over forty years. Prices
remain low, booking is essential
and service is speedy and slick.
Unlicensed but BYOB. Mains
from £7.

VIET HOA CAFÉ

72–74 Kingsland Rd ⊖ Hoxton Overground
☎ 020 7729 8293. Mon–Fri noon–3.30pm &
5.30–11.30pm, Sat & Sun 12.30–11.30pm.
MAP P.102, POCKET MAP 03

Large, chaotic Vietnamese
restaurant in a street heaving
with similar places. Big
portions and lots of spicy
noodle soups to choose from.

Pubs and bars

CALLOOH CALLAY

65 Rivington St ⊖ Old Street. Mon–Wed &
Sun 6pm–midnight, Thurs–Sat 6pm–1am.
MAP P.102, POCKET MAP N4

Hidden away off Shoreditch
High Street, this Jabberwocky-
inspired camp-kitsch cocktail
bar has a Narnia-style
wardrobe separating its wacky
rooms. You'll need to book for
the fab back room.

INDO

133 Whitechapel Rd ⊖ Aldgate East. Daily
noon–1am, Fri & Sat till 3am. MAP P.102

Small and dark bar, with an
ever-changing display of art,
good pizzas and a decent
range of beers. Despite its size,
you can often find a comfortable spot.

CALLOOH CALLAY

TEN BELLS

84 Commercial St ⊖ Shoreditch High Street. Mon–Wed & Sun noon–midnight, Thurs–Sat noon–1am. MAP P.102, POCKET MAP O5

Lively historic Spitalfields pub with beautiful Victorian tiling and a superb Modern Brit restaurant upstairs (booking essential; closed Mon & Tues).

WORSHIP STREET WHISTLING SHOP

63 Worship St ⊖ Old Street. Tues 5pm–midnight, Wed & Thurs 5pm–1am, Fri & Sat 5pm–2am. MAP P.102, POCKET MAP N4

Shabbily opulent cocktail bar with a speakeasy gin palace vibe and a menu of wildly creative cocktails.

Clubs and venues

BETHNAL GREEN WORKING MEN'S CLUB

42–44 Pollard Row ⊖ Bethnal Green ☎ 020 7739 7170, ⓦ www.workersplaytime .net. MAP P.102

At once hip and friendly, this old-school venue offers cool post-war decor and an impeccable booking policy: burlesque, disco, swing, ska, cabaret, indie, the lot.

CARGO

83 Rivington St ⊖ Old Street ☎ 020 7739 3440, ⓦ www.cargo-london .com. Mon–Thurs noon–1am, Fri & Sat noon–3am, Sun noon–midnight. MAP P.102, POCKET MAP N4

Small, popular venue in what was once a railway arch. Hosts a variety of live acts, including jazz, hip-hop, indie and folk, and an excellent line-up of club nights.

CARGO

CHARLIE WRIGHT'S MUSIC LOUNGE

45 Pitfield St ⊖ Old Street ☎ 020 7490 8345, ⓦ www.charliewrights.com. Mon & Sun 6pm–1am, Tues–Fri noon–3pm & 5pm–1am, Sat 6pm–4am. MAP P.102, POCKET MAP N4

Part of old-style – rather than trendy – Hoxton, this convivial bar-club, serving decent Thai food, has excellent jazz, swing and Latin and a late licence.

PLASTIC PEOPLE

147–149 Curtain Rd ⊖ Old Street ☎ 020 7739 6471, ⓦ www.plasticpeople.co.uk. Thurs–Sat. MAP P.102, POCKET MAP N4

Thumping basement club whose cheeringly broad booking policy stretches through techno, Afro-pop and dubstep to reggae.

XOYO

32–37 Cowper St ⊖ Old Street ☎ 020 7354 9993, ⓦ www.xoyo.co.uk. MAP P.102, POCKET MAP N4

Huge Shoreditch club whose legendary weekend club nights and regular live gigs pull in the biggest names in everything from dance music to indie rock.

The Tower and Docklands

One of the city's main tourist attractions, the Tower of London was the site of some of the goriest events in the nation's history, and is somewhere all visitors should try and get to see. Immediately to the east are the remains of what was the largest enclosed cargo-dock system in the world, built in the nineteenth century to cope with the huge volume of goods shipped in along the Thames from all over the Empire. No one thought the area could be rejuvenated when the docks closed in the 1960s, but since the 1980s, warehouses have been converted into luxury flats, waterside penthouse apartments have been built and a huge high-rise office development has sprung up around Canary Wharf.

TOWER OF LONDON

⊖ Tower Hill ☎ 0844 482 7799, ⓦ www.hrp .org.uk. March–Oct Mon & Sun 10am–5.30pm, Tues–Sat 9am–5.30pm; Nov–Feb Mon & Sun 10am–4.30pm, Tues–Sat 9am–4.30pm. £20. MAP PP.110–111, POCKET MAP 07

One of the most perfectly preserved medieval fortresses in the country, the Tower of London sits beside the Thames surrounded by a wide, dry moat. Begun by William the Conqueror, the Tower is chiefly famous as a place of imprisonment and death, though it has been used variously as a royal residence, armoury, mint, menagerie, observatory and – a function it still serves – a safe-deposit box for the Crown Jewels. Before you set off, join one of the free guided tours, given by the Tower's **Beefeaters** (officially known as Yeoman Warders). As well as giving a good introduction to the history, these ex-servicemen relish hamming up the gory stories.

Visitors today enter the Tower along Water Lane, but in times gone by most prisoners were delivered through **Traitors' Gate**, on the waterfront. The nearby **Bloody Tower** saw the murders of 12-year-old Edward V and his 9-year-old brother, and was used to imprison Walter Raleigh on three separate occasions.

The central **White Tower** is the original "Tower", begun in 1076. Now home to part of the Royal Armouries, it's worth visiting if only for the beautiful Norman Chapel of St John, on

BEEFEATER, TOWER OF LONDON

the second floor. To the west of the White Tower is the execution spot on **Tower Green** where seven highly placed but unlucky individuals were beheaded, among them Henry VIII's second and fifth wives.

The **Crown Jewels** are the major reason so many people flock to the Tower, but the moving walkways which take you past the loot are disappointingly swift, allowing you just 28 seconds' viewing during peak periods. The oldest piece of regalia is the twelfth-century Anointing Spoon, but the vast majority of exhibits, including the Imperial State Crown, postdate the Commonwealth (1649–60). Among the jewels are three of the largest cut diamonds in the world, including the legendary Koh-i-Noor, set into the Queen Mother's Crown in 1937.

TOWER BRIDGE

Tower Hill ☎ 020 7403 3761, ⓦ www .towerbridge.org.uk. Daily: April–Sept 10am–6pm; Oct–March 9.30am–5.30pm. £8. MAP PP.110–111, POCKET MAP 07

Tower Bridge ranks with Big Ben as the most famous of all London landmarks. Completed in 1894, its Neo-Gothic towers are clad in Cornish granite and Portland stone, but conceal a

Docklands Light Railway

The best way to visit Docklands is to take the Docklands Light Railway or **DLR** (☎ 020 7363 9700, ⓦ www.tfl.gov.uk/dlr), whose driverless trains run on overhead tracks, and give out great views over the cityscape. DLR trains set off from Bank tube and from Tower Gateway, close to Tower Hill tube and the Tower of London.

steel frame which, at the time, represented a considerable engineering achievement. The **raising of the bascules** (from the French for "see-saw") remains an impressive sight – phone ahead to find out when the bridge is opening (☎ 020 7940 3984). It's free to walk across the bridge, but you must pay to gain access to the **elevated walkways** linking the summits of the towers – closed from 1909 to 1982 due to their popularity with prostitutes and the suicidal. The views are pretty good and you get to visit the **Victorian Engine Rooms** on the south side of the bridge, where you can see the giant, and now defunct, coal-fired boilers and play some interactive engineering games.

TOWER BRIDGE

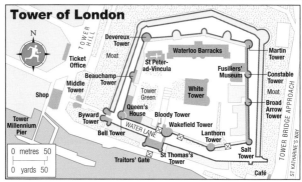

ST KATHARINE DOCKS

⊖ Tower Hill. MAP PP.110–111. POCKET MAP 07

Built in the late 1820s to relieve the congestion on the River Thames, St Katharine Docks were originally surrounded by high walls to protect the warehouses used to store luxury goods – ivory, spices, carpets and cigars – shipped in from all over the Empire. Nowadays, the docks are used as an upmarket marina, and the old warehouses house shops, pubs and restaurants. More interesting, however, are the old **swing bridges** over the basins (including one from 1828), the boats themselves – you'll often see beautiful old sailing ships and Dutch

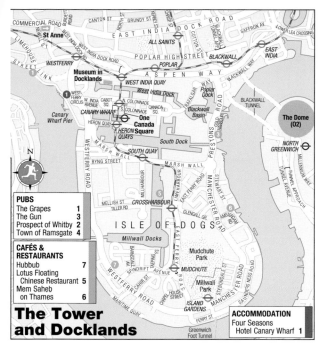

The Tower and Docklands

barges – and the attractive **Ivory House** warehouse, with its clock tower, at the centre of the three basins. At its peak this warehouse received over 200 tons of ivory annually.

WAPPING HIGH STREET

⊖ Wapping Overground. MAP PP.110–111.
Once famous for its boatyards and its three dozen riverside pubs, Wapping's Victorian atmosphere has been preserved, and as it lies just a short walk east of the Tower, this is easily the most satisfying part of Docklands to explore. Halfway along Wapping High Street is **Wapping Pier Head**, the former entrance to the London Docks, flanked by grand, curvaceous Regency terraces. Here, you'll find one of the few surviving stairs down to the river beside the **Town of Ramsgate** pub; beneath the

pub are the dungeons where convicts were chained before being deported to Australia. It was also at the *Town of Ramsgate* that "Hanging" Judge Jeffreys was captured trying to escape disguised as a collier following the victory of William of Orange in 1688.

ST ANNE'S CHURCH

5 Newell St ⊖ Westferry DLR. MAP PP.110–111.
Designed in 1714 by **Nicholas Hawksmoor**, and dominated by a gargantuan west tower, St Anne's boasts the highest church clock in London. Inside is a superb organ built for the Great Exhibition in 1851. In the graveyard Hawksmoor erected a pyramidal structure carved with masonic symbols, now hopelessly eroded; opposite is a war memorial with relief panels depicting the horrors of trench warfare.

CANARY WHARF

⊖ Canary Wharf & DLR. MAP PP.110–111

The geographical and ideological heart of the new **Docklands** is Canary Wharf, once a destination for bananas (from the Canary Islands – hence the name). Now a business district, this is the one Docklands area that you can happily stroll around, taking in the architecture, looking out for the tongue-in-cheek sculptures, and having a drink overlooking one of the old wharves. Canary Wharf's name is, of course, synonymous with Cesar Pelli's landmark tower, officially known as **One Canada Square**. It was Britain's tallest building (before the Shard) and the first skyscraper anywhere to be clad in stainless steel, it's an undeniably impressive sight, both close-up and from a distance.

MUSEUM IN DOCKLANDS

West India Quay ⊖ West India Quay ☎ 020 7001 9844, ⓦ www.museumoflondon.org.uk /docklands. Daily 10am–6pm. Free.
MAP PP.110–111

The last surviving Georgian warehouses of the West India Docks lie on the far side of a floodlit floating bridge at **West India Quay**. Amidst the dockside bars and restaurants, you'll find Warehouse No. 1, built in 1803 for storing rum,

sugar, molasses, coffee and cotton, and now home to the Museum in Docklands. Spread over several floors, the museum's exhibits chart the history of London's docks on both sides of the river from Roman times to the present day. Highlights include a model of old London Bridge, one side depicting it in 1440, the other around 1600; an eight-foot long watercolour showing the "legal quays" in the 1790s, just before the enclosed docks eased congestion; and a reconstructed warren of late nineteenth-century shops and cobbled dockland streets. Those with kids should head for Mudlarks, on the ground floor, where children can learn a bit about pulleys and ballast, drive a DLR train or simply romp around the soft play area.

THE DOME

⊖ North Greenwich. MAP PP.110–111

Clearly visible from the east bank of the Isle of Dogs, the Dome, or O2 as it's currently known (ⓦ www.theo2.co.uk) is a 23,000-seat events arena, designed by Richard Rogers for the millennium celebrations. Over half a mile in circumference, 160ft in height and held up by a dozen, 300ft-tall yellow steel masts, it's the largest of its kind in the world.

THE DOME

Cafés and restaurants

HUBBUB

269 Westferry Rd ⊖ Mudchute DLR.
Mon–Wed noon–11pm, Thurs & Fri noon–
midnight, Sat 10am–midnight, Sun
10am–10.30pm. MAP PP.110-111

A real oasis in the Docklands
desert, this café-bar is housed
in a former church, now arts
centre, and does decent
fry-ups, sandwiches and tapas.

LOTUS FLOATING CHINESE RESTAURANT

9 Oakland Quay ⊖ Crossharbour DLR
☎ 020 7515 6445. Tues–Sun noon–10.30pm.
MAP PP.110-111

This floating Chinese restaurant
moored in Millwall Docks
specializes in steaming hot
fresh dim sum (£2.60–5), duck
and hotpots.

MEM SAHEB ON THAMES

65–67 Amsterdam Rd ⊖ Crossharbour DLR
☎ 020 7538 3008. Mon–Fri noon–3pm &
6–11pm, Sat 6–11pm, Sun noon–4pm &
6–10pm. MAP PP.110-111

Decent riverside Indian
restaurant a short walk from
the business area of Docklands,
with a superb view over the
river. Mains £8–18.

Pubs

THE GRAPES

76 Narrow St ⊖ Westferry DLR.
Mon–Wed noon–3pm & 5.30–11pm,
Thurs–Sat noon–11pm, Sun noon–10.30pm.
MAP PP.110-111

A lovely, narrow little pub
on a quiet street, with lots
of seafaring paraphernalia
and a great riverside balcony
out back. The ales are good
and there's an expensive
restaurant upstairs.

HUBBUB

THE GUN

27 Coldharbour ⊖ Canary Wharf or
South Quay or Blackwall DLR. Mon–Sat
11am–midnight, Sun 11am–11pm.
MAP PP.110-111

Legendary dockers' pub, once
the haunt of Lord Nelson, and
now a classy gastropub. Its cosy
back bar has a couple of snugs,
and the outside deck offers an
unrivalled view of the O2.

PROSPECT OF WHITBY

57 Wapping Wall ⊖ Wapping Overground.
Mon–Thurs noon–11pm, Fri & Sat noon–
midnight, Sun noon–10.30pm. MAP PP.110-111

Steeped in history, this is
London's most famous riverside
pub, with a pewter bar,
flagstone floor, ancient timber
beams and stacks of maritime
memorabilia. Decent beers and
terrific views too.

TOWN OF RAMSGATE

62 Wapping High St ⊖ Wapping
Overground. Daily noon–midnight.
MAP PP.110-111

Dark, narrow, medieval pub
located by Wapping Old Stairs,
which once led down to
Execution Dock. Admiral Bligh
and Fletcher Christian were
regular drinking partners here
in pre-Mutiny days.

South Bank and around

The South Bank has a lot going for it. As well as the massive waterside arts centre, it's home to a host of tourist attractions including the enormously popular London Eye. With most of London's key sights sitting on the north bank of the Thames, the views from here are the best on the river, and thanks to the wide, traffic-free riverside boulevard, the whole area can be happily explored on foot. And a short walk from the South Bank lie one or two lesser-known but nonetheless absorbing sights such as the Imperial War Museum, which contains the country's only permanent exhibition devoted to the Holocaust.

SOUTHBANK CENTRE

Waterloo. MAP P.115, POCKET MAP J17

The Southbank Centre is home to a whole variety of artistic institutions, the most attractive of which is the **Royal Festival Hall**, built in 1951 for the Festival of Britain and one of London's chief concert venues. Even the centre's most architecturally depressing parts are softened by their riverside location, the avenue of trees, fluttering banners, buskers and skateboarders, and the weekend food stalls and secondhand bookstalls outside the nearby **BFI Southbank**, the city's chief arts cinema. It also runs

Mediathèque (Tues–Sun noon–8pm; free), where you can settle into one of the viewing stations and choose from a selective archive of British films, TV programmes and documentaries. For more on the venues within the Southbank Centre see the "Venues" listings on p.119.

NATIONAL THEATRE

Waterloo. MAP P.115, POCKET MAP K17

Looking like a multistorey car park, the National Theatre is an institution first mooted in 1848 but sadly only realized in 1976. It has received endless flak for its architecture, but

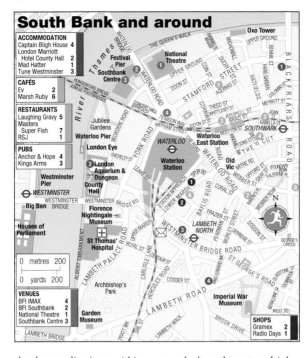

South Bank and around

ACCOMMODATION
Captain Bligh House 4
London Marriott
County Hall 2
Mad Hatter 1
Tune Westminster 3

CAFÉS
Ev 2
Marsh Ruby 6

RESTAURANTS
Laughing Gravy 5
Masters
Super Fish 7
RSJ 1

PUBS
Anchor & Hope 4
Kings Arms 3

VENUES
BFI IMAX 4
BFI Southbank 2
National Theatre 1
Southbank Centre 3

SHOPS
Gramex 2
Radio Days 1

the three auditoriums within are superb and can be visited on excellent **backstage tours** (1hr; £8.50; ☏020 7452 3400), for which you should book in advance.

OXO TOWER

⊖ Southwark. MAP P.115, POCKET MAP L7

The Oxo Tower started life as a Victorian power station before being converted in the 1930s into a meat-packing factory for the company that makes Oxo stock cubes – the lettering is spelt out in the windows of the main tower. The building now contains an **exhibition space** on the ground floor (daily 11am–6pm), plus flats for local residents, sandwiched between a series of retail workshops for designers on the first and second floors, and a swanky restaurant, bar and brasserie on the top floor. To enjoy the view,

you don't need to eat or drink here, however: you can simply take the lift to the eighth-floor **public viewing gallery** (daily 10am–10pm).

STROLLING ALONG THE SOUTH BANK

LONDON EYE

🚇 Waterloo or Westminster ☎ 0871 781 3000, 🌐 www.ba-londoneye.com. Daily 10am–8.30pm, later April–Aug. From £18 online. MAP P.115, POCKET MAP J18

The London Eye is now one of the city's most famous landmarks. Standing an impressive 443ft high, it's the largest **Ferris wheel** in Europe, weighing over 2000 tonnes, yet as simple and delicate as a bicycle wheel. It's constantly in slow motion, which means a full-circle "flight" in one of its 32 pods should take around thirty minutes – that may seem a long time, but in fact it passes incredibly quickly. Book in advance (and online to save money) as on arrival you'll still have to queue to be loaded on.

LONDON AQUARIUM

County Hall, Riverside Walk 🚇 Waterloo or Westminster ☎ 0871 663 1678, 🌐 www.sealife.co.uk. Mon–Thurs 10am–6pm, Fri–Sun 10am–7pm. From £16 online. MAP P.115, POCKET MAP J18

The most popular attraction in County Hall, the vast former council building by the

LONDON AQUARIUM

London Eye, is the London Aquarium, laid out on two subterranean levels. With some super-large tanks, and everything from dog-face puffers and piranhas to robot fish (seriously), this is an attraction that's pretty much guaranteed to please kids. The Touch Pool, where children can stroke the (non-sting) rays, is particularly popular. Impressive in scale, the aquarium also has a walk-through underwater tunnel. Ask at the main desk for the times of presentations.

LONDON DUNGEON

County Hall, Westminster Bridge Rd 🚇 Waterloo or Westminster ☎ 0871 423 2240 🌐 www.thedungeons.com. Mon–Wed & Fri 10am–5pm, Thurs 11am–5pm, Sat & Sun 10am–6pm; longer hours in school holidays. From £17.50 online. MAP P.115, POCKET MAP J18

The newest arrival to County Hall is the ever-popular horror-fest, the London Dungeon. Young teenagers and the credulous probably get the most out of this life-sized tableaux of folk being hanged, drawn and quartered and tortured, the general hysteria being boosted by actors in period garb. Visitors are led through a series of live-action period scenarios, dwelling on the most gruesome London legends from Sweeney Todd to the inevitable Jack the Ripper section, ending with the "Drop Ride to Doom".

FLORENCE NIGHTINGALE MUSEUM

Lambeth Palace Road 🚇 Waterloo or Westminster ☎ 020 7620 0374, 🌐 www.florence-nightingale.co.uk. Daily 10am–5pm; £7.80. MAP P.115, POCKET MAP J19

Hidden among the outbuildings of **St Thomas' Hospital**, the Florence Nightingale

Museum celebrates the devout woman who revolutionized the nursing profession by establishing the first school of nursing at St Thomas' in 1860 and publishing her *Notes on Nursing*, which emphasized the importance of hygiene, decorum and discipline Exhibits include the white lantern that earned her the nickname "The Lady with the Lamp"; Athena, her stuffed pet owl, and a long overdue section on the remarkable **Mary Seacole**, the Jamaican nurse who nursed soldiers in the Crimea itself.

GARDEN MUSEUM

Lambeth Palace Rd ⊖ Westminster or Lambeth North ☎ 020 7401 8865, ⊛ www.gardenmuseum.org.uk. Mon–Sat 10.30am–5pm, Sun 10.30am–4pm. £7.50. MAP P.115 POCKET MAP J9

Housed in the former church of **St Mary-at-Lambeth**, this unpretentious museum puts on excellent exhibitions on a horticultural theme in the ground floor galleries, and has a small permanent exhibition in the belvedere, reached by a new wooden staircase. Two interesting sarcophagi lurk among the foliage of the small

graveyard: one belongs to Captain Bligh, the commander of the *Bounty*; more unusual is the memorial to John Tradescant, gardener to James I and Charles I, depicting, among other things, a seven-headed griffin and several crocodiles.

IMPERIAL WAR MUSEUM

Lambeth Rd ⊖ Lambeth North ☎ 020 7416 5000, ⊛ www.iwm.org.uk. Daily 10am–6pm. Free. MAP P.115, POCKET MAP L9

Housed in a domed building that was, until 1930, the central portion of the infamous "Bedlam" lunatic asylum, the Imperial War Museum holds by far the best collection of militaria in the capital. The treatment of the subject matter is impressively wide-ranging and fairly sober, with the main hall's milita-ristic display of guns, tanks and fighter planes offset by the lower-ground-floor array of documents and images attesting to the human damage of the last century of war. In addition to the static displays, there's a walk-through **World War I trench** and a section telling the story of family life during the Blitz. The museum's **art galleries** on the second floor are well worth a visit for their superb exhibitions of war artists, official and unofficial. Entered from the third floor, the harrowing **Holocaust Exhibition** (not recom-mended for children under 14) pulls few punches, and has made a valiant attempt to avoid depicting the victims of the Holocaust as nameless masses by focusing on individual cases, interspersing the archive footage with eyewitness accounts from contemporary survivors.

Shops

GRAMEX

25 Lower Marsh ⊖ Waterloo. Mon–Sat
11am–7pm. MAP P.115, POCKET MAP K19

This new and second-hand
record store features classical
CDs and vinyl, with some jazz,
and comfy leather armchairs to
sample or discuss your finds
at leisure.

RADIO DAYS

87 Lower Marsh ⊖ Waterloo. Mon–Sat
10am–6pm (Fri until 7pm). MAP P.115,
POCKET MAP K19

Fantastic collection of
memorabilia and accessories
from the 1920s to the 1980s,
including shoes, shot-glass
collections, cosmetics, vintage
magazines and clothes.

Cafés

EV

97–99 Isabella St ⊖ Southwark. Mon–Sat
noon–11.30pm, Sun noon–10.30pm. MAP P.115,
POCKET MAP L7

Ev is a busy, buzzy Turkish
enterprise with a lovely
spacious garden terrace. You
can choose between snacking
in the deli or going for the
full-on restaurant.

MARSH RUBY

30 Lower Marsh ⊖ Waterloo. Mon–Fri
11.30am–3pm. MAP P.115, POCKET MAP K19

Terrific, filling lunchtime
curries for around a fiver: the
food is largely organic/free
range and there's a basic but
cheery communal dining area
at the back.

Restaurants

LAUGHING GRAVY

154 Blackfriars Rd ⊖ Southwark
☎ 020 7998 1701. Mon–Thurs noon–3pm &
5–10pm, Fri noon–3pm & 5–10.30pm, Sat
noon–4pm & 5–10.30pm, Sun noon–4.30pm.
MAP P.115, POCKET MAP L8

Warm, welcoming brasserie
serving a menu of robust
modern English and
Mediterranean food in a
brick-lined dining room with
a cosy, neighbourhood vibe.
Mains £11–21.

MASTERS SUPER FISH

191 Waterloo Rd ⊖ Waterloo ☎ 020 7928
6924. Mon 4.30–10.30pm, Tues–Sat
noon–3pm & 4.30–10.30pm. MAP P.115,
POCKET MAP L8

An old-fashioned, unpretentious fish and chip restaurant,
which serves up huge portions
with all the trimmings:
gherkins, pickled onions,
coleslaw and a few compli-
mentary prawns. Mains
£7.50–13.

RSJ

13a Coin St ⊖ Waterloo ☎ 020 7928 4554.
Mon–Fri noon–2.30pm & 5.30–11pm,
Sat 5.30–11pm. MAP P.115, POCKET MAP K17

Regularly high standards of
Anglo-French cooking make
this a good spot for a meal after
or before an evening at a South
Bank theatre or concert hall.
Mains £12–23.

ANCHOR & HOPE

Pubs

ANCHOR & HOPE

36 The Cut ⊖ Southwark. Mon 5–11pm,
Tues–Sat 11am–11pm, Sun 12.30–5pm.
MAP P.115, POCKET MAP L8

Gastropub that dishes up truly
excellent, yet simple grub:
Modern European and creative,
with mouthwatering puds. You
can't book a table, except for
Sunday lunch.

KINGS ARMS

25 Roupell St ⊖ Waterloo. Mon–Fri
11am–11pm, Sat noon–11pm, Sun
noon–10.30pm. MAP P.115, POCKET MAP K8

Terrific local on a quiet
Victorian terraced street: the
front part is a traditional
drinking area, while the
tastefully cluttered rear is a
glass and wood conservatory-
style space where they serve
good-value and tasty Thai food.

Venues

BFI IMAX

1 Charlie Chaplin Walk ⊖ Waterloo
☎ 0330 333 7878, ⓦ www.bfi.org.uk. MAP P.115,
POCKET MAP K17

Remarkable glazed drum
housing Europe's largest
screen, showing 2D and 3D
films, but like all IMAX
cinemas it suffers from the fact
that very few movies are shot
on 70mm film.

BFI SOUTHBANK

South Bank ⊖ Waterloo ☎ 020 7928 3232,
ⓦ www.bfi.org.uk. MAP P.115, POCKET MAP K17

Known for its attentive
audiences and an exhaustive,
eclectic programme that
includes directors' seasons,
talks and themed series.
Around eight films daily are
shown in the vast NFT1 and
three smaller screens.

NATIONAL THEATRE

NATIONAL THEATRE

South Bank ⊖ Waterloo ☎ 020 7452 3000,
ⓦ www.nationaltheatre.org.uk. MAP P.115,
POCKET MAP K17

The NT consists of three
separate theatres – the
1150-seater Olivier, the
proscenium-arched Lyttelton
and the experimental Dorfman
– and puts on a programme
ranging from Greek tragedies
to Broadway musicals. Some
productions sell out months
in advance, but cheap day seats
go on sale at 9.30am on the
morning of each performance
– get there by 8am for the
popular shows.

SOUTHBANK CENTRE

South Bank ⊖ Waterloo ☎ 0844 875 0073,
ⓦ www.southbankcentre.co.uk. MAP P.115,
POCKET MAP J17

The SBC has three concert
venues. The gargantuan Royal
Festival Hall (RFH) is
tailor-made for large-scale
choral and orchestral works,
and is home to the Philhar-
monia and the London
Philharmonic. The lugubrious
Queen Elizabeth Hall (QEH)
is used for chamber concerts,
solo recitals and contemporary
work, while the Purcell Room
is the most intimate venue.

Bankside and Southwark

In Tudor and Stuart London, the chief reason for crossing the Thames to Southwark was to visit the then disreputable Bankside entertainment district around the south end of London Bridge. Four hundred years on, Londoners have rediscovered the area, thanks to wholesale regeneration that has engendered a wealth of new attractions along the riverside between Blackfriars and Tower bridges and beyond – with the charge led by the mighty Tate Modern. And with a traffic-free, riverside path connecting most of the sights, this is easily one of the most enjoyable areas of London in which to hang out.

MILLENNIUM BRIDGE

Southwark. MAP PP.122-123, POCKET MAP L6-L7

The first new bridge to be built across the Thames since Tower Bridge opened in 1894, the sleek, stainless-steel Millennium Bridge is London's sole pedestrian-only river crossing. A suspension bridge of innovative design, it famously bounced up and down when it first opened and had to be closed immediately for two years for repairs. It still wobbles a bit, but most people are too busy enjoying the spectacular views across to St Paul's Cathedral and Tate Modern to notice.

TATE MODERN

Bankside ⊖ Southwark ☎ 020 7887 8888, Ⓦ www.tate.org.uk. Daily 10am–6pm (Fri & Sat until 10pm). Free. MAP PP.122-123, POCKET MAP L7

Bankside is dominated by the austere power station transformed by the Swiss duo Herzog & de Meuron into Tate Modern, where the Tate shows off its vast collection of international modern art. The best way to enter is down the ramp from the west, so you get the full effect of the stupendously large **turbine hall**, used to display one huge, mind-blowing installation. Given that Tate Modern is the world's

MILLENNIUM BRIDGE

TATE MODERN

largest modern art gallery, you need to devote the best part of a day to do it justice – or be very selective. It's easy enough to find your way around: pick up a plan (and, for an extra £4, a multimedia guide), and take the escalator to level 2. This, and levels 3 and 4, display the **permanent collection**; levels 2 and 3 are also used for fee-paying temporary exhibitions, and level 6 has a rooftop restaurant with a great view over the Thames.

The curators have eschewed the usual chronological approach and gone instead for hanging works according to -isms. On the whole this works very well, though the early twentieth-century canvases, in their gilded frames, do struggle when made to compete with the attention-grabbing conceptual stuff.

Although the displays change every six months or so, you're still pretty much guaranteed to see at least some works by **Monet** and Bonnard, Modigliani, Cubist pioneers **Picasso** and Braque, Surrealists such as **Dalí**, abstract artists like **Mondrian**, Bridget Riley and Jackson Pollock, and Pop supremos **Warhol** and Lichtenstein. There are seminal works such as a replica of the **Duchamp**'s urinal entitled *Fountain* and signed "R. Mutt", Yves Klein's totally blue paintings, and Carl André's infamous "Bricks" (officially entitled *Equivalent VIII*). And such is the space here that several artists get whole rooms to themselves, among them **Joseph Beuys** and his shamanistic wax and furs, and **Mark Rothko**, whose abstract *Seagram Murals*, originally destined for a posh restaurant in New York, have their own shrine-like room in the heart of the collection. There's usually a few surprises, too, such as sections on Soviet graphics or Vienna's violent *Aktionismus* movement, plus plenty of video installations by contemporary artists. You'll also find quite a bit of overlap with Tate Britain, with works by British artists such as Stanley Spencer, Francis Bacon, David Hockney, Barbara Hepworth, Henry Moore and Lucian Freud.

Tate to Tate

The **Tate Boat** shuttles between Tate Britain and Tate Modern every forty minutes; journey time is twenty minutes (£6.50).

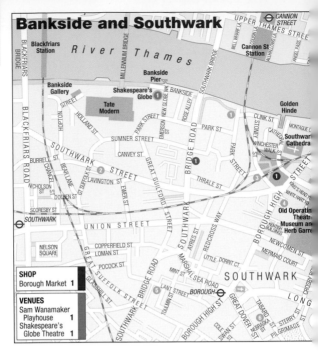

Bankside and Southwark

SHAKESPEARE'S GLOBE THEATRE

21 New Globe Walk ⊖ Southwark or
London Bridge ☎ 020 7902 1400, ⓦ www
.shakespearesglobe.com. Daily 9am–5.30pm.
Exhibition £13.50. MAP PP.122-123, POCKET MAP M7

Dwarfed by the Tate Modern,
but equally remarkable in its
own way, Shakespeare's Globe
Theatre is an open-air
reconstruction of the
polygonal playhouse where
most of the Bard's later works
were first performed. Sporting
the first new thatched roof in
central London since the 1666
Great Fire, the theatre puts on
plays by Shakespeare and his
contemporaries, both outside
and in the new indoor
candle-lit theatre (see p.127).
To find out more about
Shakespeare and Bankside,
visit the Globe's stylish
exhibition, whose imaginative
hands-on displays really hit
the spot. Visitors also get

taken on an informative
half-hour **guided tour** round
the theatre itself, except in the
afternoons during the summer
season, when you can only
visit the exhibition (for a
reduced fee).

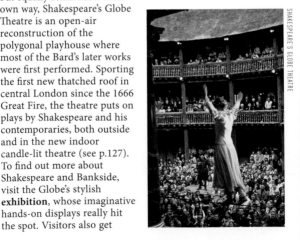

SHAKESPEARE'S GLOBE THEATRE

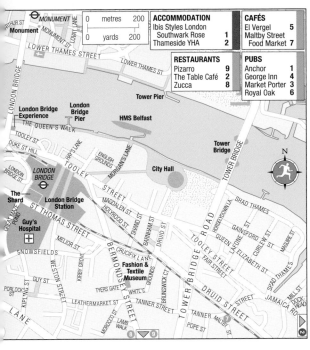

ACCOMMODATION
Ibis Styles London
Southwark Rose 1
Thameside YHA 2

CAFÉS
El Vergel 5
Maltby Street
Food Market 7

RESTAURANTS
Pizarro 9
The Table Café 2
Zucca 8

PUBS
Anchor 1
George Inn 4
Market Porter 3
Royal Oak 6

GOLDEN HINDE

St Mary Overie Dock, Cathedral St
⊖ London Bridge ☎ 020 7403 0123,
ⓦ www.goldenhinde.com. Daily 10am–5.30pm.
£6. MAP PP.122–123, POCKET MAP M7

An exact replica of the galleon in which **Francis Drake** sailed around the world from 1577 to 1580, this modern version of the *Golden Hinde* circumnavigated the globe for some twenty years before eventually settling permanently in Southwark. The ship is surprisingly small, and its original crew of eighty-plus must have been cramped to say the least. There's a lack of interpretive panels, so it's worth booking yourself on a guided tour, during which costumed guides show you the ropes, so to speak, and demonstrate activities such as firing a cannon or using the ship's toilet.

CLINK PRISON MUSEUM

1 Clink St ⊖ London Bridge ☎ 020 7403 0900, ⓦ clink.co.uk. July–Sept daily 10am–9pm; Oct–June Mon–Fri 10am–6pm, Sat & Sun 10am–7.30pm. £7.50.
MAP PP.122–123, POCKET MAP N7

Housed in the suitably dismal confines of an old cellar, this museum explores the history of the former **Clink Prison**, which once stood close by. The prison began as a medieval dungeon for disobedient clerics under the Bishop of Winchester's Palace – the rose window of the Great Hall has survived just east of the museum – and later became a dumping ground for Bankside lowlife, before being burnt to the ground by rioters in 1780. The exhibition features a handful of prison-life tableaux and plenty of graphic descriptions of the torture and horror experienced by the prisoners.

SOUTHWARK CATHEDRAL

Cathedral St ⊖ London Bridge ☎ 020 7367
6734, ⓦ www.southwarkcathedral.org.uk.
Mon–Fri 8am–6pm, Sat & Sun 11am–5pm.
Free. MAP PP.122–123, POCKET MAP M7

Of the original thirteenth-
century Augustinian priory
church of St Mary Overie, only
the choir and retrochoir now
remain, separated by a tall and
beautiful stone Tudor screen;
they're thought to be the oldest
Gothic structures left in
London. The nave was rebuilt
in the nineteenth century, but
the cathedral contains
numerous interesting
monuments, from a thirteenth-
century oak effigy of a knight
to an early twentieth-century
memorial to Shakespeare (his
brother is buried here). Above
the memorial is a stained-glass
window featuring a whole cast
of characters from the plays.

OLD OPERATING THEATRE, MUSEUM AND HERB GARRET

9a St Thomas St ⊖ London Bridge
☎ 020 7188 2679, ⓦ www.thegarret.org.uk.
Daily 10.30am–5pm. £6.50. MAP PP.122–123,
POCKET MAP N7

By far the most educational –
and strangest – of Southwark's

HMS BELFAST

museums is the Old Operating
Theatre. Visitors must climb up
to the attic of a former church
tower, which houses an old
hospital **apothecary**, with
displays explaining the painful
truth about pre-anaesthetic
operations. These took place in
the adjacent women's **operating
theatre**, designed in 1821 "in
the round", literally like a
theatre, so that students (and
members of high society) could
view the proceedings.

THE SHARD

32 London Bridge ⊖ London Bridge
☎ 0844 499 7111, ⓦ theviewfromtheshard
.com. Daily 9am–10pm. From £25 online.
MAP PP.122–123, POCKET MAP N7

It's hard to justify the hubristic
(Qatari-funded) **Shard**,
London's – and the country's
– tallest building, which
houses a mixture of flats,
restaurants, at hotel and a
viewing platform. Even less
justifiable are the ticket prices
to reach the top floors of
Renzo Piano's 1016ft-high,
tapered, glass-clad skyscraper.
Still, once you're there, if you
can ignore the New Age
muzak, the views are sublime,
making everything else in
London look small, from the
unicycle of the London Eye to
the tiny box that is St Paul's
Cathedral, while the model
railway of London Bridge is
played out below you.

LONDON BRIDGE EXPERIENCE

2–4 Tooley St ⊖ London Bridge ☎ 0800
0434 666, ⓦ thelondonbridgeexperience.com.
Mon–Fri & Sun 10am–5pm, Sat 10am–6pm.
From £18 online. MAP PP.122–123, POCKET MAP M7

With the London Dungeon
now in County Hall (see
p.116), Gothic horror fans
should head instead to this
slightly more historically
pertinent scarefest. First off,
it's a theatrical trot through the

CITY HALL

history of London Bridge, with
guides in period garb hamming
up the gory bits. Then, in case
you're not scared enough yet,
in the **London Tombs** section
(no under 11s), more actors,
dressed as zombies and
murderers, leap out of the fog
to frighten the wits out of you.

HMS BELFAST

The Queen's Walk ⊖ London Bridge ☎ 020
7940 6300, ⓦ hmsbelfast.iwm.org.uk. Daily:
March–Oct 10am–6pm; Nov–Feb 10am–5pm.
£14. MAP PP.122-123, POCKET MAP N7

An 11,550-ton **Royal Navy
cruiser**, HMS *Belfast* saw
action both in World War II
and in the Korean War, and has
been permanently moored on
the Thames since 1971. The
most enjoyable aspect of a visit
is exploring the maze of cabins
and scrambling up and down
the vertiginous ladders. If you
want to know more about the
ship's history, head for the
Exhibition Flat in Zone 5; in
the adjacent Life at Sea room,
you can practise your Morse
code and knots and listen to
accounts of naval life on board.

CITY HALL

The Queen's Walk ⊖ London Bridge or
Tower Hill ☎ 020 7983 4000, ⓦ www
.london.gov.uk. Mon–Thurs 8.30am–6pm, Fri
8.30am–5.30pm, plus occasional weekends.
Free. MAP PP.122-123, POCKET MAP N7

Bearing a striking resem-
blance to a giant car headlight,
Norman Foster's startling
glass-encased City Hall is the
headquarters for the **Greater
London Authority** and the
Mayor of London. Visitors
are welcome to stroll up the
helical walkway, visit the café
and watch proceedings from
the second floor. Contact in
advance for access to
"London's Living Room"
on the ninth floor, which
boasts the best views over
the Thames.

FASHION & TEXTILE MUSEUM

83 Bermondsey St ⊖ London Bridge or
Borough ☎ 020 7407 8664, ⓦ ftmlondon
.org. Tues–Sat 11am–6pm, Thurs until 8pm,
Sun 11am–5pm. £8.80. MAP PP.122-123,
POCKET MAP N8

Lifelong dream of Zandra
Rhodes, fashion's *grande dame
extraordinaire*, the FTM is an
arresting sight – daubed in
yellow, pink and orange – on
an otherwise drab street
architecturally. Rhodes
opened her first boutique in
the 1960s and reached her
peak of popularity during the
punk era. Her won sartorial
taste hasn't changed much
since, but thankfully the
museum's exhibitions are
more wide-ranging and are
often drawn from her own
vast collection.

Shop

BOROUGH MARKET

8 Southwark St ⊖ London Bridge. Wed & Thurs 10am–5pm, Fri 10am–6pm, Sat 8am–5pm. MAP PP.122-123, POCKET MAP M7

Fine-food heaven, with suppliers from all over the UK converging to sell organic and artisan goodies from around the world. The Victorian structure, with its slender wrought-iron columns, is lovely. Prices are high and Saturdays can be a crush; arrive early.

Cafés

EL VERGEL

132 Webber St ⊖ Borough. Mon–Fri 8am–3pm, Sat & Sun 10am–4pm. MAP PP.122-123, POCKET MAP M8

Small, very busy café that does all the usual lunchtime takeaways, but you're really here to sample the Latin American specialities such as empanadas (pasties filled with meat and spices or spinach and feta).

MALTBY STREET FOOD MARKET

Maltby St ⊖ Tower Bridge. Sat 9am–4pm, Sun 11am–4pm. MAP PP.122-123, POCKET MAP O8

BOROUGH MARKET

Edgier and less expensive than nearby Borough Market, this street food hot spot huddles under the railway arches near Tower Bridge. Most action is on the lively Ropewalk, with its pop-up bars, cafés and snack stalls.

Restaurants

PIZARRO

194 Bermondsey St ⊖ London Bridge ☎ 020 7378 9455. Mon–Fri noon–3pm & 6–11pm, Sat noon–11pm, Sun noon–10pm. MAP PP.122-123, POCKET MAP N8

Fabulous restaurant run by José Pizarro, one of London's finest Spanish chefs – his sherry/tapas bar, *José*, nearby at number 104, is also terrific. With its short menu of unfussy, beautifully executed food, Spanish wines and sherries, it's at the heart of Bermondsey's foodie scene. Tapas, coffee and pastries served all day. Mains from £13.

THE TABLE CAFÉ

83 Southwark St ⊖ London Bridge ☎ 020 7401 2760. Mon 7.30am–4.30pm, Tues–Fri 7.30am–10.30pm, Sat & Sun 8.30am–4pm. MAP PP.122-123, POCKET MAP L7

Contemporary, casual, canteen-style restaurant, handy for the Tate, serving modern, seasonal food using sustainable, ethically sourced ingredients. The breakfasts and brunches are a real highlight. Mains from £7.50.

ZUCCA

184 Bermondsey St ⊖ London Bridge ☎ 020 7378 6809. Tues–Fri noon–3pm & 6–10pm, Sat noon–3.30pm & 6–10pm, Sun noon–4pm. MAP PP.122-123, POCKET MAP N8

Exceptional modern Italian food, made with the freshest seasonal ingredients, and with huge portions. Mains £11–17.

Pubs

ANCHOR

54 Park St ⊖ London Bridge. Mon–Wed 11am–11pm, Thurs–Sat 11am–midnight, Sun noon–11pm. MAP PP.122–123, POCKET MAP M7

First built in 1770, this sprawling pub retains only a few vestiges of the past, but it does boast a rare central riverside terrace – inevitably it's often mobbed by tourists.

GEORGE INN

77 Borough High St ⊖ London Bridge. Daily 11am–11pm. MAP PP.122–123. POCKET MAP M7

London's only surviving galleried coaching inn, dating from the seventeenth century, and now owned by the National Trust. Expect lots of wonky flooring, half-timbering, a good range of real ales and a fair smattering of tourists.

MARKET PORTER

9 Stoney St ⊖ London Bridge. Mon–Fri 6–8.30am & 11am–11pm, Sat noon–11pm, Sun noon–10.30pm. MAP PP.122–123. POCKET MAP M7

Handsome corner pub by Borough Market, with an interesting range of real ales and decent food. Outrageously popular, as evidenced by the masses that spill out onto the surrounding pavements.

ROYAL OAK

44 Tabard St ⊖ Borough. Mon–Fri 11am–11pm, Sat noon–11pm, Sun noon–9pm. MAP PP.122–123, POCKET MAP M8

Beautiful, lovingly restored Victorian pub that eschews jukeboxes and one-armed bandits, and opts simply for serving a superb stock of real ales (mild, pale and old) from Harveys Brewery in Sussex and some good old-fashioned pub grub.

ROYAL OAK

Venues

SAM WANAMAKER PLAYHOUSE

21 New Globe Walk ⊖ Blackfriars or Mansion House ☎ 020 7401 9919, ⓦ www .shakespearesglobe.com. MAP PP.122–123. POCKET MAP M7

Attached to Shakespeare's Globe theatre, this Jacobean-syle indoor venue presents an intriguing programme of concerts, early theatre and music events – all in an intimate and atmospheric, candlelit space.

SHAKESPEARE'S GLOBE THEATRE

21 New Globe Walk ⊖ Blackfriars or Mansion House ☎ 020 7401 9919, ⓦ www .shakespearesglobe.com. May–Sept. MAP PP.122–123, POCKET MAP M7

This thatch-roofed replica of the famous Elizabethan theatre (see p.122) uses only natural light and the minimum of scenery, and puts on fun, historically authentic and, more often than not, critically acclaimed plays by Shakespeare and his contem-poraries, with "groundling" tickets (standing-room only) for under a tenner.

Kensington and Chelsea

London's wealthiest district, the Royal Borough of Kensington and Chelsea is particularly well-to-do in the area south of Hyde Park. The moneyed feel here is evident in the flash shops and swanky bars as well as the plush houses and apartments. The most popular area for tourists, meanwhile, is South Kensington, where three of London's top museums stand side by side. Further south, Chelsea has a slightly more bohemian pedigree, although these days, it's really just another wealthy west London suburb. To the north, Notting Hill is rammed solid with trendy – but wealthy – media folk, yet retains a strong Moroccan and Portuguese presence, as well as vestiges of the African-Caribbean community who initiated – and still run – Carnival, the city's largest street party.

WELLINGTON ARCH

Hyde Park Corner ⊖ Hyde Park Corner
☎ 020 7930 2726, ⓦ www.english-heritage
.org.uk. Daily: April–Sept 10am–6pm; Oct
10am–5pm; Nov–March 10am–4pm. £4.20.
MAP PP.130–131, POCKET MAP B18

Standing in the midst of one of London's busiest traffic interchanges, Wellington Arch was erected in 1828 to commemorate Wellington's

WELLINGTON ARCH

victories in the Napoleonic Wars. In 1846, it was topped by an equestrian statue of the Duke himself, which was later replaced by Peace driving a four-horse chariot. Inside, you can view an informative exhibition on London's outdoor sculpture and take a lift to the top of the monument, where the exterior balconies offer a bird's-eye view of the surrounding area.

APSLEY HOUSE

Hyde Park Corner ⊖ Hyde Park Corner
☎ 020 7499 5676, ⓦ www.english-heritage
.org.uk. Wed–Sun; April–Oct 11am–5pm;
Nov–March 11am–4pm. £6.90. MAP PP.130–131,
POCKET MAP B18

The former London residence of the "Iron Duke", Apsley House has housed the **Wellington Museum** since 1952. However unless you're a keen fan of the Duke (or the building's architect, Benjamin Wyatt), the highlight here is the **art collection**, much of which used to belong to the King of Spain. Among the best pieces,

displayed in the Waterloo Gallery on the first floor, are works by de Hooch, van Dyck, Velázquez, Goya, Rubens and Murillo. The famous, more than twice life-size, nude statue of Napoleon by Antonio Canova stands at the foot of the main staircase. It was disliked by the sitter, not least for the figure of Victory in the emperor's hand, which appears to be trying to fly away.

HYDE PARK

ⓦ www.royalparks.gov.uk. Daily 5am–midnight.
MAP PP.130–131, POCKET MAP E7

Seized from the Church by Henry VIII to satisfy his desire for yet more hunting grounds, Hyde Park was first opened to the public by James I, when refreshments available included "milk from a red cow". Hangings, muggings and duels, the **1851 Great Exhibition** and numerous public events have all taken place here – and it's still a popular gathering point or destination for political demonstrations. For the most part, however, Hyde Park is simply a leisure ground – a wonderful open space that allows you to lose all sight of the city beyond a few persistent tower blocks.

At the treeless northeastern corner is **Marble Arch**, erected in 1828 as a triumphal entry to Buckingham Palace but now stranded on a ferociously busy traffic island at the west end of Oxford Street. This is the most historically charged spot in Hyde Park, as it marks the site of Tyburn gallows, the city's main location for public executions until 1783, when the action moved to Newgate. It's also the location of **Speakers' Corner**, a peculiarly English Sunday tradition, featuring an assembly of soap-box orators, religious extremists and hecklers.

At the centre of the park is the curvaceous lake of the **Serpentine**. Rowing boats and pedalos can be rented (Easter–Oct daily 10am until dusk; £12/hr) from the boathouse on the north bank, while the lake's popular **Lido** (May Sat & Sun 10am–6pm; June till mid-Sept daily 10am–6pm; £4.50) is situated on the south bank. Nearby is the **Diana Memorial Fountain** (daily: March and Oct 10am–6pm; April–Aug 10am–8pm; Sept 10am–7pm; Nov–Feb 10am–4pm; free), less of a fountain, and more of a giant oval-shaped mini-moat, in which kids can dabble their feet.

Kensington and Chelsea

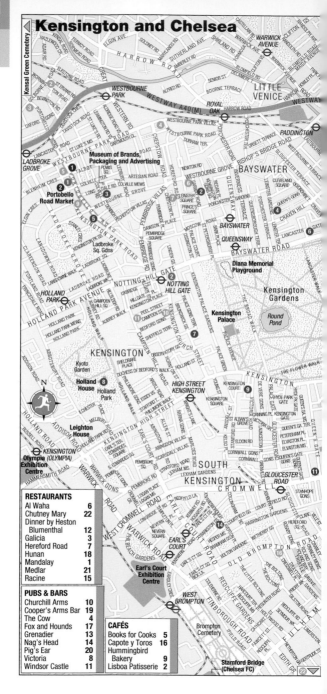

RESTAURANTS

Al Waha	6
Chutney Mary	22
Dinner by Heston Blumenthal	12
Galicia	3
Hereford Road	7
Hunan	18
Mandalay	1
Medlar	21
Racine	15

PUBS & BARS

Churchill Arms	10
Cooper's Arms Bar	19
The Cow	4
Fox and Hounds	17
Grenadier	13
Nag's Head	14
Pig's Ear	20
Victoria	8
Windsor Castle	11

CAFÉS

Books for Cooks	5
Capote y Toros	16
Hummingbird Bakery	9
Lisboa Patisserie	2

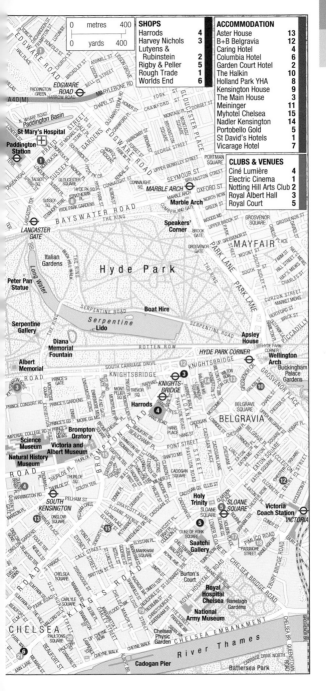

SHOPS	
Harrods	4
Harvey Nichols	3
Lutyens & Rubinstein	2
Rigby & Peller	5
Rough Trade	1
Worlds End	6

ACCOMMODATION	
Aster House	13
B+B Belgravia	12
Caring Hotel	4
Columbia Hotel	6
Garden Court Hotel	2
The Halkin	10
Holland Park YHA	8
Kensington House	9
The Main House	3
Meininger	11
Myhotel Chelsea	15
Nadler Kensington	14
Portobello Gold	5
St David's Hotels	1
Vicarage Hotel	7

CLUBS & VENUES	
Ciné Lumière	4
Electric Cinema	1
Notting Hill Arts Club	2
Royal Albert Hall	3
Royal Court	5

KENSINGTON GARDENS

⊖ Queensway, Lancaster Gate or High Street Kensington Ⓦ www.royalparks.gov.uk. Daily 6am–dusk. MAP PP.130–131, POCKET MAP C7

The more tranquil, leafier half of Hyde Park, Kensington Gardens is home to **Long Water**, the pretty upper section of the Serpentine and the **Italian Gardens**, a group of five fountains laid out symmetrically in front of an Italianate loggia.

One of the park's best-loved monuments is **Peter Pan**, the fictional character who enters London along the Serpentine in the eponymous tale. The book's author, J.M. Barrie, used to walk his dog in Kensington Gardens, and it was here that he met the five pretty, upper-class Llewellyn Davies boys, who wore "blue blouses and bright red tam o'shanters". They were the inspiration for the book's "Lost Boys", and he eventually became their guardian. Barrie himself paid for the statue, which was erected in secret during the night in 1912. More fun for kids (and also inspired by Peter Pan), is the nearby excellent **Diana Memorial Playground**.

To the south of Peter Pan is the **Serpentine Gallery** (daily 10am–6pm; free; Ⓦ www .serpentinegallery.org), which has a reputation for lively and often controversial contemporary art exhibitions. The gallery also commissions a leading architect each year to design a summer **teahouse pavilion**.

The park's most impressive monument by far, however, is the **Albert Memorial**, erected in 1876. It's as much a hymn to the glorious achievements of the British Empire as to its subject, Queen Victoria's husband (he died of typhoid in 1861), whose gilded image sits under its central canopy, clutching a catalogue for the 1851 Great Exhibition. If you want to learn more about the 169 life-sized depictions of long-gone artists (all men) around the pediment, and the various other allegorical sculptures, join one of the monthly guided tours (March–Dec first Sun of month 2pm and 3pm; 45min; £7).

KENSINGTON PALACE

Kensington Gardens ⊖ Queensway or High Street Kensington ☎ 020 3166 6000. Ⓦ www.hrp.org.uk. Easter–Oct daily 10am–6pm; Nov–Easter 10am–5pm. From £15.40 online. MAP PP.130–131, POCKET MAP B8

ALBERT MEMORIAL

Bought by William and Mary in 1689, the modestly proportioned Jacobean brick mansion of Kensington Palace was the chief royal residence for the next fifty years. KP, as it's fondly known in royal circles, is best known today as the place where **Princess Diana** lived from her marriage until her death in 1997. Today, it's the official residence of a number of royals including Prince William and Kate Middleton.

The palace is home to the **Royal Ceremonial Dress Collection**, which means you usually get to see a few of the frocks worn by Diana, as well as several of the Queen's dresses. The highlights of the **King's State Apartment**s are the trompe-l'oeil ceiling paintings by William Kent, particularly those in the Cupola Room, and the paintings in the King's Gallery by, among others, Tintoretto. Also of interest in the King's Gallery is the wind dial above the fireplace, connected to the palace weather vane, which was built for William III and is still fully functioning.

In the more modest Queen's state apartments, the curators have stepped up the multimedia theatrics to tell the sad story of **Queen Anne**, whose eighteen children all pre-deceased her. On the ground floor, you can learn about **Queen Victoria, who** spent an unhappy childhood, under the steely gaze of her strict German mother. According to her diary, her best friends were the palace's numerous "black beetles".

BROMPTON ORATORY

Brompton Rd ⊖ South Kensington ☎ 020 7808 0900. ⓦ www.bromptonoratory.com. Mon–Sat 6.30am–8pm, Sun 7.30am–8pm. Free. MAP PP.130–131, POCKET MAP D9

London's most flamboyant Roman Catholic church, Brompton Oratory was completed in 1886 and modelled on the Gesù church in Rome. The ornate Italianate interior is filled with gilded mosaics and stuffed with sculpture, much of it genuine Italian Baroque, while the pulpit is a superb piece of Neo-Baroque from the 1930s; note the high cherub count on the tester. And true to its architecture, the church practises "smells and bells" Catholicism, with daily Mass in Latin.

NATURAL HISTORY MUSEUM

Cromwell Rd ⊖ South Kensington
☎ 020/7942 5000, ⓦ www.nhm.ac.uk. Daily
10am–5.50pm. Free. MAP PP.130–131,
POCKET MAP D9

With its 675-foot terracotta
facade, Alfred Waterhouse's
purpose-built mock-
Romanesque 1881 colossus
ensures the Natural History
Museum's status as London's
most handsome museum. The
collections are as much an
important resource for serious
zoologists as they are a
popular attraction.

The main entrance leads to
the vast **Central Hall**
dominated by an 85ft-long
plaster cast of a Diplodocus
skeleton. To one side, you'll
find the **Dinosaur** gallery,
where a raised walkway leads
straight to the highlight for
many kids, the grisly life-sized
animatronic dinosaur tableau,
currently a roaring
Tyrannosaurus rex. Other
child-friendly sections include
the **Creepy-Crawlies** room,
which features a live colony of
leaf-cutter ants and the old-
fashioned **Mammals** gallery
with its life-size model of a
blue whale.

For a visually exciting romp
through evolution, head for the
Red Zone (once the Geology
Museum); popular sections
include the slightly tasteless
Kobe earthquake simulator,
and the spectacular display
of gems and crystals in the
Earth's Treasury.

Little visited compared to the
rest of the museum, the **Orange
Zone** is dominated by the
Cocoon, a giant concrete egg
encased within the Darwin
Centre's atrium, and home to
over 20-million specimens. On
the seventh floor visitors can
learn more about the history of
the collection, and, in the
nearby Zoology spirit building,
view a small selection of bits
and bobs pickled in glass jars –
everything from silkworm
larvae to a jar of parasitic
worms from a sperm whale's
stomach.

SCIENCE MUSEUM

Exhibition Rd ⊖ South Kensington
☎ 0870/870 4868, ⓦ www.sciencemuseum
.org.uk. Daily 10am–6pm, till 7pm in school
holidays. Free. MAP PP.130–131, POCKET MAP D9

The Science Museum is
undeniably impressive, filling
seven floors with items drawn
from every conceivable area of
science, including space travel,
telecommunications, time
measurement, chemistry,

measurement, chemistry, photography and medicine. The museum also puts on lively daily demonstrations to show that not all science teaching has to be deathly dry.

First off, ask at the information desk in the Power Hall for details of the day's (usually free) events and demonstrations. Most people will want to head for the four-floor **Wellcome Wing**, with its interactive computers and IMAX cinema (tickets £10). To get there, you must pass through the **Making the Modern World**, a display of iconic inventions from Robert Stephenson's *Rocket* steam train of 1829 to the Ford Model T, the world's first mass-produced car.

If you've got kids, head for the **Launch Pad**, the museum's chief interactive gallery where they can experiment with water, waves, light and sound and build a catenary arch (and knock it down again); "explainers" are on hand to try and impart some educational input.

VICTORIA AND ALBERT MUSEUM

Cromwell Rd ⊖ South Kensington
☏ 020 7942 2000, ⓦ www.vam.ac.uk. Daily 10am–5.45pm (Fri until 10pm). Free.
MAP PP.130–131, POCKET MAP D9

In terms of sheer variety and scale, the **V&A** is the greatest museum of applied arts in the world. Beautifully but haphazardly displayed across a seven-mile, four-storey maze of halls and corridors, the V&A's treasures are impossible to survey in a single visit. Floor plans from the information desks can help you decide which areas to concentrate on.

The most celebrated of the V&A's exhibits are the **Raphael Cartoons**, seven vast biblical paintings that served as designs for a set of tapestries destined for the Sistine Chapel. Close by, you can view highlights from the UK's largest dress collection and the world's biggest collection of Indian art outside India. In addition, there are extensive Chinese, Islamic and Japanese galleries; a gallery of twentieth-century **objets d'art** to rival the Design Museum; and more Constable **paintings** than Tate Britain. And the V&A's temporary shows – for which you have to pay – are among the best in Britain.

Wading through the huge collection of European sculpture, you come to the surreal **plaster casts** gallery, filled with copies of European art's greatest hits, from Michelangelo's *David* to Trajan's Column from the forum in Rome (sawn in half to make it fit). Before you leave, make sure you check out the museum's trio of original refreshment rooms (now back to their original use), the **Morris, Gamble & Poynter Rooms**, at the back of the main galleries.

CAST COURTS V&A

HOLY TRINITY CHURCH

Sloane Square ⊖ Sloane Square ☎ 020 7730 7270, ⓦ www.holytrinitysloanesquare.co.uk. Mon–Sat 8.30am–5.30pm, Sun 8.30am–1.30pm. Free. MAP PP.130–131, POCKET MAP F9

An architectural masterpiece created in 1890, Holy Trinity is probably the finest **Arts and Crafts** church in London. The east window is the most glorious of the furnishings, a vast, 48-panel extravaganza designed by Edward Burne-Jones, and the largest ever made by Morris & Co. Holy Trinity is very High Church, filled with the smell of incense, statues of the Virgin Mary, and confessionals.

SAATCHI GALLERY

King's Rd ⊖ Sloane Square ☎ 020 7811 3070, ⓦ www.saatchi-gallery.co.uk. Daily 10am–6pm. Free. MAP PP.130–131, POCKET MAP E10

On the south side of King's Road, a short stroll from Sloane Square, are the former **Duke of York's Barracks**, now housing upmarket shops and cafés. The main building, erected in 1801 and fronted by a solid-looking Tuscan portico, is home to the privately-run Saatchi Gallery. Its fifteen whitewashed rooms – "a study in blandness" according to one art critic – host changing exhibitions of contemporary art.

ROYAL HOSPITAL CHELSEA

Royal Hospital Rd ⊖ Sloane Square ☎ 020 7881 5200, ⓦ www.chelsea-pensioners.co.uk. Mon–Sat 10am–noon & 2–4pm, Sun 2–4pm. Free. MAP PP.130–131, POCKET MAP F10

Founded as a retirement home for army veterans by Charles II in 1682 and still going strong, the Wren-designed Royal Hospital is worth a visit for the vast, barrel-vaulted **chapel**, with its colourful apse fresco, and the equally grand, wood-panelled **dining hall**, opposite, with its allegorical mural of Charles II and his hospital. In the Secretary's Office, on the east side of the hospital, there's a small **museum**, displaying Pensioners' uniforms, medals and two German bombs.

NATIONAL ARMY MUSEUM

Royal Hospital Rd ⊖ Sloane Square ☎ 020 7881 6606, ⓦ www.nam.ac.uk. Daily 10am–5.30pm. Free. MAP PP.130–131, POCKET MAP E11

Appropriately housed in a sort of concrete bunker, the National Army Museum harbours interesting historical artefacts, plus an impressive array of uniforms and medals (though for a more balanced view of war, you're better off visiting the Imperial War Museum; see p.117). Highlights

SAATCHI GALLERY

include a vast spot-lit model of the **Battle of Waterloo** (at 7pm before the Prussians arrived to save the day); the skeleton of Marengo, Napoleon's charger at the battle; the saw used to amputate the Earl of Uxbridge's leg; a paper lantern used by Florence Nightingale; and Richard Caton-Woodville's famous painting of *The Charge of the Light Brigade*.

CHELSEA PHYSIC GARDEN

Royal Hospital Rd ⊖ Sloane Square
☎ 020 7352 5646, ⓦ www.chelseaphysic garden.co.uk. April–Oct Tues–Fri & Sun 11am–6pm. £9. MAP PP.130–131, POCKET MAP E11

Hidden from the road by a high wall, Chelsea Physic Garden is a charming little inner-city escape. Founded in 1673, it's the second oldest botanic garden in the country: England's first rock garden was constructed here in 1773, and the walled garden contains Britain's oldest olive tree. Unfortunately, it's also rather small, and a little too close to Chelsea Embankment to be a peaceful oasis, but keen botanists will enjoy it nevertheless. There's also a café, which serves afternoon tea and delicious home-made cakes.

PORTOBELLO ROAD MARKET

⊖ Notting Hill Gate or Ladbroke Grove. Main market Mon–Sat 9am–6pm; antiques Sat 8am–6pm. MAP PP.130–131, POCKET MAP A6

Situated in one of the wealthiest, celebrity-saturated parts of town, Portobello Road Market is probably London's trendiest, yet it's always a great spot for a browse and a bargain. Things kick off, at the intersection with Chepstow Villas, with junky antique stalls and classier, pricier antique shops. After a brief switch to fruit and veg around the 1910 **Electric Cinema**, the market

MUSEUM OF BRANDS

gets a lot more fun and funky at Portobello Green under the Westway flyover, where the emphasis switches to retro clothes and jewellery, odd trinkets, records and books. Further up again, the secondhand material becomes pure boot-sale, laid out on rugs on the road. Beyond Portobello Green, **Golborne Road market** (same times as Portobello) is cheaper and less crowded, with some very attractive antique and retro furniture.

MUSEUM OF BRANDS, PACKAGING AND ADVERTISING

2 Colville Mews, off Lonsdale Rd
⊖ Notting Hill Gate ☎ 020 7908 0880, ⓦ www.museumofbrands.com. Tues–Sat 10am–6pm, Sun 11am–5pm. £6.50. MAP PP.130–131, POCKET MAP A6

Despite its rather unwieldy title, it's definitely worth popping into this museum, which is based on the private collection of Robert Opie, a Scot whose compulsive collecting disorder has left him with ten thousand yoghurt pots alone. From Victorian ceramic pots of anchovy paste to the alcopops of the 1990s, the displays provide a fascinating social commentary on the times.

LEIGHTON HOUSE

12 Holland Park Rd ⊖ High Street Kensington ☎ 020 7602 3316, ⓦ www.rbkc .gov.uk/museums. Daily except Tues 10am–5.30pm. £7. MAP PP.130–131, POCKET MAP A9

Leighton House was built by the architect George Aitchison for Frederic Leighton, President of the Royal Academy and the only artist ever to be made a peer (albeit on his deathbed). "It will be opulence, it will be sincerity", the artist opined before construction commenced in the 1860s. The big attraction is its domed **Arab Hall**. Based on the banqueting hall of a Moorish palace in Palermo, it has a central black marble fountain, and is decorated with Saracen tiles, gilded mosaics and latticework drawn from all over the Islamic world. The other rooms are less spectacular but in compensation are hung with excellent paintings by Lord Leighton and his Pre-Raphaelite friends Edward Burne-Jones, Lawrence Alma-Tadema and John Everett Millais.

HOLLAND PARK

⊖ Holland Park or High Street Kensington. Daily 7.30am–dusk. MAP PP.130–131, POCKET MAP A8

Holland Park is laid out in the former grounds of the Jacobean mansion of Holland House – sadly only the east wing survived the war, but it's enough to give an idea of what the place looked like. Several formal gardens are laid out before the house, drifting down in terraces to a café, a restaurant (the former Garden Ballroom) and an art gallery. The most unusual of the gardens is the **Kyoto Garden**, a Japanese-style sanctuary to the northwest of the house, peppered with modern sculpture and complete with koi carp and peacocks.

KENSAL GREEN CEMETERY

Harrow Rd ⊖ Kensal Green ☎ 020 8969 0152, ⓦ www.kensalgreencemetery.com. Daily: April–Sept Mon–Sat 9am–6pm, Sun 10am–6pm; Oct–March Mon–Sat 9am–5pm, Sun 10am–5pm. Free. MAP PP.130–131.

Opened in 1833, Kensal Green Cemetery was the first of the city's commercial graveyards, and contains some of London's most extravagant Gothic tombs. The cemetery is vast, so it makes sense to join one of the **guided tours** that take place most Sundays at 2pm (£7), and include a visit to the catacombs (bring a torch) on the first and third Sunday of the month. Graves of the more famous incumbents – Thackeray, Trollope, Siemens and the Brunels – are less interesting architecturally than those on either side of the **Centre Avenue**, which leads from the eastern entrance on Harrow Road. Worth looking out for are Major-General Casement's bier, held up by four grim-looking turbaned Indians; circus manager Andrew Ducrow's conglomeration of beehive, sphinx and angels; and artist William Mulready's neo-Renaissance extravaganza.

MAJOR-GENERAL CASEMENT'S BIER, KENSAL GREEN CEMETERY

Shops

HARRODS

87–135 Brompton Rd ⊖ Knightsbridge.
Mon–Sat 10am–8pm, Sun noon–6pm.
MAP PP.130–131, POCKET MAP E8

London's most famous
department store is an
enduring landmark of quirks
and pretensions – not least its
draconian dress code (no
clothing revealing intimate
parts of the the body; no
backpacks to be worn on backs,
etc). It's notable for its Art
Nouveau tiled food hall, its
Dodi & Di statue, the huge toy
department and its range of
designer labels.

HARVEY NICHOLS

109–125 Knightsbridge ⊖ Knightsbridge.
Mon–Sat 10am–8pm, Sun noon–6pm.
MAP PP.130–131, POCKET MAP A19

Absolutely fabulous, darling,
with all the latest designer
collections and shop assistants
who look like models. The
gorgeous cosmetics department
is frequented by A- and
Z-listers alike, while the
fifth-floor food hall offers
frivolous goodies at high prices.

LUTYENS & RUBINSTEIN

21 Kensington Park Rd ⊖ Ladbroke Grove.
Mon & Sat 10am–6pm, Tues–Fri
10am–6.30pm, Sun 11am–5pm. MAP P.130–131

Classy bookshop with a
hand-selected array of classics,
titles in translation, poetry, art
books and literary gifts. A
bibliophiles' dream.

RIGBY & PELLER

13 King's Rd ⊖ Sloane Square. Mon–Sat
10am–7pm (Wed until 8pm), Sun noon–6pm.
MAP PP.130–131, POCKET MAP E10

Corsetières to HM the Queen,
if that can be counted as a
recommendation, this store
stocks a wide range of beautiful
lingerie and swimwear, with

HARRODS

designer names as well as its
own range, for all shapes and
sizes. The personal fitting
service is deemed to be
London's best.

ROUGH TRADE

130 Talbot Rd ⊖ Ladbroke Grove. Mon–Sat
10am–6.30pm, Sun 11am–5pm. MAP PP.130–131,
POCKET MAP A6

Legendary indie music
specialist shop, first opened in
1976 at the height of punk/new
wave, with knowledgeable,
friendly staff and a dizzying
array of genres from indie-pop
and electronica to country
and beyond.

WORLDS END

430 King's Rd ⊖ Sloane Square. Mon–Sat
10am–6pm. MAP PP.130–131, POCKET MAP D11

Iconic Vivienne Westwood
outlet, on the shabby end of the
King's Road, from which she
sells clothes, shoes and
accessories from her Anglo-
mania label. In a previous
incarnation, when it was
co-owned by Malcolm McLaren,
it sold proto-punk fetishist gear,
and became a magnet for the
young punks who went on to
form the Sex Pistols.

Cafés

BOOKS FOR COOKS

4 Blenheim Crescent ⊖ Ladbroke Grove.
Tues–Sat 10am–6pm. MAP PP.130–131
Tiny café within London's
top cookery bookshop. It's
cramped but friendly; this is
an experience not to be
missed, with a tasty dishes at
low prices. Make sure you get
there in time to grab a table
for the set-menu lunch
(noon–1.30pm).

CAPOTE Y TOROS

157 Old Brompton Rd ⊖ Gloucester Road
or South Kensington. Tues–Sat 6–11.30pm.
MAP PP.130–131, POCKET MAP C10
Sunny bar with emphasis on
sherries (more than forty
available by the glass), and
interesting tapas (£4.50–12).

HUMMINGBIRD BAKERY

133 Portobello Rd ⊖ Notting Hill Gate.
Mon–Fri 10am–6pm, Sat 9am–6.30pm, Sun
11am–5pm. MAP PP.130–131, POCKET MAP A6
A cute and kitsch place,
this was one of the
forerunners in London's
cupcake craze, and still
specializes in pretty cupcakes
and sumptuous sponges to
take away.

BOOKS FOR COOKS

LISBOA PATISSERIE

57 Golborne Rd ⊖ Ladbroke Grove. Daily
7.30am–7.30pm. MAP PP.130–131
Authentic Portuguese
pastelaria, with the best *pasteis
de nata* (custard tarts) this side
of Lisbon – also coffee, cakes
and a friendly atmosphere.

Restaurants

AL WAHA

75 Westbourne Grove ⊖ Bayswater or
Queensway ☏ 020 7229 0806. Daily noon–
midnight. MAP PP.130–131, POCKET MAP B6
Arguably London's most
authentic Lebanese restaurant;
courteous service and delicious
meze, but also mouth-watering
main course dishes such as
grilled chicken and lamb, sea
bass and red mullet. Mains
£10–17.

CHUTNEY MARY

535 King's Rd ⊖ Fulham Broadway
☏ 020 7351 3113. Mon–Fri 6.30–11.30pm,
Sat 12.30–2.45pm & 6.30–11.30pm, Sun
12.30–2.30pm & 6.30–10.30pm. MAP PP.130–131
Come here for gourmet Indian
food with a modern twist.
Mains £17.50–25; Sunday lunch
buffet £26.

DINNER BY HESTON BLUMENTHAL

Mandarin Oriental Hotel, 66 Knightsbridge
⊖ Knightsbridge ☏ 020 7201 3833. Daily
noon–2.30pm & 6.30–10.30pm. MAP PP.130–131,
POCKET MAP A19
Heston doesn't actually cook
here, but one of his former
Fat Duck chefs serves wildly
imaginative food, using old
English recipes that give you a
once-in-a-lifetime experience.
Mains £28–42.

GALICIA

323 Portobello Rd ⊖ Ladbroke Grove or
Westbourne Park ☏ 020 8969 3539. Tues–Sat
noon–3pm & 7–11.30pm, Sun noon–3pm &
7–10.30pm. MAP PP.130–131

Authentic Spanish restaurant without pretension and with a regular Iberian clientele who enjoy the traditional Galician tapas (£3–7) at the bar. Mains from £8.

HEREFORD ROAD

3 Hereford Rd ⊖ Bayswater or Notting Hill Gate ☎ 020 7727 1144. Mon–Sat noon–3pm & 6–10.30pm, Sun noon–4pm & 6–10pm. MAP P.130-131, POCKET MAP B6

Highly accomplished English cooking focusing on simple, old-fashioned excellence and seasonal produce. Mains from £11.50, and set meals, from £9.50, on weekday lunchtimes.

HUNAN

51 Pimlico Rd ⊖ Sloane Square ☎ 020 7730 5712 Mon–Sat 12.30–2pm & 6.30–11pm. MAP PP.130-131, POCKET MAP F10

Despite the name, this serves Taiwanese/Chinese fusion food. There's no menu: tell them how spicy you like things, and they will bring you a vast array of small dishes. Lunch £32.80, dinner £50.80.

MANDALAY

444 Edgware Rd ⊖ Edgware Road ☎ 020 7258 3696. Mon–Sat noon–2.30pm & 6–10.30pm. MAP PP.130-131, POCKET MAP D5

Pure and unexpurgated Burmese cuisine – a melange of Thai, Malaysian and a lot of Indian. The portions are huge, the service friendly and the prices low. Booking advised in the evening. Mains £4–8.

MEDLAR

438 Kings Rd ⊖ Fulham Broadway ☎ 020 7349 1900. Daily noon–3pm & 6.30–10.30pm. MAP P.130-131, POCKET MAP C11

A lovely Michelin-starred place offering French-influenced Modern British food in a relaxed, welcoming dining room. It's all prix fixe, and excellent value. Three-course lunch £27 Mon–Fri, £30 Sat, £35 Sun; three-course dinner £45 (£35 on Sun).

RACINE

239 Brompton Rd ⊖ Knightsbridge or South Kensington ☎ 020 7584 4477. Mon–Fri noon–3pm & 6–10.30pm, Sat noon–10.30pm, Sun noon–10pm. MAP PP.130-131, POCKET MAP D9

A modern take on a traditional French bistro, serving an array of delicious, nostalgic dishes from the glory days of French cooking. Booking is advised. Mains £13–30; menus from £16.50.

Pubs and bars

CHURCHILL ARMS

119 Kensington Church St ⊖ Notting Hill Gate. Mon–Wed 11am–11pm, Thurs–Sat 11am–midnight, Sun noon–10.30pm. MAP PP.130–131, POCKET MAP B7

Very cosy, quirky, flower-festooned pub serving Fuller's beers, Guinness and good Thai food.

COOPER'S ARMS BAR

87 Flood St ⊖ Sloane Square. Daily noon–11pm. MAP PP.130–131, POCKET MAP E11

Popular, easy-going neighbourhood pub, offering first-rate beer and posh British pub grub. The gussied-up interior features vintage travel posters and a grandfather clock.

THE COW

89 Westbourne Park Rd ⊖ Westbourne Park or Royal Oak. Mon–Thurs noon–11pm, Fri & Sat noon–midnight, Sun noon–10.30pm. MAP PP.130–131, POCKET MAP B5

Owned by Tom Conran, son of gastro-magnate Terence, this boho pub pulls a lively crowd, due in part to its spectacular food, which includes a daily supply of fresh oysters.

THE COW

FOX AND HOUNDS

29 Passmore St ⊖ Sloane Square. Daily noon–11pm. MAP PP.130–131, POCKET MAP F10

On a quiet street near Sloane Square, this tiny Young's pub provides a perfect winter retreat. With its open fire, faux books, oil paintings and relaxed, neighbourhood feel, it's a world away from the glitzier options in these parts.

GRENADIER

18 Wilton Row ⊖ Hyde Park Corner or Knightsbridge. Mon–Sat noon–11pm, Sun noon–10.30pm. MAP PP.130–131, POCKET MAP B19

Located in a cobbled mews, this quaint little pub was Wellington's local (his horse mounting block survives outside) and his officers' mess; the original pewter bar survives and the wood-panelled interior is cosy. Serves real ales and pricey food.

NAG'S HEAD

53 Kinnerton St ⊖ Hyde Park Corner or Knightsbridge. Mon–Sat 11am–11pm, Sun noon–10.30pm. MAP PP.130–131, POCKET MAP A19

A convivial, quirky and raffish little pub in a posh mews, with dark wood-panelling, a mobile phone ban, and a wealth of nostalgic bric-a-brac attesting to its bohemian credentials. The sunken backroom has a flagstone floor. Live jazz performances on Sundays.

PIG'S EAR

35 Old Church St ⊖ Sloane Square. Daily noon–11pm. MAP PP.130–131, POCKET MAP D11

Deep in Chelsea village, *The Pig's Ear* is a lively, stylish panelled gastropub, where you can enjoy excellent craft ales and seriously good British/French food too.

VICTORIA

10a Strathearn Place ⊖ Lancaster Gate
or Paddington. Mon–Sat 11am–11pm,
Sun noon–10.30pm. MAP PP.130–131,
POCKET MAP D6

Fabulously ornate corner pub,
with two open fires, much
Victorian brass and tilework,
and gold-trimmed mirrors.
The Fuller's beer here is
excellent, too.

WINDSOR CASTLE

114 Campden Hill Rd ⊖ Notting Hill Gate.
Mon–Sat 11am–11pm, Sun noon–10.30pm.
MAP PP.130–131, POCKET MAP A7

Popular, pretty, early Victorian
wood-panelled pub with a
large courtyard. Good ales
and classy pub grub – it's a
welcoming spot to come
across, tucked away in the
backstreets of one of
London's poshest residential
neighbourhoods.

Clubs and venues

CINÉ LUMIÈRE

17 Queensberry Place ⊖ South
Kensington ☎ 020 7871 3515, ⓦ www
.institut-francais.org.uk. MAP PP.130–131,
POCKET MAP D9

Predominantly, but by no
means exclusively, French films,
both old and new (sometimes
with subtitles), put on by the
Institut Français.

ELECTRIC CINEMA

191 Portobello Rd ⊖ Ladbroke Grove
☎ 020 7908 9696, ⓦ www.electriccinema
.co.uk. MAP PP.130–131, POCKET MAP A6

One of the oldest cinemas in
the country (opened 1911),
the Electric has been filled
out with luxury leather
armchairs, footstools,
two-seater sofas and an
excellent bar.

NOTTING HILL ARTS CLUB

NOTTING HILL ARTS CLUB

21 Notting Hill Gate ⊖ Notting Hill Gate
☎ 020 7460 4459, ⓦ www.nottinghillartsclub
.com. MAP PP.130–131, POCKET MAP B7

Groovy, arty basement club
that's popular for everything
from Latin-inspired funk, jazz
and disco through to soul,
house and indie.

ROYAL ALBERT HALL

Kensington Gore ⊖ South Kensington or
High Street Kensington ☎ 020 7589 8212,
ⓦ www.royalalberthall.com. MAP PP.130–131,
POCKET MAP C8

Splendid red-brick, terracotta
and marble concert hall built in
1871 that serves as the main
venue for the annual BBC Proms
summer festival of classical
music (ⓦ www.bbc.co.uk
/proms), and also the place for a
whole range of spectacular
popular shows from opera to
pop concerts. Guided tours of
the opulent building itself are
also available (daily: April–Sept
9.30am–4.30pm; £12).

ROYAL COURT

Sloane Square ⊖ Sloane Square ☎ 020
7565 5000, ⓦ www.royalcourttheatre.com.
MAP PP.130–131, POCKET MAP F10

One of the best places in
London to catch radical new
writing, either in the prosce-
nium arch Theatre Downstairs,
or the smaller-scale Theatre
Upstairs studio space.

Regent's Park and Camden

Framed by dazzling Nash-designed, magnolia-stuccoed terraces, and home to London Zoo, Regent's Park is a very civilized and well-maintained spot. Nearby Camden, by contrast, has a scruffy feel to it, despite its many well-to-do residential streets. This is partly due to the chaos and fall-out from the area's perennially popular weekend market, centred around Camden Lock on the Regent's Canal. A warren of stalls with an alternative past still manifest in its quirky wares, street fashion, books, records and ethnic goods, the market remains one of the city's best-known off-beat attractions.

REGENT'S PARK

⊖ Regent's Park, Great Portland Street or Baker Street ⓦ www.royalparks.org.uk. MAP P.145, POCKET MAP E4–F4

It was under the Prince Regent (later George IV) that Regent's Park began to take its current form – hence its official title – and the public weren't allowed in until 1845 (and even then for just two days of the week). According to John Nash's 1811 masterplan, the park was to be girded by a continuous belt of terraces, and sprinkled with a total of 56 villas, including a magnificent pleasure palace for the prince himself. The plan was never fully realized, but enough was built to create something of the idealized garden city that Nash and the Prince Regent envisaged. Pristine, mostly Neoclassical terraces form a near-unbroken horseshoe around the Outer Circle, which marks the park's perimeter along with a handful of handsome villas.

By far the prettiest section of the park is **Queen Mary's Gardens**, within the central Inner Circle. As well as a pond replete with exotic ducks, and a

REGENT'S PARK

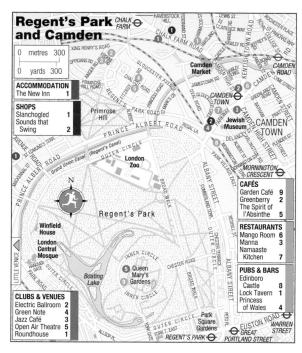

Regent's Park and Camden

CHALK FARM
HAVERSTOCK HILL

| 0 | metres | 300 |
| 0 | yards | 300 |

ACCOMMODATION
The New Inn ... 1

SHOPS
Slanchogled ... 1
Sounds that Swing ... 2

Primrose Hill

Camden Market

CAMDEN TOWN

Jewish Museum

CAMDEN TOWN

London Zoo

Regent's Park

MORNINGTON CRESCENT

Winfield House

London Central Mosque

Queen Mary's Gardens

Boating Lake

CAFÉS
Garden Café ... 9
Greenberry ... 2
The Spirit of l'Absinthe ... 5

RESTAURANTS
Mango Room ... 6
Manna ... 3
Namaaste Kitchen ... 7

PUBS & BARS
Edinboro Castle ... 8
Lock Tavern ... 1
Princess of Wales ... 4

CLUBS & VENUES
Electric Ballroom ... 2
Green Note ... 4
Jazz Café ... 3
Open Air Theatre ... 5
Roundhouse ... 1

Park Square Gardens

REGENT'S PARK

WARREN STREET

EUSTON ROAD

GREAT PORTLAND STREET

handsomely landscaped giant rockery, a large slice of the gardens is taken up with a glorious **rose garden**, featuring some 400 varieties surrounded by a ring of ramblers. Along the eastern edge of the park, the tree-lined **Broad Walk** forms a stately approach (much appreciated by rollerbladers) to the park's most popular attraction, London Zoo.

LONDON CENTRAL MOSQUE

146 Park Rd, Regent's Park ⊖ St John's Wood or Marylebone ☎ 020 7725 2212. ⓦ www.iccuk.org. MAP P.145, POCKET MAP E4

Prominent on the Regent's Park skyline is the shiny copper dome and minaret of the London Central Mosque, an entirely appropriate addition to the park given the Prince Regent's taste for the Orient. Non-Muslim visitors are welcome to look in

at the permanent exhibition on Islam, and glimpse at the beautiful chandelier inside the hall of worship, which is packed out with a diversity of communities for the Friday lunchtime prayers.

LONDON CENTRAL MOSQUE

Regent's Canal by boat

Three companies run daily boat services on the Regent's Canal between Camden and Little Venice, passing through the Maida Hill tunnel. The narrowboat **Jenny Wren** (March Sat & Sun; April–Oct daily; ☎020 7485 4433, ⓦwww.walkersquay.com) starts off at Camden, goes through a canal lock and heads for Little Venice, while **Jason's** narrowboats (April–Oct daily; ☎020 7286 3428, ⓦwww.jasons.co.uk) start off at Little Venice (both have live commentary); the **London Waterbus Company** (April–Sept daily; Oct Thurs–Sun only; Nov–March Sat & Sun; ☎020 7482 2550, ⓦwww.londonwaterbus.com) sets off from both places and calls in at London Zoo en route. Whichever you choose, you can board at either end; tickets cost around £12 return, and journey time is 45 minutes one-way.

REGENT'S CANAL

⊖ Warwick Avenue or Camden Town.
MAP P.145, POCKET MAP J2–A4

The Regent's Canal, completed in 1820, was constructed as part of a direct link from Birmingham to the newly built London Docks. After an initial period of heavy usage it was overtaken by the railway, and never really paid its way as its investors had hoped. By some miracle, however, it survived, and its nine miles, 42 bridges, twelve locks and two tunnels stand as a reminder of another age. The lock-less stretch of the canal between Little Venice and Camden Town is the busiest, most attractive section, tunnelling through to Lisson Grove, skirting Regent's Park, offering views of London Zoo, and passing straight through the heart of Camden Market. It's also the one section that's served by scheduled narrowboats (see box above). Alternatively, you can cycle, walk or jog along the towpath.

LONDON ZOO

Outer Circle, Regent's Park ⊖ Camden Town ☎ 0844 225 1826, ⓦ www.zsl.org /zsl-london-zoo. Daily: March–Oct 10am–6pm; Nov–Feb 10am–4pm. £22. MAP P.145, POCKET MAP F3

The northeastern corner of Regent's Park, is occupied by London Zoo. Founded in 1826 with the remnants of the royal menagerie, the enclosures here are as humane as any inner-city zoo could make them, and kids usually enjoy themselves. In particular they love **Animal Adventure**, the children's zoo (and playground) where they can actually handle the animals, and the regular "Animals in Action" live shows. The invertebrate house, now known as **BUGS**, the **Gorilla Kingdom**, the **African Bird Safari** and the walk-through rainforest and monkey enclosure are also guaranteed winners. The zoo boasts some striking architectural features, too, such as the 1930s modernist, spiral-ramped concrete former **penguin pool** (where Penguin Books' original colophon was sketched), designed by the Tecton partnership, led by Berthold Lubetkin, who also made the zoo's Round House. The **Giraffe House**, by contrast, was designed in Neoclassical style by Decimus Burton, who was also responsible for the mock-Tudor Clock Tower. Other landmark features are the mountainous **Mappin Terraces**, from just before World War I, and the colossal tetrahedral aluminium-framed tent of Lord Snowdon's modern **aviary**.

GORILLA KINGDOM, LONDON ZOO

CAMDEN MARKET

⊖ Camden Town ⓦ www.camdenlock.net. Most stalls open daily 9.30am–5.30pm. MAP P.145, POCKET MAP F1–G2

For all its tourist popularity, Camden Market (in actual fact, a conglomeration of markets) remains a genuinely offbeat place. The tiny crafts market, which began in the 1970s in the cobbled courtyard by **Camden Lock**, has since mushroomed out of all proportion, with everyone trying to grab a piece of the action on both sides of Camden High Street and Chalk Farm Road. More than 100,000 shoppers turn up here each weekend, and some stalls now stay open all week long, alongside a crop of shops, cafés and bistros. The overabundance of cheap leather goods, hats, trainers, incense and naff jewellery is compensated for by the sheer variety of what's on offer: everything from bootleg tapes to furniture and mountain bikes, alongside a mass of clubwear and street-fashion stalls. And there are plenty of takeaway food outlets ready to fuel hungry shoppers with wok-fried noodles, bowls of paella, burgers, kebabs, cakes and smoothies.

JEWISH MUSEUM

129 Albert St ⊖ Camden Town ☎ 020 7284 7384, ⓦ www.jewishmuseum.org.uk. Mon–Thurs & Sun 10am–5pm, Fri 10am–2pm. £7.50. MAP P.145, POCKET MAP G2

Despite having no significant Jewish associations, Camden is home to London's purpose-built Jewish Museum. On the first floor, there's an engaging exhibition explaining Jewish practices and illustrated by cabinets of Judaica. On the second floor, there's a special Holocaust gallery, which tells the story of Leon Greenman (1920–2008), one of only two British Jews who suffered and survived Auschwitz. The museum also puts on a lively programme of special exhibitions, discussions and concerts, and has a café on the ground floor.

Shops

SLANCHOGLED

66 Chalk Farm Rd ⊖ Chalk Farm.
Mon–Sat 10am–6pm, Sun 11am–6pm.
MAP P.145, POCKET MAP F1

Unusual, sunny shop selling arts and crafts materials – paper and inks, ribbons and transfers, anything you can imagine – with lots of creative ideas to inspire.

SOUNDS THAT SWING

88 Parkway ⊖ Camden Town. Mon–Sat 11am–6pm, Sun noon–6pm. MAP P.145, POCKET MAP G2

The bricks-and-mortar store of No Hit Records offers an impeccable selection of retro rockabilly, blues, gospel, ska and the like on vinyl.

Cafés

GARDEN CAFÉ

Inner Circle, Regent's Park ⊖ Baker Street.
Daily 9am–8pm. MAP P.145, POCKET MAP F4

Classic 1960s modernist building with lots of outdoor seating. It's run by the classy Benugo group and serves Modern European café food.

GREENBERRY

101 Regents Park Rd ⊖ Chalk Farm.
Tues–Sat 9am–10pm, Sun & Mon 9am–4pm.
MAP P.145, POCKET MAP E1

This buzzy neighbourhood bistro serves fresh, creative food with global influences, plus home-made ice cream. Dishes £5–20.

THE SPIRIT OF L'ABSINTHE

41 Chalcot Rd ⊖ Chalk Farm. Mon–Fri 8am–6pm, Sat 9am–4pm. MAP P.145, POCKET MAP F2

Pretty little French café (with restaurant attached) offering scrumptious baguettes, tarts, patisserie and *croques monsieurs*. On Sundays the restaurant serves breakfast (till noon).

Restaurants

MANGO ROOM

10 Kentish Town Rd ⊖ Camden Town
☎ 020 7482 5065. Daily noon–11pm.
MAP P.145, POCKET MAP G2

An engaging, laid-back Caribbean place dishing up smart versions of ackee and saltfish, curried goat and jerk chicken. Mains £10–16.

MANNA

4 Erskine Rd ⊖ Chalk Farm ☎ 020 7722 8028. Tues–Fri noon–3pm & 6.30–10pm, Sat noon–3pm & 6–10pm, Sun noon–8.30pm.
MAP P.145, POCKET MAP E1

Smart restaurant serving large portions of very good veggie and vegan food from around the world. Mains £12–14.

NAMAASTE KITCHEN

64 Parkway ⊖ Camden Town ☎ 020 7485 5977. Mon–Thurs noon–2.30pm & 5.30–11.30pm, Fri & Sat noon–11.30pm, Sun noon–11pm. MAP P.145, POCKET MAP G2

Superb modern Indian restaurant presenting unusual dishes such as wild rabbit *achari*. Mains £9–17, thalis £7.50.

Pubs and bars

EDINBORO CASTLE

57 Mornington Terrace ⊖ Camden Town.
Mon–Sat noon–11pm, Sun noon–10.30pm.
MAP P.145, POCKET MAP G2

A huge pub with a gastro menu and a large, leafy beer garden which hosts summer weekend barbecues.

LOCK TAVERN

35 Chalk Farm Rd ⊖ Chalk Farm. Mon–Thurs noon–midnight, Fri & Sat noon–1am, Sun noon–11pm. MAP P.145, POCKET MAP F1

Rambling pub with comfy sofas, a leafy terrace upstairs and beer garden below, hipster pub grub and DJs playing anything from punk, funk and electro to avant-country.

PRINCESS OF WALES

22 Chalcot Rd ⊖ Chalk Farm. Mon–Sat 9am–midnight, Sun 9am–11.30pm. MAP P.145, POCKET MAP F2

Smart, popular gastropub with excellent food and regular live jazz. Get here early to eat in the pub, or book a table in the dining room or lovely garden.

Clubs and venues

ELECTRIC BALLROOM

184 Camden High St ⊖ Camden Town
☎ 020 7485 9006, Ⓦ www.electricballroom
.co.uk. MAP P.145, POCKET MAP G2

Long-running, grungy club that hosts rock and metal, disco nights (Sat), and several gigs a week.

GREEN NOTE

106 Parkway ⊖ Camden Town ☎ 020 7485 9899, Ⓦ www.greennote.co.uk. MAP P.145, POCKET MAP G2

Intimate music venue that punches way above its weight

OPEN AIR THEATRE, REGENT'S PARK

with its excellent roots, folk and world music.

JAZZ CAFÉ

5 Parkway ⊖ Camden Town ☎ 020 7485 6834, Ⓦ www.mamacolive.com/thejazzcafe. Daily 7pm–2am. Entry from £10. MAP P.145, POCKET MAP G2

Buzzing venue whose adventurous music policy explores Latin, funk and hip-hop, as well as jazz. If you fancy a sit-down book a seat at one of the restaurant tables. Late-night club sessions start at 10.30pm on Fri and Sat.

OPEN AIR THEATRE

Regent's Park, Inner Circle ⊖ Baker Street ☎ 0844 826 4242, Ⓦ www.openairtheatre.com. MAP P.145, POCKET MAP F4

This beautiful space in Regent's Park hosts a tourist-friendly summer programme of Shakespeare, musicals, plays and concerts; perfect when the weather's good.

ROUNDHOUSE

Chalk Farm Rd ⊖ Chalk Farm ☎ 0844 482 8008, Ⓦ www.roundhouse.org.uk. MAP P.145, POCKET MAP F1

Camden's barn-like former engine shed puts on a variety of theatrical spectacles, circus performances and live gigs.

Hampstead and Highgate

The high points of north London, both geographically and aesthetically, the elegant, largely eighteenth-century developments of Hampstead and Highgate have managed to cling on to their village origins. Of the two, Highgate is slightly sleepier and more aloof, Hampstead busier and buzzier, with high-profile intelligentsia and discerning pop stars among its residents. Both benefit from direct access to one of London's wildest patches of greenery, Hampstead Heath, where you can enjoy stupendous views over London, as well as outdoor concerts and high art in and around the country mansion of Kenwood House.

HAMPSTEAD HEATH

Gospel Oak or Hampstead Heath Overground, or ⊖ Hampstead or Golders Green.
MAP PP.152–153

Hampstead Heath is the city's most enjoyable public park, with a wonderful variety of bucolic scenery across its 800 acres. At the park's southern end are the rolling green pastures of **Parliament Hill**, north London's premier spot for kite-flying. On either side are numerous **ponds**, three of which – one for men, one for women and one mixed – you can swim in (daily 7am–9pm or dusk). The thickest woodland is to be found in the West Heath, also the site of the most formal section, **Hill Garden**, a secretive and romantic little gem with eccentric balustraded terraces and a ruined pergola. Beyond lies **Golders Hill Park**, where you can gaze at pygmy goats and fallow deer, and inspect the impeccably maintained aviaries, home to flamingos, cranes and other exotic birds.

The Heath's most celebrated sight is the whitewashed Neoclassical mansion of **Kenwood House** (daily 10am–5pm; free; Ⓦwww .english-heritage.org.uk), set in its own magnificently landscaped grounds at the high point of the Heath. The house is

KENWOOD HOUSE, HAMPSTEAD HEATH

home to a superlative collection of seventeenth- and eighteenth-century art, including masterpieces by Vermeer, Rembrandt, Boucher, Gainsborough and Reynolds. Of the period interiors, the most spectacular is Robert Adam's sky-blue and gold library, its book-filled apses separated from the central entertaining area by paired columns.

FENTON HOUSE

KEATS HOUSE

Keats Grove ⊖ Hampstead or Hampstead Heath Overground ☎ 020 7332 3868, ⓦ www.cityoflondon.gov.uk. March–Oct Tues–Sun 1–5pm; Nov–Feb Fri–Sun 1–5pm. £5.50. MAP PP.152–153

An elegant, whitewashed Regency double villa, Keats House is a shrine to Hampstead's most lustrous figure. Inspired by the tranquillity of the area and by his passion for girl-next-door Fanny Brawne (whose house is also part of the museum), Keats wrote some of his most famous works here before leaving for Rome, where he died of consumption in 1821 aged just 25. The neat, rather staid interior contains books and letters, Fanny's engagement ring and the four-poster bed in which the poet first coughed up blood.

2 WILLOW ROAD

⊖ Hampstead or Hampstead Heath Overground ☎ 020 7435 6166, ⓦ www.nationaltrust.org.uk. March–Nov Wed–Sun 11am–5pm. £6. MAP PP.152–153

An unassuming red-brick terraced house built in the 1930s by the Hungarian-born architect **Ernö Goldfinger** (1902–87), 2 Willow Road gives a fascinating insight into the modernist mindset. This was a state-of-the-art pad when Goldfinger moved in, and as he changed little during

the following fifty years, what you see today is a 1930s avant-garde dwelling preserved in aspic, a house at once both modern and old-fashioned. An added bonus is that the rooms are packed with **works of art** by the likes of Bridget Riley, Duchamp, Henry Moore and Man Ray. Before 3pm, visits are by hour-long guided tour only (noon, 1 and 2pm); after 3pm the public has unguided, unrestricted access.

FENTON HOUSE

Windmill Hill ⊖ Hampstead ☎ 020 7435 3471, ⓦ www.nationaltrust.org.uk. March–Nov Wed–Sun 11am–5pm. £6.50. MAP PP.152–153

Decorated in the eighteenth-century taste, grand Fenton House is home to a collection of European and Oriental ceramics, as well as a superb collection of **early musical instruments**. Experienced keyboard players are occasionally let loose on some of the instruments during the day and you can book tickets for one of the occasional **concerts**. Tickets for the house also allow you to take a stroll in the beautiful orchard, kitchen garden and formal **garden** (garden only; £2), which features some top-class topiary and herbaceous borders.

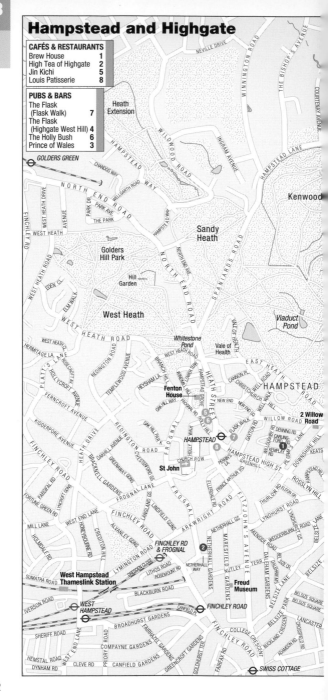

Hampstead and Highgate

CAFÉS & RESTAURANTS
Brew House	1
High Tea of Highgate	2
Jin Kichi	5
Louis Patisserie	8

PUBS & BARS
The Flask (Flask Walk)	7
The Flask (Highgate West Hill)	4
The Holly Bush	6
Prince of Wales	3

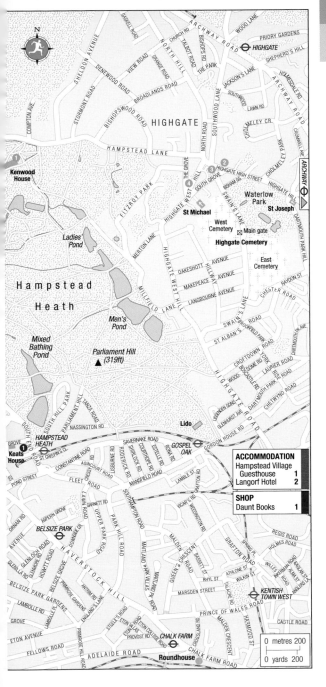

FREUD MUSEUM

20 Maresfield Gardens ⊖ Finchley Road. ☎ 020 7435 2002, ⓦ www.freud.org.uk. Wed–Sun noon–5pm. £7. MAP PP.152–153.

Hidden away in the leafy streets of south Hampstead, the Freud Museum is one of the most poignant of London's museums. Having lived in Vienna for his entire adult life, **Sigmund Freud** was forced to flee the Nazis, and arrived in London during the summer of 1938 as a semi-invalid (he died within a year). The ground-floor study and library look exactly as they did when Freud lived here – the collection of erotic antiquities and the famous couch, sumptuously draped in Persian carpets, were all brought here from Vienna. Upstairs, home movies of family life in Vienna are shown continually, and a small room is dedicated to his daughter, Anna, herself an influential child analyst, who lived in the house until her death in 1982.

HIGHGATE CEMETERY

Swain's Lane ⊖ Archway ☎ 020 8340 1834, ⓦ www.highgatecemetery.org. MAP PP.152–153.

Receiving far more visitors than Highgate itself, Highgate Cemetery is London's most famous graveyard. The most illustrious incumbent of the **East Cemetery** (April–Oct Mon–Fri 10am–5pm, Sat and Sun 11am–5pm; Nov–March closes 4pm; £4) is **Karl Marx**. Erected by the Communist movement in 1954, his vulgar bronze bust surmounting a granite plinth is a far cry from the unfussy memorial he had requested; close by lies the much simpler grave of the author George Eliot. The East Cemetery's lack of atmosphere is in part compensated for by the fact that you can wander at will through its maze of circuitous paths.

On the other side of Swain's Lane, the overgrown **West Cemetery**, with its spooky Egyptian Avenue and terraced catacombs, is the ultimate Hammer Horror graveyard, and one of the city's most impressive sights. Visitors can only enter by way of a **guided tour** (March–Nov Mon–Fri 1.45pm, Sat and Sun every 30min 11am–4pm; £12; no under 8s) – get there early on summer Sundays. Among the prominent graves usually visited are those of artist Dante Gabriel Rossetti, and of lesbian novelist Radclyffe Hall.

Shop

DAUNT BOOKS

51 South End Rd ⊖ Hampstead Heath.
Mon–Sat 9am–6pm, Sun 11am–6pm.
MAP PP.152–153

Hampstead branch of this
excellent bookshop, which is
strong on guidebooks, travel
writing and fiction, and has a
good kids' section.

Cafés and restaurants

BREW HOUSE

Kenwood House, Hampstead Heath. Bus
#210 from ⊖ Archway. Daily: spring &
summer 9am–6pm; autumn & winter
9am–4pm. MAP PP.152–153

Everything from full English
breakfast to lunches, cakes and
teas, either served in the old
laundry at Kenwood, or enjoyed
in the sunny garden courtyard.

HIGH TEA OF HIGHGATE

50 Highgate High St. Bus #210 from
⊖ Archway. Tues 1–6pm, Wed, Thurs,
Sat & Sun 11am–6pm, Fri 8.30am–6pm.
MAP PP.152–153

Half-modern, half-retro
tearoom serving proper
loose-leaf tea and gorgeous
home-made cakes.

JIN KICHI

73 Heath St ⊖ Hampstead ☎ 020 7794
6158. Tues–Sun 12.30–2pm & 6–10.45pm,
Sun closes 10pm. MAP PP.152–153

Cramped, homely and very
busy (so book ahead), *Jin Kichi*
has a vast menu with almost
every Japanese dish, though it
specializes in grilled skewers of
meat. Mains £6–12.

LOUIS PATISSERIE

32 Heath St ⊖ Hampstead. Daily 9am–6pm.
MAP PP.152–153

This tiny, understated,
old-fashioned Hungarian
tearoom/patisserie has long
been serving sticky cakes, tea
and coffee to a mixed crowd.

Pubs

THE FLASK

14 Flask Walk ⊖ Hampstead. Mon–Thurs
11am–11pm, Fri & Sat 11am–midnight, Sun
noon–10.30pm. MAP PP.152–153

Convivial Young's pub, tucked
down one of Hampstead's
more atmospheric lanes, that
retains much of its original
Victorian interior.

THE FLASK

77 Highgate West Hill. Bus #210 from
⊖ Archway. Mon–Sat noon–11pm, Sun
noon–10.30pm. MAP PP.152–153

Ideally situated at the heart
of Highgate village green,
this pub has a rambling,
low-ceilinged interior and a
summer terrace – as a result,
it's very, very popular on
the weekend.

THE HOLLY BUSH

22 Holly Mount ⊖ Hampstead.
Mon–Sat noon–11pm, Sun noon–10.30pm.
MAP PP.152–153

A lovely old pub, with a cosy
real fire in winter and a
charming wooden interior,
tucked away in the steep
backstreets of Hampstead
village. Some fine real ales on
offer, as well as decent food
(particularly the sausages and
pies), though it can get a bit too
mobbed at weekends.

PRINCE OF WALES

53 Highgate High St ⊖ Archway. Mon–Thurs
noon–11pm, Fri & Sat noon–midnight, Sun
noon–10.30pm. MAP PP.152–153

If *The Flask* is too full, this is
a great alternative: a cosy, tiny
local with good real ales and
a nice terrace out the back.

Greenwich

Greenwich is one of London's most beguiling spots. Its nautical associations are trumpeted by the likes of the magnificent *Cutty Sark* tea clipper and the National Maritime Museum; its architecture, especially the Old Royal Naval College and the Queen's House, is some of the finest on the river; and its Observatory is renowned throughout the world. With the added attractions of riverside pubs and walks, a large and well-maintained park with superb views across the river and to Docklands, plus a popular weekend arts and crafts market, you can see why Greenwich is the one place in southeast London that draws large numbers of visitors.

OLD ROYAL NAVAL COLLEGE

Romney Rd ⊖ Cutty Sark DLR ☎ 020/8269 4747, ⓦ www.ornc.org. Daily 10am–5pm. Free. MAP P.158

It's entirely appropriate that the Old Royal Naval College is the one London building that makes the most of its riverbank location. Initially intended as a royal palace, Wren's beautifully symmetrical Baroque ensemble was eventually converted into a hospital for disabled seamen in the eighteenth century. From 1873 until 1998 it was home to the Royal Naval College, but now houses the University of Greenwich and the Trinity College of Music.

The two grandest rooms, situated underneath Wren's twin domes, are magnificently opulent and well worth visiting. The **Chapel**'s exquisite pastel-shaded plasterwork and spectacular decorative ceiling detail were designed by James "Athenian" Stuart, after a fire in 1799 destroyed the original interior. The magnificent **Painted Hall** features trompe-l'oeil fluted pilasters, and James Thornhill's gargantuan allegorical ceiling painting depicting William and Mary handing down Peace and Liberty to Europe, with a vanquished Louis XIV clutching a broken sword below them.

OLD ROYAL NAVAL COLLEGE

NATIONAL MARITIME MUSEUM AND QUEEN'S HOUSE

Romney Rd ⊖ Cutty Sark DLR ☎ 020 8858 4422, ⓦ www.rmg.co.uk. Daily 10am–5pm. Free. MAP P.158.

The excellent **National Maritime Museum** houses a vast collection of boats and nauticalia, imaginatively displayed in modern, interactive galleries designed to appeal to visitors of all ages. The glass-roofed central courtyard houses the museum's largest artefacts, among them the splendid 63ft-long gilded **Royal Barge**, designed in Rococo style for Prince Frederick, the much unloved eldest son of George II.

The numerous themed galleries of the museum proper are superbly designed to appeal to visitors of all ages, but if you have kids in tow, head for Floor 2, where you'll find the **Children's Gallery**, which gives a taste of life at sea, loading miniature cargo, firing a cannon, learning to use Morse Code and so forth. Older children and adults alike will enjoy honing their ship handling skills on the **Ship Simulator** next door.

A bright white Palladian villa flanked by colonnades, the **Queen's House** is the focal point of Greenwich's riverside architectural ensemble and an integral part of the Maritime Museum. Inside, one or two features survive from Stuart times, most notably the cuboid Great Hall, and the beautiful cantilevered Tulip Staircase. The rooms now provide a permanent home for the museum's vast maritime **art collection**, including works by Reynolds, Hogarth, Gainsborough and Turner.

Getting to Greenwich

The most scenic and leisurely way to reach Greenwich is to take a **boat** from one of the piers in central London. Greenwich can also be reached by **train** from Charing Cross, Waterloo East or London Bridge (every 15–30min), or by **Docklands Light Railway** (DLR) from Bank or Tower Gateway direct to Cutty Sark. For the best view of the Wren buildings, get out at Island Gardens station to admire the view across the river, and then take the Greenwich Foot Tunnel under the Thames.

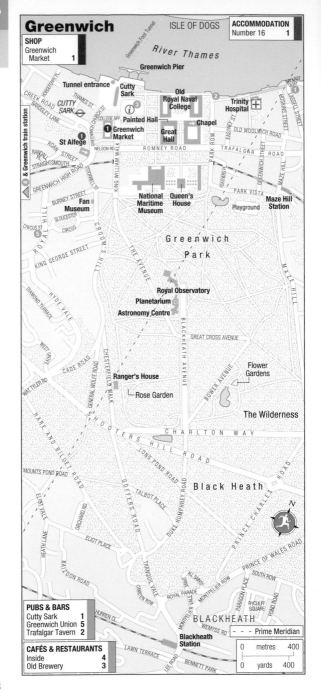

Greenwich

ISLE OF DOGS

ACCOMMODATION
Number 16   1

SHOP
Greenwich Market   1

Greenwich Foot Tunnel

River Thames

Greenwich Pier

Tunnel entrance
Cutty Sark

CREEK ROAD
CUTTY SARK
THAMES ST
GREENWICH CHURCH ST

Old Royal Naval College

Trinity Hospital

BRIDGE ST
BELLOT ST
LASSELL ST
EASTNEY ST
ROSSNS STREET
OLD WOOLWICH ROAD

Painted Hall

Chapel

St Alfege

Greenwich Market

Great Hall

ROMNEY ROAD
PARK ROW
TRAFALGAR   ROAD
GREENWICH HIGH RD
MAZE HILL

COLLEGE APP.
KING WILLIAM WALK
NELSON RD
FEATHERS PL

BARDSLEY LANE
CREEK RD
ROAD
STRAIGHTSMOUTH
RANDALL PL
STOCKWELL ST

Fan Museum

BURNEY STREET
GLOUCESTER
CIRCUS
PARK VISTA

National Maritime Museum

Queen's House

Maze Hill Station

Playground

CIRCUS ST
ROYAL HILL
CROOM'S HILL

Greenwich Park

KING GEORGE STREET

THE AVENUE

HYDE VALE

DIAMOND TERRACE
WEST GROVE

CROOM'S HILL

Royal Observatory

Planetarium

Astronomy Centre

BLACKHEATH AVENUE

GREAT CROSS AVENUE

MAZE HILL

CADE ROAD
CHESTERFIELD WALK

Ranger's House

Rose Garden

GENERAL WOLFE ROAD
HOOTER'S HILL ROAD
BOWER AVENUE

Flower Gardens

The Wilderness

WAT TYLER RD
HARE AND BILLET ROAD

CHARLTON   WAY

Black Heath

MOUNTS POND ROAD
LONG POND ROAD
GOFFERS ROAD
TALBOT PLACE
DUKE HUMPHREY ROAD
PRINCE CHARLES ROAD

ELIOT VALE
HEATH LANE
ORCHARD RD
ELIOT PLACE

BALZOON ROAD
TRANQUIL VALE
CAMDEN ROW

N

PRINCE OF WALES ROAD
SOUTH ROW

KIDBROOKE
ROYAL PARADE
MONTPELIER ROW
PARAGON PLACE
RYCULFF SQUARE
POND ROAD

PUBS & BARS
Cutty Sark   1
Greenwich Union   5
Trafalgar Tavern   2

HURREN CL
MONTPELIER VALE
WEMYSS RD

BLACKHEATH

- - - Prime Meridian

CAFÉS & RESTAURANTS
Inside   4
Old Brewery   3

LAWN TERRACE
LEE ROAD

Blackheath Station

BENNETT PARK

| 0 | metres | 400 |
| 0 | yards | 400 |

CUTTY SARK

King William Walk ⊖ Cutty Sark DLR
☎ 020 8312 6608, Ⓦ www.rmg.co.uk. Daily
10am–5pm. £12. MAP P.158.

Wedged in a dry dock by the Greenwich Foot Tunnel is the majestic *Cutty Sark*, the world's last surviving **tea clipper**. Launched from the Clydeside shipyards in 1869, the *Cutty Sark* was more famous in its day as a wool clipper, returning from Australia in just 72 days. The vessel's name comes from Robert Burns' *Tam O'Shanter*, in which Tam, a drunken farmer, is chased by Nannie, an angry witch in a short Paisley linen dress, or "cutty sark"; the clipper's figurehead shows her clutching the hair from the tail of Tam's horse. After a devastating fire in 2007, the ship has been beautifully restored and now includes a museum beneath the ship's copper-lined keel displaying a collection of more than eighty ships' figureheads.

GREENWICH PARK

⊖ Cutty Sark DLR Ⓦ www.royalparks.gov.uk.
Daily dawn–dusk. MAP P.158

A welcome escape from the traffic and crowds, Greenwich Park is a great place to have a picnic or collapse under the shade of one of the giant plane trees. The chief delight, though, is the superb view from the steep hill crowned by the Royal Observatory (see p.160), from which Canary Wharf looms large over Docklands and the Dome. The park is also celebrated for its rare and ancient trees, its royal deer enclosure in "The Wilderness" and its semicircular rose garden.

FAN MUSEUM

12 Crooms Hill ⊖ Greenwich DLR ☎ 020 8305
1441, Ⓦ www.thefanmuseum.org.uk. Tues–Sat
11am–5pm, Sun noon–5pm. £4. MAP P.158.

The Fan Museum is a fascinating little place (and an extremely beautiful house) to the west of Greenwich Park, revealing the importance of the fan as a social and political document. The permanent exhibition on the ground floor traces the history of the fan and the materials employed, from peacock feathers to straw, while the temporary exhibitions on the first floor explore conditions of production, the fan's link with the Empire and changing fashion. Outside, there's a tearoom, housed in the kitsch, hand-painted orangery, with afternoon tea served (Tues & Sun 2.15 & 3.45pm).

ROYAL OBSERVATORY

Greenwich Park ⊖ Cutty Sark DLR
☎ 020 8312 6565, ⓦ www.rmg.co.uk. Daily
10am–5pm. £7. MAP P.158

Established in 1675 by Charles II to house the first Astronomer Royal, John Flamsteed, the Royal Observatory perches on the crest of Greenwich Park's highest hill. The oldest part of the complex is the rather dinky Wren-built red-brick building, whose northeastern turret sports a bright-red time-ball that climbs the mast at 12.58pm and drops at 1pm GMT precisely; it was added in 1833 to allow ships on the Thames to set their clocks. On the house's balcony overlooking the Thames, you can take a look at a **Camera Obscura**, of the kind which Flamsteed used to make safe observations of the sun.

Flamsteed's chief task was to study the night sky in order to discover an astronomical method of finding the

ROYAL OBSERVATORY

longitude of a ship at sea, the lack of which was causing enormous problems for the emerging British Empire. Greenwich's greatest claim to fame, nowadays, is as the home of **Greenwich Mean Time** (GMT) and the Prime Meridian. Since 1884, Greenwich has occupied zero longitude – hence the world sets its clocks by GMT.

Astronomers continued to work here until the postwar smog forced them to decamp; the old observatory, meanwhile, is now a very popular **museum**. First off, you can see Flamsteed's restored apartments and the Octagon Room, where the king used to show off to his guests. The Time galleries beyond display four of the fabulous marine clocks designed by **John Harrison**, including "H4", which helped him win the Longitude Prize in 1763. In the Meridian Building, you get to see several meridians, including the present-day Greenwich Meridian fixed by the cross hairs in Airy's "Transit Circle", the astronomical instrument that dominates the last room.

In the **Astronomy Centre**, housed in the fanciful, domed terracotta South Building, the high-tech galleries give a brief rundown of the Big Bang theory of the universe, allow you to conduct some hands-on experiments to explain concepts such as gravity and spectroscopy, and then invite you to consider the big questions of astronomy today. You can also choose to watch one of the thirty-minute presentations in the state-of-the-art **Planetarium** (daily noon–4pm; £6.50), introduced by a Royal Observatory astronomer.

Shop

GREENWICH MARKET

Greenwich High Rd ⊖ Cutty Sark or
Greenwich DLR & Greenwich train station.
Stalls Tues–Sun 10am–5.30pm; many shops
open daily. MAP P.158

Sprawling flea market selling
everything from bric-a-brac to
furniture. Tuesday, Wednesday
and Friday to Sunday are best
for arts, crafts and food; for
antiques and vintage come on
Tuesday, Thursday or Friday.
Independent shops nearby offer
further treasures.

Cafés and restaurants

INSIDE

19 Greenwich South St ⊖ Greenwich DLR &
train station ☎ 020 8265 5060. Tues–Fri
noon–2.30pm & 6–10pm, Sat noon–3pm &
6–10pm, Sun noon–3pm. MAP P.158

Prepared using seasonal
ingredients, the Modern
European food served at this
classy local restaurant is causing
quite a buzz. Mains from £14,
set weekday lunches from £14.

OLD BREWERY

Pepys Building, Old Royal Naval College
⊖ Cutty Sark DLR ☎ 020 3327 1280. Daily
10am–11pm. MAP P.158

The café of the Meantime craft
brewery serves light meals
during the day before
transforming into a more
expensive Modern British
brasserie in the evening..

Pubs and bars

CUTTY SARK

Ballast Quay, off Lassell St ⊖ Cutty Sark DLR.
Mon–Sat 11am–11pm, Sun noon–10.30pm.
MAP P.158

TRAFALGAR TAVERN

This Georgian pub is the best
one along Greenwich's
riverside, with friendly staff,
an appropriately nautical
flavour, a good range of real
ales and posh pub grub
served all day.

GREENWICH UNION

56 Royal Hill ⊖ Greenwich DLR &
train station. Mon–Fri noon–11pm,
Sat 11am–11pm, Sun 11.30am–10.30pm.
MAP P.158

Owned by the Meantime
brewery, this relaxed pub
offers delicious Meantime
craft brews, guest ales and a
gastropub menu that includes
gourmet burgers.

TRAFALGAR TAVERN

5 Park Row ⊖ Cutty Sark DLR. Mon–Thurs
noon–11pm, Fri & Sat noon–midnight, Sun
noon–10.30pm. MAP P.158

Frequented by the likes of
Dickens (and mentioned in
Our Mutual Friend), William
Thackeray and Wilkie Collins,
this Regency-style inn is a
firm tourist favourite. It has a
great riverside position and
serves good snacks.

Kew and Richmond

The wealthy suburbs of Kew and Richmond like to think of themselves as apart from the rest of London, and in many ways they are. Both have a distinctly rural feel: Kew, thanks to its outstanding botanic gardens; Richmond, owing to its picturesque riverside setting and its gigantic park. Taking the leafy towpath from Richmond Bridge to one of the nearby stately homes, or soaking in the view from Richmond Park, you'd be forgiven for thinking you were in the countryside. Both Kew and Richmond are an easy tube ride from the centre, but the most pleasant way to reach them is to take one of the boats that plough up the Thames from Westminster.

SYON PARK

Twickenham Rd. Syon Lane train station from Waterloo ☎ 020 8560 0881, ⓦ www.syonpark .info. House: Easter–Oct Wed, Thurs & Sun 11am–5pm. Gardens: Easter–Oct daily 10.30am–5pm, Nov–Feb Sat & Sun 10.30am–4pm. House & gardens £11.50; gardens only £6.50. MAP P.163

From its rather plain, castellated exterior, you'd never guess that **Syon House** boasts London's most opulent eighteenth-century interior. The splendour of Robert Adam's refurbishment is immediately revealed in the pristine Great Hall, an apsed double cube with a screen of Doric columns at one end and classical statuary dotted around the edges. There are several more Adam-designed rooms to admire, and a smattering of works by van Dyck, Lely, Gainsborough and Reynolds adorn the walls. While Adam beautified Syon House, Capability Brown laid out its **gardens** around an artificial lake, surrounding the water with oaks, beeches, limes and cedars. The gardens' real highlight, however, is the crescent-shaped Great Conservatory.

GREAT CONSERVATORY, SYON HOUSE

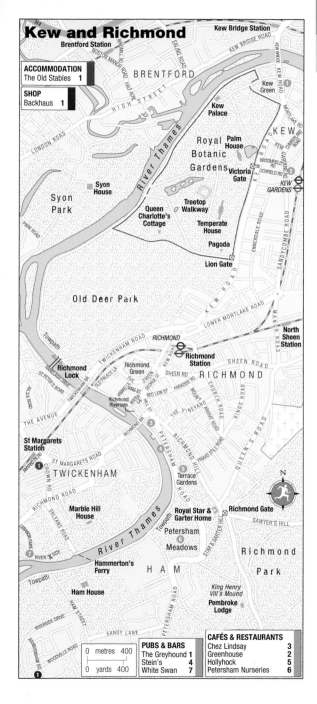

Kew and Richmond

ACCOMMODATION
The Old Stables **1**

SHOP
Backhaus **1**

M4
WHITTON ROAD
BOSTON MANOR ROAD
EALING ROAD
BRENTFORD
HIGH STREET
LONDON ROAD
PARK ROAD
Syon House
Syon Park
River Thames
Towpath

Kew Palace
Royal Botanic Gardens
Palm House
Victoria Gate
Queen Charlotte's Cottage
Treetop Walkway
Temperate House
Pagoda
Lion Gate
ENNERDALE ROAD
SANDYCOMBE ROAD
BROOMFIELD RD
LICHFIELD RD
KEW GARDENS
KEW
Kew Green
MORTLAKE RD
KEW ROAD
KEW BRIDGE ROAD
KEW BRIDGE
KEW CUMBERLAND ROAD

Old Deer Park
LOWER MORTLAKE ROAD
MANOR ROAD
North Sheen Station
KEW ROAD
TWICKENHAM ROAD
Richmond Lock
Towpath
RICHMOND
RICHMOND BRIDGE
Richmond Green
Richmond Station
Richmond Riverside
OLD PALACE LA
KING'S ROAD
THE GREEN
SHEEN RD
SHEEN ROAD
RED LION ST
PARADISE RD
CHURCH ROAD
MOUNT ARARAT ROAD
QUEEN'S ROAD
RICHMOND
THE VINEYARD
FRIARS STILE ROAD

ST MARGARETS GROVE
ST PETER'S ROAD
AILSA ROAD
THE AVENUE
St Margarets Station
ARAGON RD
CROWN RD
TWICKENHAM
RICHMOND ROAD
ST MARGARETS ROAD
ORLEANS ROAD
Marble Hill House
LEBANON PARK
RIVERSIDE
RIVER X
Hammerton's Ferry
Ham House
Towpath
HAM
MAY STREET
RIVERSIDE DRIVE
ASHBURNHAM RD
WOODVILLE ROAD
SANDY LANE
PETERSHAM ROAD
Petersham Meadows
Royal Star & Garter Home
Terrace Gardens
RICHMOND HILL
STAR & GARTER HILL
Richmond Gate
SAWYER'S HILL
Richmond Park
King Henry VIII's Mound
Pembroke Lodge

River Thames

N

| 0 | metres | 400 |
| 0 | yards | 400 |

PUBS & BARS
The Greyhound **1**
Stein's **4**
White Swan **7**

CAFÉS & RESTAURANTS
Chez Lindsay	**3**
Greenhouse	**2**
Hollyhock	**5**
Petersham Nurseries	**6**

163

KEW GARDENS

⊖ Kew Gardens ☎ 020 8332 5655,
Ⓦ www.kew.org. Daily 9.30am–6.30pm or
dusk. £14.50. MAP P.163

Established in 1759, Kew's
Royal Botanic Gardens have
grown from their original
eight acres into a 300-acre
site in which more than
33,000 species are grown in
plantations and glasshouses.
The display attracts nearly two
million visitors every year, who
come to enjoy the beautiful
landscaped parkland and
steamy palmhouses. There's
always something to see,
whatever the season, but to
get the most out of the place,
come sometime between spring
and autumn, bring a picnic and
stay for the day.

The majority of people arrive
at Kew Gardens tube and train
station, a few minutes' walk
east of the Victoria Gate.
Immediately opposite the
Victoria Gate, the **Palm House**
is by far the most celebrated of
the glasshouses, a curvaceous
mound of glass and wrought-
iron designed by Decimus
Burton in the 1840s. Its
drippingly humid atmosphere
nurtures most of the known
palm species, while there's a
small but excellent tropical
aquarium in the basement.
South of here is the largest of
the glasshouses, the **Temperate
House**, which contains plants
from every continent, including

TREETOP WALKWAY, KEW GARDENS

the sixty-foot Chilean Wine
Palm, one of the largest indoor
palms in the world. Nearby is
the **Treetop Walkway**, which
lifts you 60ft off the ground,
and gives you a novel view of
the tree canopy.

Elsewhere in the park,
Kew's origins as an eighteenth-
century royal pleasure garden
are evident in the diminutive
royal residence, **Kew Palace**
(Easter–Sept daily
10am–5.30pm; free), bought
by George II as a nursery for
his umpteen children. There
are numerous follies dotted
about the gardens, the most
conspicuous of which is the
ten-storey, 163-foot-high
Pagoda, visible to the south of
the Temperate House. A sure

River transport

From April to October, **Westminster Passenger Services** (☎ 020 7930
2062, Ⓦ www.wpsa.co.uk) runs a scheduled service from Westminster
Pier to Kew, Richmond and Hampton Court. The full trip takes three
hours one-way, and costs £15 single, £22.50 return. In addition, **Turks**
(☎ 020 8546 2434, Ⓦ www.turks.co.uk) runs a regular service from
Richmond to Hampton Court (April to mid-Sept Tues–Sun), which costs £8
single or £9.50 return. For the latest on boat services on the Thames, see
Ⓦ www.tfl.gov.uk.

way to lose the crowds is to head for the thickly wooded, southwestern section of the park around **Queen Charlotte's Cottage** (April–Sept Sat & Sun 11am–4pm; free), a tiny thatched summerhouse built in the 1770s as a royal picnic spot for George III's queen.

RICHMOND

Richmond & Richmond train station.
MAP P.163

Pedestrianized, terraced and redeveloped in the 1980s, Richmond's **riverside** is a neo-Georgian pastiche for the most part, and a popular one at that. The real joy of the waterfront, though, is **Richmond Bridge**, an elegant span of five arches made from Purbeck stone in 1777 and cleverly widened in the 1930s, thus preserving what is London's oldest extant Thames bridge. From April to October you can rent rowing boats from the nearby jetties, or take a boat trip to Hampton Court or Westminster. Alternatively, simply head south down the towpath, past the terraced gardens which give out great views over the river. On either side are the wooded banks of the Thames: to the left cows graze on Petersham Meadows; beyond lies Ham House.

HAM HOUSE

Ham St. Bus #371 or #65 from
Richmond & Richmond train station
020 8940 1950, www.nationaltrust.org.uk/hamhouse. March–Oct daily except Fri noon–4pm; June–Sept until 5pm. £10.
MAP P.163

Expensively furnished in the seventeenth century but little altered since then, Ham House boasts one of the finest Stuart interiors in the country, from the stupendously ornate Great Staircase to the Long Gallery, featuring six "Court Beauties" by Peter Lely. Elsewhere, there are several fine Verrio ceiling paintings, some exquisite parquet flooring, lavish plasterwork and silverwork, and paintings by van Dyck and Reynolds. A bonus is the formal **gardens** (daily: March–Oct 10am–5pm; Nov–Feb 10am–4pm; £4), especially the Cherry Garden, with a lavender parterre surrounded by yew hedges and pleached hornbeam arbours. The Orangery, overlooking the original kitchen garden, serves as a tearoom.

RICHMOND RIVERSIDE

MARBLE HILL HOUSE

Marble Hill Park, Richmond Rd. St Margarets train station from Waterloo ☎ 020 8892 5115, ⓦ www.english-heritage .org.uk. April–Oct Sat & Sun 10am–5pm. £5.90. MAP P.163

This stuccoed Palladian villa, set in rolling green parkland, was built in 1729 for the **Countess of Suffolk**, mistress of George II for some twenty years and, conveniently, also a lady-in-waiting to his wife, Queen Caroline. She was renowned for her wit and intelligence and she entertained the Twickenham Club of Pope, Gay and Horace Walpole. The few original furnishings are enhanced with reproductions, giving the place something of the feel of an eighteenth-century villa. **The Great Room**, on the piano nobile, is a perfect cube whose coved ceiling carries on up into the top-floor apartments. Copies of van Dycks decorate the walls as they did in Lady Suffolk's day, but the highlight is **Lady Suffolk's Bedchamber**, with its Ionic columned recess – a classic Palladian device – where she died in 1767 at the age of 79. In the grounds, there are occasional **open-air concerts** on summer evenings.

RICHMOND PARK

Bus #371 from ⊖ Richmond ☎ 0300 061 2200, ⓦ www.royalparks.gov.uk. Daily: March–Sept 7.30am–dusk; Oct–Feb 7.30am–dusk. Free. MAP P.163

Richmond's greatest attraction is its enormous park, at the top of Richmond Hill – 2500 acres of undulating grassland and bracken, dotted with coppiced ancient woodland. Eight miles across at its widest point, this is Europe's largest city park, famed for its red and fallow deer, which roam freely, and for its venerable oaks. For the most part untamed, the park does have a couple of deliberately landscaped areas. The most popular spot is **Isabella Plantation**, a carefully landscaped woodland park, with a little rivulet running through it, two small artificial ponds, and spectacular rhododendrons and azaleas in the spring. For refreshment, head for **Pembroke Lodge**, once the childhood home of the philosopher Bertrand Russell, and now a teahouse at the park's highest point, affording wonderful views up the Thames valley. Tradition has it that Henry VIII waited here for the flare that signalled the execution of his second wife, Anne Boleyn.

RICHMOND PARK

Shop

BACKHAUS

175 Ashburnham Rd, Richmond. Bus #371
from ⊖ Richmond. Mon–Fri 7.30am–5pm,
Sat 7.30am–4pm. MAP P.163
Top German bakery making
authentic cheesecakes, Stollen
and to-die-for rye breads, with
an adjacent deli selling sausages
and cheese.

Cafés and restaurants

CHEZ LINDSAY

11 Hill Rise ⊖ Richmond ☎ 020 8948 7473.
Mon–Sat noon–11pm, Sun noon–10pm. MAP P.163
There's a wide choice of galettes
(from £5) or more formal
French main courses, including
lots of fresh fish and shellfish,
at this bright, authentic Breton
creperie. Mains £11–23.

GREENHOUSE

1 Station Parade ⊖ Kew Gardens. Daily
8am–5.30pm. MAP P.163
A deliciously old-fashioned
and pretty place near Kew
Gardens, with cream teas and
good veggie food.

HOLLYHOCK

Terrace Gardens ⊖ Richmond.
Daily 9am–dusk. MAP P.163
Laidback, fair-trade veggie café,
perfect for tea and cakes on the
terrace overlooking the gardens
and the river.

PETERSHAM NURSERIES

Off Petersham Rd. Bus #371 or #65 from
Richmond ☎ 020 8940 5230. Tues–Sun
noon–3pm. MAP P.163
Expect fresh, organic,
expensive food at this
restaurant, hidden away in
a posh garden centre. There's
a cheaper tea room too.

STEIN'S

Pubs

THE GREYHOUNND

82 Kew Green ⊖ Kew Gardens. Daily
9am–11.30pm. MAP P.163
One of a handful of good
options on and around Kew
Green – the *Botanist* and
Coach and Horses are also
good – this light, contemporary gastropub offers tasty
food and real ales.

STEIN'S

Richmond Towpath ⊖ Richmond. May to
mid-Oct daily noon–10pm; mid-Oct to April
Sat & Sun noon–dusk. MAP P.163
An authentic Bavarian beer
garden, serving up wurst
and sauerkraut washed down
with *echt* beers (no beer
without food). Outdoor
seating only; the place is
closed in wet weather.

WHITE SWAN

Riverside. Twickenham train station from
Waterloo. Mon–Fri 11am–11pm, Sat
10am–11pm, Sun 11am–10.30pm. MAP P.163
Filling pub food, draught beer
and a quiet riverside location
– except on rugby match days
– make this a good halt on
any towpath ramble. The
summer Sunday barbecues are
a big draw.

Hampton Court

Hampton Court Palace is the finest of England's royal abodes and well worth the trip out from central London. A wonderfully imposing, sprawling red-brick ensemble on the banks of the Thames, it was built in 1516 by the upwardly mobile Cardinal Wolsey, Henry VIII's Lord Chancellor, only to be purloined by Henry himself after Wolsey fell from favour. Charles II laid out the gardens, inspired by what he had seen at Versailles, while King William III and Queen Mary II had large sections of the palace remodelled by Wren. With so much to see, both inside and outside the palace, you're best off devoting the best part of a day to the place, taking a picnic with you to have in the grounds.

STATE APARTMENTS

☏ 0844 482 7777, ⊛ www.hrp.org.uk.
April–Oct daily 10am–6pm; Nov–March closes 4.30pm. £16.50. MAP P.169

The palace's Tudor west front may no longer be moated but it positively prickles with turrets, castellations, chimneypots and pinnacles. Its impressive **Great Gatehouse** would have been five storeys high in its day. King Henry lavished more money on Hampton Court than any other palace, yet the only major survival from Tudor times in **Henry VIII's Apartments** is his Great Hall, which features a glorious double hammerbeam ceiling. The **Haunted Gallery** is home to the ghost of Henry's fifth wife, 19-year-old Catherine Howard, who ran down the gallery to plead for the king's mercy – only to be dragged kicking and screaming back to her chambers. Another highlight is the superbly ornate **Chapel Royal**, one of the most memorable sights in the whole palace, with its colourful plasterwork vaulting, heavy with pendants of gilded music-making cherubs.

HAMPTON COURT PALACE

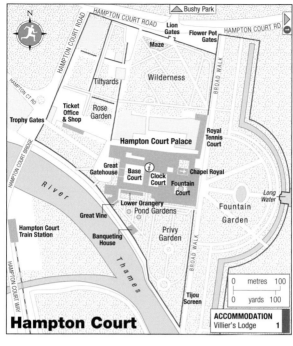

Hampton Court

The Queen's State Apartments boast wonderful trompe-l'oeil frescoes on the grandiose Queen's Staircase and in the Queen's Drawing Room, where Anne's husband is depicted riding naked and wigless on the back of a "dolphin". The gem, though, is in fact the Wolsey Closet, a tiny Tudor room that gives a tantalizing glimpse of the splendour of the original palace. Next door is the Communication Gallery, linking William and Mary's apartments, now lined with Lely's "Windsor Beauties", flattering portraits of the best-looking women in the court of Charles II. William III's Apartments, built at the same time as Mary II's, are even more grand, particularly the militaristic trompe-l'oeil paintings on the King's Staircase and the King's Great Bedchamber, which boasts a superb vertical Gibbons frieze and ceiling paintings by Verrio.

Several early Tudor rooms, with striking linenfold panelling and gilded strapwork ceilings, are now used to display Young Henry VIII's Story. This is a worthy attempt by the palace to portray Henry in his virile youth, during his happy, twenty-year marriage to his first wife, Catherine of Aragon. Last, but not least, are the earthy and evocative Henry VIII's Kitchens, large sections of which have survived to this day and have been restored and embellished with historical reconstructions. To make the most of this route, you really do need to use the free audioguide, which helps to bring the scene to life with contemporary accounts.

Getting to and around the palace

Trains from Waterloo take around half an hour to reach Hampton Court train station, which is just across the river from the palace.

The State Apartments are divided into six thematic **walking tours**, which are numbered and colour-coded. There's not a lot of information in any of the rooms, but **guided tours**, each lasting half an hour or so, take place throughout the State Apartments; all are led by period-costumed historians, who do a fine job of bringing the place to life. In addition, **audioguides** are available for all the walking tours from the information centre on the east side of Clock Court.

If your energy is lacking – and Hampton Court is a huge complex – the most rewarding sections are Henry VIII's Apartments, William III's Apartments and Henry VIII's Kitchens. And be sure not to miss out on the splendid Maze.

THE GARDENS AND THE MAZE

MAP P.169

If you're coming from the State Apartments, you'll probably emerge onto the magnificent Broad Walk, which runs along Wren's austere east front and is lined with superbly maintained herbaceous borders. Halfway along is the indoor **Royal Tennis Court**, established here by Henry VIII – if you're lucky, you might catch a game of this arcane precursor of modern tennis.

Fanning out from the Broad Walk is the **Fountain Garden**, a grand, semicircular parterre featuring conical, overgrown dwarf yew trees. To the south of the palace is the more formal **Privy Garden** (£5.20; free with palace ticket) which features magnificent wrought-iron riverside railings by Jean Tijou. The **Pond Gardens**, originally constructed as ornamental fish ponds stocked with freshwater fish for the kitchens, feature some of the gardens' most spectacularly colourful flowerbeds. Further along, protected by glass, is the palace's celebrated **Great Vine**, grown from a cutting in 1768 by Capability Brown and averaging about seven hundred pounds of Black Hamburg grapes per year (sold at the palace in September).

HAMPTON COURT MAZE

BUSHY PARK

Close by stands the Wren-built **Lower Orangery**, now home to Andrea Mantegna's luminous richly coloured masterpiece, *The Triumphs of Caesar*. Painted around 1486 for the Ducal Palace in Mantua, these heroic paintings are among his best works, characterized by an accomplished use of perspective and an obsessive interest in archeological and historical accuracy. Access to the Lower Orangery is from the Base Court.

The most famous feature of the palace gardens, however, is the deceptively tricky trapezoidal yew hedge **Maze** (£4; free with palace ticket), planted in the 1690s. Mazes, or labyrinths as they were called at the time, were originally designed for pilgrims, who used to crawl along on hands and knees reciting prayers as penance for not making a pilgrimage to the Holy Land. They were all the rage among the eighteenth-century nobility, who used them primarily for amusement, secret conversations and flirtation. The maze was originally planted with hornbeam, but with the onset of the tourist boom in the 1960s the hornbeam took quite a battering and had to be replaced with yew.

BUSHY PARK

MAP P.169

Beyond the Lion Gates to the north of the Maze and across Hampton Court Road lies **Bushy Park**, the palace's semi-wild enclosure of over a thousand acres, which sustains copious herds of fallow and red deer. Wren's mile-long royal road, **Chestnut Avenue**, cuts through the park, and is at its best in May when the trees are in blossom. The park's main architectural feature is the **Diana Fountain**, situated a third of the way along to help break the monotony. The statue – which, in fact, depicts Arethusa – was commissioned by Charles II from Francesco Fanelli and originally graced the Privy Garden; stranded in the centre of this vast pond, she looks ill-proportioned and a bit forlorn.

Off to the west, a little further up the avenue, you'll come upon the **Waterhouse Woodland Gardens**, which are at their most colourful each spring when the rhododendrons, azaleas and camellias are in bloom. The crowds are fairly thin even here, but if you really want to escape the visitors make for the park's wilder western section, which is home to abundant wildlife.

Hotels, B&Bs and hostels

There's no getting away from the fact that accommodation in London is expensive. Compared with most European cities, you pay over the odds in every category. The cheapest option is to go to one of the independent hostels, where dorm beds start at around £20. Going up a notch, even the most basic B&Bs struggle to bring their tariffs below £90 for a double with shared facilities, which is why so many people head for the budget chain hotels. For a really decent hotel room, you shouldn't expect much change out of £100 a night. Most B&Bs and many hotels are housed in former residential properties, which means that rooms tend to be on the small side. That said, even the most basic rooms tend to have TVs, and breakfast is nearly always included in the price. Though hostels normally don't provide breakfast, they do usually have cooking facilities – exceptions are mentioned in the text. The prices quoted are for the cheapest double room or dorm bed in high season, though rates often vary online and according to availability (see box opposite).

Whitehall and Westminster

THE GRAND > 8 Northumberland Avenue ⊖ Charing Cross ☏ 020 7839 8877, ⓦ www.thegrandattrafalgarsquare.com. MAP P.37, POCKET MAP G17. Grandiloquent Victorian building in a fantastic location just off Trafalgar Square, efficiently run, with fully equipped, modern rooms and free wi-fi. There's on-site dining, too, and a fitness room. **£200**

LUNA & SIMONE HOTEL > 47–49 Belgrave Rd ⊖ Victoria ☏ 020 7834 5897, ⓦ www.lunasimonehotel.com. MAP P.40, POCKET MAP G10. B&B with a bright foyer, very friendly staff and plain, well-maintained en-suite rooms. Big breakfasts. **£140**

SANCTUARY HOUSE > 33 Tothill St ⊖ St James's Park ☏ 020 7799 4044, ⓦ www.sanctuaryhousehotel.com. MAP P.40, POCKET MAP F19. A Fuller's hotel above a Fuller's pub, decked out in uncontroversial modern style. Breakfast is extra, and is served in the pub, but the location by St James's Park is terrific. Rates vary – ask about the special deals. **£160**

St James's

THE STAFFORD > 16–18 St James's Place ⊖ Green Park ☏ 020 7493 0111, ⓦ www.kempinski.com. MAP P.47, POCKET MAP D17. Tucked into a quiet backstreet off St James's Street, *The Stafford* provides high-class rooms in the main building, the unique Carriage House, a luxuriously converted row of eighteenth-century stables, and in the upmarket Mews Suites. The *American Bar* was founded to provide cocktails for American visitors in the 1930s, and its courtyard terrace remains a delight. **£270**

Booking a room

Demand for beds is so great that London doesn't really have a low season. Look online well in advance to get the best price – you may be able to shave £50–100 off room rates at some of the more upmarket hotels.

London's **tourist offices** (see p.193) operate a room-booking service, for which a small fee is levied (they also take the first night's fee in advance). There are also **British Hotel Reservation Centre** (BHRC; 24hr helpline ☎ 020 7592 3055, ⓦ www.bhrc.co.uk) desks at Heathrow airport, St Pancras and Victoria train stations, Victoria coach station and Trafalgar Sqaure. BHRC desks are open daily from early till late, and there's no booking fee – they can also get big discounts at the more upmarket hotels.

You can book accommodation for free **online** at ⓦ www.londontown.com; payment is made directly to the hotel and they offer very good discounts. Other useful websites for last-minute offers include ⓦ www.laterooms. com and ⓦ www.lastminute.com. ⓦ www.londonbb.com sources classy **B&B** options, while ⓦ www.couchsurfing.org puts travellers in touch with people to stay with for free and ⓦ ww.airbandb.co.uk offers interesting self-catering options.

Mayfair and Marylebone

CENTRAL YHA > 104 Bolsover St ⊖ Great Portland Street ☎ 0845 371 9154, ⓦ www.yha.org.uk. MAP P.59, POCKET MAP D12. Excellent three-hundred-bed hostel in a quiet West End spot, with a kitchen and café-bar. Dorms are mostly en suite. No groups. Free wi-fi for members. **Dorms £33**

GROSVENOR HOUSE > Park Lane ⊖ Marble Arch ☎ 020 7499 6363, ⓦ londongrosvenorhouse.co.uk. MAP P.53, POCKET MAP A16. Open since 1929, this is one of the capital's *grandes dames* – the Queen learnt to skate in the hotel's ice rink (now the Great Hall). It's now a Marriott, with high rack rates, but there are discounts to be had. Breakfast not included. **£450**

LINCOLN HOUSE HOTEL > 33 Gloucester Place ⊖ Marble Arch or Baker Street ☎ 020 7486 7630, ⓦ www.lincoln-house-hotel.co.uk. MAP P.59, POCKET MAP A14. Dark wood panelling gives this Georgian B&B in Marylebone a ship's-cabin feel. All the rooms are en suite and well equipped; rates vary according to the size of the bed and length of stay. Breakfast not included. Free wi-fi. **£105**

SUMNER HOTEL > 54 Upper Berkeley St ⊖ Marble Arch ☎ 020 7723 2244, ⓦ thesumner.com MAP P.59, POCKET MAP E6. A spruce B&B – with the feel of a boutique hotel – in a Georgian townhouse. Rooms vary in size and style – the best are light and modern, some have tiny balconies, those facing the street can be noisy – but all are tasteful and comfortable, and there's a tranquil sitting room. Breakfast is a buffet. Free wi-fi. **£210**

Soho and Covent Garden

DEAN STREET TOWNHOUSE > 69–71 Dean St ⊖ Tottenham Court Road ☎ 020 7434 1775, ⓦ deanstreettownhouse.com. MAP PP.66–67, POCKET MAP F15. This 1730s beauty, owned by the Soho House club, has rooms ranging from "tiny" right up to "bigger", where you'll have plenty of space. All are luxurious with gorgeous details. Free wi-fi. **£210**

Budget chain hotels

Chain hotels have pretty much got the budget hotel market sewn up. B&Bs may be able to offer a more personal touch and more character in the decor, but the franchises are often in unbeatable central locations. Although they will never really be more than perfunctory places to stay, on the whole they can be guaranteed to provide clean if anonymous rooms.

Bumping along at the bottom are **easyHotel** (ⓦwww.easyhotel.com), whose prices start at just £33 for an en-suite double – if you want a window, TV use or room cleaning, it's extra; there are branches in Victoria, South Ken, Paddington, Old Street and Earl's Court. Serious bargains can also be had at the **Tune** chain, which works in a similar way, offering minimal rooms in Westminster, Liverpool Street, Paddington and King's Cross (ⓦwww.tunehotels.com). **Travelodge** has some very handily situated hotels; rooms are unexciting, but if you book online well in advance, en-suite doubles can cost less than £60. **Premier Inn** is generally considered a cut above Travelodge (and it doesn't have quite the online bargains); the rest of the chain gang aren't worth considering as you can get better value elsewhere.

THE FIELDING HOTEL > 4 Broad Court, Bow St ⊖Covent Garden ☎020 7836 8305, ⓦwww.thefielding hotel.co.uk. MAP PP.66–67, POCKET MAP H15. Quietly situated on a traffic-free court, this excellent hotel is one of Covent Garden's hidden gems. Its en-suite rooms are a firm favourite with visiting performers, since it's just a few yards from the Royal Opera House. No lift and no breakfast. Free wi-fi. **£140**

HAZLITT'S > 6 Frith St ⊖Tottenham Court Road ☎020 7434 1771, ⓦwww.hazlittshotel .com. MAP PP.66–67, POCKET MAP F14. Located off the south side of Soho Square, this early eighteenth-century building is a hotel of real character and discreet charm, offering en-suite rooms exquisitely decorated with period furniture. Breakfast (served in the rooms) is not included. Free wi-fi. **£205**

NADLER SOHO > 10 Carlisle St ⊖Tottenham Court Road ☎020 3697 3697, ⓦwww.thenadler.com. MAP PP.66–67, POCKET MAP F14. Glossy hotel offering good value.

Rooms are modern and high-tech, if unexciting (the cheapest are pretty small), and each has a microwave, fridge and kettle – and an espresso machine – so you could effectively self-cater. **£160**

OXFORD STREET YHA > 14 Noel St ⊖Oxford Circus or Tottenham Court Road ☎0845 371 9133, ⓦwww.yha.org.uk. MAP PP.66–67, POCKET MAP E14. The Soho location and relatively modest size mean this hostel tends to fill quickly. The atmosphere is party central rather than family-friendly. Private rooms available. Free wi-fi for members. **Dorms £36, doubles £80**

SEVEN DIALS HOTEL > 7 Monmouth St ⊖Covent Garden ☎020 7681 0791, ⓦwww.sevendialshotellondon .com. MAP PP.66–67, POCKET MAP G14. Pleasant family-run B&B hotel on a lovely street in the heart of the West End. The staircase is narrow and steep (no lift) and the rooms are small – most are en suite, some have private toilets, but all have a TV, tea/coffee-making facilities and free wi-fi. **£95**

Bloomsbury

ALHAMBRA HOTEL > 17 Argyle St ⊖King's Cross St Pancras ☎020 7631 4115, ⓦwww.alhambrahotel .com. MAP P.80, POCKET MAP J3. Clean, friendly, budget hotel a stone's throw from St Pancras. Cheapest rooms have shared facilities and there's no lift, but breakfast and wi-fi are free. **£85**

AROSFA HOTEL > 83 Gower St ⊖Goodge Street or Euston Square ☎020 7636 2115, ⓦwww .arosfalondon.com. MAP PP.80, POCKET MAP F12. Fifteen en-suite B&B rooms. Some are tiny, but it's clean, comfy and reliable. Full breakfast and free wi-fi in the lounge. **£115**

CLINK 261 HOSTEL > 261–265 Gray's Inn Rd ⊖King's Cross St Pancras ☎020 7833 9400, ⓦwww.clinkhostels .com. MAP P.80, POCKET MAP J3. A clean and friendly boutique hostel in a converted office block near King's Cross station, with laundry and kitchen facilities. Breakfast included. Private rooms available. **Dorms from £17; doubles £60**

CLINK 78 HOSTEL > 78 King's Cross Rd ⊖King's Cross St Pancras ☎020 7183 9400, ⓦwww.clink hostels.com. MAP P.80, POCKET MAP K3. This party hostel has funky decor, some pod beds, and plenty of period features from the days when it was a Victorian courthouse – you can even stay in one of the old cells. Breakfast included; kitchen facilities from noon; 4- to 16-bed dorms available, some en suite, plus private rooms. **Dorms from £16.50; doubles £65**

GENERATOR > 37 Tavistock Place ⊖Russell Square ☎020 7388 7666, ⓦwww.generatorhostels.com. MAP P.80, POCKET MAP J4. A huge party hostel, with over 800 beds, in a converted police barracks tucked away down a cobbled street. The decor is colourful and hip, and there's a young, sociable atmosphere with themed nights in the late-night bar. Free wi-fi, laundry, but no kitchen; breakfast and snacks available in the café. Groups welcome. **Dorms from £20; doubles £75**

RIDGEMOUNT HOTEL > 65–67 Gower St ⊖Goodge Street ☎020 7636 1141, ⓦwww .ridgemounthotel.co.uk. MAP P.80, POCKET MAP F12. Very friendly, old-fashioned, family-run place, with small rooms (half with shared facilities), a garden and free hot drinks machine. A reliable, basic bargain option. Full breakfast and free wi-fi. **£82**

ROUGH LUXE >1 Birkenhead St ⊖King's St Pancras ☎020 7837 5338, ⓦroughluxe.co.uk. MAP P.80, POCKET MAP J3. This gorgeously quirky six-room hotel offers warmth, comfort and shabby chic opulence in the unlikely setting of King's Cross. The arty, nostalgic aesthetic is stronger in some rooms than others, so check the photos online. **£180**

ST PANCRAS YHA > 79–81 Euston Rd ⊖King's Cross St Pancras ☎0845 371 9344, ⓦwww.yha.org. uk. MAP P.80, POCKET MAP J4. Modern hostel opposite the Eurostar terminal on the busy Euston Road; rooms are very clean, bright, triple-glazed and air-conditioned. All rooms are en suite and family rooms are available. No groups. They don't have a kitchen but there's a café. Free wi-fi for members. **Dorms from £28; doubles £80**

The City

APEX CITY OF LONDON HOTEL > 1 Seething Lane ⊖Tower Hill ☎020 7977 9593, ⓦwww.apexhotels .co.uk. MAP PP.86–87, POCKET MAP N6. A swish hotel on a secluded City street, designed for corporate clientele. Rooms are modern and well appointed; the pricier ones enjoy more light and better views. Rates vary enormously according to availability, so book early. On-site gym, restaurant and bar, plus free wi-fi. **£160**

DOUBLETREE BY HILTON – TOWER OF LONDON > 7 Pepys St ⊖ Tower Hill ☎ 020 7709 1000, ⓦ doubletree1 .hilton.com. MAP P.86–87, POCKET MAP O6. Large, bright, modern hotel with nearly 600 rooms – all with iMacs. The rooftop bar, *Skylounge*, offers amazing views. Free wi-fi. **£200**

THE KING'S WARDROBE > 6 Wardrobe Place, Carter Lane ⊖ St Paul's ☎ 020 7792 2222, ⓦ www.bridgestreet.com. MAP PP.86–87, POCKET MAP L6. In a quiet courtyard just behind St Paul's Cathedral, this place is part of an international chain that caters largely for a business clientele. The apartments offer fully equipped kitchens and workstations, a concierge service and housekeeping. Though the building is Georgian and occupies the site of the medieval Royal Wardrobe, the interior is modern. **£185**

THE ROOKERY > 12 Peter's Lane, Cowcross St ⊖ Farringdon ☎ 020 7336 0931, ⓦ www.rookeryhotel.com. MAP PP.86–87, POCKET MAP L5. Rambling Georgian townhouse on the edge of the City that makes a fantastically discreet little hideaway. It's as charming as can be with its panelled walls, flagstone floors and creaky, timeworn floorboards; rooms offer faded Baroque glam with antique fittings, lovely rugs and super bathrooms. **£165**

ST PAUL'S YHA > 36 Carter Lane ⊖ St Paul's ☎ 0845 371 9012, ⓦ www.yha.org.uk. MAP PP.86–87, POCKET MAP L6. Large 215-bed hostel in a superb location opposite St Paul's Cathedral. Breakfast included and a café for dinner, but no kitchen. Small groups only. Dorms, twins and family rooms. **Dorms £32; doubles £65**

THE ZETTER HOTEL > 86–88 Clerkenwell Rd ⊖ Farringdon ☎ 020 7324 4444, ⓦ www.thezetter.com. MAP PP.86–87, POCKET MAP L4. A warehouse converted with real style and a dash of 1960s glamour. Rooms are funky and colourful, and there's a popular on-site brasserie. Ask for a room at the back, overlooking quiet, cobbled St John's Square. Water for guests is supplied from *The Zetter*'s own well, beneath the building. **£130**

The East End

HOXTON HOTEL > 81 Great Eastern St ⊖ Old Street ☎ 020 7550 1000, ⓦ www.hoxtonhotels.com. MAP P.102, POCKET MAP N4. Self-consciously trendy hotel in über-hip Hoxton, with contemporary art on the walls and fashionably lugubrious decor in the rooms. The facilities are good, with flat-screen TVs and duck-down duvets. A light breakfast is delivered to your room. Free wi-fi and cheap phone calls. The brasserie is a destination in itself. **£80**

SHOREDITCH ROOMS > Shoreditch House, Ebor St ⊖ Shoreditch High Street Overground ☎ 020 7739 5040, ⓦ shoreditchrooms.com. MAP P.102, POCKET MAP O4. Hip little place with 26 rooms from "tiny" to "small-plus", some with minuscule balconies. Lots of tongue-and-groove and fresh, sunbleached colours, old school desks and vintage tiled bathrooms. Free wi-fi. **£165**

Tower and Docklands

FOUR SEASONS HOTEL CANARY WHARF > 46 Westferry Circus ⊖ Canary Wharf ☎ 020 7510 1999, ⓦ www.fourseasons.com. MAP PP.110–111. A spectacular riverfront setting, modern interiors and good links to the City have made this hotel very popular with business folk, but weekend rates, which can bring prices down, mean that it's an equally good base for sightseeing. Several rooms have superb Thames views. Guests have acess to a pool, fitness centre, spa and tennis courts, and the option of taking a boat into town. **£300**

South Bank and around

CAPTAIN BLIGH HOUSE > 100 Lambeth Rd ⊖ Lambeth North ⓦ www .captainblighhouse.co.uk. MAP P.115, POCKET MAP K9. The former home of Captain Bligh (of *Bounty* fame) is now a nautically flavoured Georgian B&B, a short walk from the South Bank, run by a friendly, unobtrusive couple. There are just a handful of rooms and an apartment, all with self-catering facilities; breakfast is taken in your room. Four-night minimum. **£115**

LONDON MARRIOTT HOTEL COUNTY HALL > County Hall ⊖ Waterloo ☎ 020 7928 5200, Ⓦ www.marriott.com. MAP P.115, POCKET MAP J19. The Marriott has taken over some of the finest rooms in historic County Hall, former home to London's government, with over three-quarters offering river views, and many with small balconies. It's all suitably pompous inside, and there's a full-sized indoor pool and well-equipped gym. **£275**

MAD HATTER > 3–7 Stamford St ⊖ Southwark or Blackfriars ☎ 020 7401 9222, Ⓦ www .madhatterhotel.co.uk. MAP P.115, POCKET MAP L7. Good-value Fuller's hotel with thirty clean and comfy en-suite rooms, above a Fuller's pub in an old hat factory. This is a great location, a short walk from Tate Modern and the South Bank, and staff are friendly. Free wi-fi. **£150**

TUNE WESTMINSTER > 118–120 Westminster Bridge Rd ⊖ Lambeth North or Waterloo Ⓦ tunehotels .com. MAP P.115, POCKET MAP K19. The Southeast Asian cheapie chain has brought their down-to-earth pricing policy – "Five-star beds at one-star prices" – to the UK. By doing away with things like tables, chairs and closets, prices stay low and you simply opt to pay for extras including towels, TV, hairdryers and wi-fi, on the hotel's website. **£60**

Bankside and Southwark

IBIS STYLES LONDON SOUTHWARK ROSE > 43–47 Southwark Bridge Rd ⊖ London Bridge ☎ 020 7015 1480, Ⓦ www.ibis.com. MAP PP.122–123, POCKET MAP M7. The *Southwark Rose* is a good central, budget option with contemporary design touches that raise the ambience a little above the other bland chain hotels in this area. Rooms are generally comfortable and clean and a buffet breakfast is included in rates, which vary widely depending on availability. Free wi-fi. **£120**

THAMESIDE YHA > 20 Salter Rd ⊖ Rotherhithe ☎ 0845 371 9756, Ⓦ www.yha.org.uk. MAP PP.122–123. London's largest YHA hostel, with 320 beds, is in a quiet spot near the river. It can feel a bit of a trek from the centre, but it often has space and there's a good pub next door. Self-catering is available, and there's a restaurant serving breakfast and dinner. Free wi-fi for members. Dorms **£25**; doubles **£50**

Kensington and Chelsea

ASTER HOUSE > 3 Sumner Place ⊖ South Kensington ☎ 020 7581 5888, Ⓦ www.asterhouse.com. MAP PP.130–131, POCKET MAP D10. Pleasant, award-winning B&B in a luxurious, white-stuccoed South Ken street with a lovely garden at the back and a large conservatory where breakfast is served. **£200**

B+B BELGRAVIA > 64–66 Ebury St ⊖ Victoria ☎ 020 7259 8570, Ⓦ www .bb-belgravia.com. MAP PP.130–131, POCKET MAP F9. Very close to the train and coach station, this is a real rarity in this neck of the woods – a B&B with flair. The rooms are comfortable, with original features as well as stylish modern touches. Communal spaces are light and well designed, and staff welcoming and enthusiastic. Free wi-fi and bike loan. **£100**

CARING HOTEL > 24 Craven Hill Gardens ⊖ Bayswater, Queensway or Lancaster Gate ☎ 020 7262 8708, Ⓦ www.caringhotel.co.uk. MAP PP.130–131, POCKET MAP C6. This large guesthouse, in a quiet street, is a popular, reliable choice. Rooms are clean and functional: some have shared facilities, some showers only, and others are en suite. Free wi-fi in public areas and free continental breakfast. **£70**

COLUMBIA HOTEL > 95–99
Lancaster Gate ⊖ Lancaster Gate
☎ 020 7402 0021, ⓦ www.columbia
hotel.co.uk. MAP PP.130–131,
POCKET MAP C7. This large hotel, once
five Victorian houses, offers singles,
doubles, triples and quads, some with
views over Hyde Park. It's all a bit dated
but the cocktail bar, with its vaguely
Art Deco feel, has a certain faded
charm. **£105**

GARDEN COURT HOTEL >
30–31 Kensington Gardens Square
⊖ Bayswater or Queensway
☎ 020 7229 2553, ⓦ www.garden
courthotel.co.uk. MAP PP.130–131,
POCKET MAP B6. Unfussy hotel close
to Portobello Market; rooms are
small, and the cheaper ones have
shared facilities. Buffet breakfast. Free
wi-fi. **£130**

THE HALKIN > 5 Halkin St
⊖ Hyde Park Corner ☎ 020 7333
1000, ⓦ www.comohotels.com.
MAP PP.130–131, POCKET MAP B19.
A luxury hotel that spurns the chintzy
country-house theme: elegant,
East-meets-West minimalism
prevails in each of the 41 rooms.
The high-end dining options include
Michelin-starred Basque restaurant
Amesta. **£320**

HOLLAND PARK YHA >
Holland Walk ⊖ Holland Park or
High Street Kensington ☎ 0845
371 9122, ⓦ www.yha.org.uk.
MAP PP.130–131, POCKET MAP A8.
Idyllically situated in Holland Park and
fairly convenient for the centre. There
is a kitchen and a café. Popular with
groups. **Dorms £22**

KENSINGTON HOUSE >
15–16 Prince of Wales Terrace
⊖ High Street Kensington ☎ 020
7937 2345, ⓦ www.kenhouse.com.
MAP PP.130–131, POCKET MAP C8.
Independent hotel in a nineteenth-
century townhouse. The en-suite rooms
are smallish and worn in places, but
clean and contemporary, and some
even have balconies. Free continental
breakfast. **£120**

THE MAIN HOUSE > 6 Colville Rd
⊖ Ladbroke Grove or Notting Hill
Gate ☎ 020 7221 9691, ⓦ www
.themainhouse.co.uk. MAP PP.130–131,
POCKET MAP A6. Three enormous suites
that are both homely – thanks to some
lovely period furniture – and chic.
Perfectly placed for Portobello Road.
Tea and coffee are brought to your room.
Three-night minimum stay. **£130**

MEININGER > Baden Powell House,
65–67 Queen's Gate ⊖ Gloucester Road
or South Kensington ☎ 020 3318 1407,
ⓦ www.meininger-hostels.com.
MAP PP.130–131, POCKET MAP C9. Bright
and cheerful modern hostel, part of a
German chain, run with Teutonic efficiency
and located near the South Ken museums.
Free wi-fi. No kitchen; breakfast available.
Dorms (4–12 beds), plus private rooms.
Dorms £40; doubles £62

MYHOTEL CHELSEA > 35 Ixworth
Place ⊖ South Kensington ☎ 020 7225
7500, ⓦ www.myhotels.com. MAP
PP.130–131, POCKET MAP D10. Though
the decor – "Where Sex and the City
meets Brideshead Revisited" – isn't to
everyone's taste, rooms in this friendly
small hotel are well equipped and the
atmosphere is peaceful. Good online
deals. **£150**

NADLER KENSINGTON > 25
Courtfield Gardens ⊖ Earl's Court
☎ 020 7244 2255, ⓦ thenadler
.com. MAP P.130–131, POCKET MAP B10.
Excellent-value budget boutique hotel.
Rooms range from "bijou singles" to
"deluxe"; all are comfortable, clean
and quiet, modern and attractive, with
mini-kitchens and free wi-fi. **£130**

PORTOBELLO GOLD > 95–97
Portobello Rd ⊖ Notting Hill Gate
or Ladbroke Grove ☎ 020 7460 4910,
ⓦ www.portobellogold.com.
MAP PP.130–131, POCKET MAP A6.
A friendly, basic option above a pub and
casual restaurant. The five rooms are
plain and some are tiny, with miniature
en-suite bathrooms, but the hotel also
has an apartment (sleeps 6 – at a bit of
a pinch), with a roof terrace (and putting
green). Breakfast not included. **£75**

ST DAVID'S HOTELS > 14–20 Norfolk Square ⊖ Paddington ☎ 020 7723 3856, Ⓦ www .stdavidshotels.com. MAP PP.130–131, POCKET MAP D6. Inexpensive guesthouse famed for its substantial English breakfast. Most rooms are en suite, and the large family rooms make it a good option for families on a budget. **£80**

VICARAGE HOTEL > 10 Vicarage Gate ⊖ High Street Kensington or Notting Hill Gate ☎ 020 7229 4030, Ⓦ www.londonvicaragehotel.com. MAP PP.130–131, POCKET MAP B8. Ideally located B&B on a quiet street a step away from Kensington Gardens. Clean rooms, some en suite; full English breakfast included. **£112**

Regent's Park and Camden

THE NEW INN > 2 Allitsen Rd ⊖ St John's Wood ☎ 020 7722 0726, Ⓦ www.newinnlondon.co.uk. MAP P.145, POCKET MAP D3. Excellent guesthouse with five en-suite rooms – two of them huge – above a gastropub in a quiet street a few minutes' walk from the north edge of Regent's Park. Breakfast costs extra. **£120**

Hampstead and Highgate

HAMPSTEAD VILLAGE GUESTHOUSE > 2 Kemplay Rd ⊖ Hampstead or Hampstead Heath Overground ☎ 020 7435 8679, Ⓦ www.hampsteadguesthouse.com. MAP PP.152–153. Unconventional B&B in a freestanding Victorian house on a quiet backstreet between Hampstead village and the Heath. Rooms (most en suite)

are characterful, crammed with books, pictures and handmade and antique furniture. Breakfast costs extra. **£105**

LANGORF HOTEL > 20 Frognal ⊖ Finchley Road or Finchley Road & Frognal Overground ☎ 020 7794 4483, Ⓦ www.langorfhotel.com. MAP PP.152–153. Pristinely maintained if rather old-fashioned hotel in a trio of red-brick Victorian mansions, with a walled garden. Apartments (sleeping 3–4) also available. **£115**

Greenwich

NUMBER 16 > 16 St Alfeges Passage ⊖ Cutty Sark DLR ☎ 020 8853 4337, Ⓦ www.st-alfeges.co.uk. MAP PP.158. Stylish three-room B&B – owned by a flamboyant ex-antique dealer/actor – offering a warm welcome and offbeat touches. **£125**

Kew and Richmond

THE OLD STABLES > 1 Bridle Lane, Twickenham. St Margarets train station from Waterloo ☎ 020 8892 4507, Ⓦ www.oldstables.com. MAP P.163. Three bedrooms and one apartment in a house in a quiet street by the train station; walking distance to Richmond and the Thames. No on-site staff, but the manager is a phone call away and breakfast is provided. **£87**

Hampton Court

VILLIERS LODGE > 1 Cranes Park, Surbiton. Surbiton train station from Waterloo ☎ 020 8399 6000, Ⓦ villierslodgesurbiton.co.uk. MAP P.169. This large, luxurious Victorian house – convenient for Hampton Court – has been converted into a spotless, sunny B&B with five doubles and two singles. Breakfast included. Free wi-fi. **£105**

Arrival

The majority of visitors arrive in London at one of its five airports, all but one of which can involve an expensive trip to the centre. Those arriving by train or bus are dropped right in the middle of the city, with easy access to public transport.

By plane

Flying into London, you'll arrive at Heathrow, Gatwick, Stansted, Luton or City **airport**, each of which is less than an hour from the city centre.

HEATHROW

Heathrow Airport (☎ 0844 335 1801, ⓦ www.heathrowairport.com) lies around fifteen miles west of central London, and is the city's busiest airport, with five terminals and three train/tube stations: one for terminals 1, 2 and 3, and separate ones for terminals 4 and 5. The fastest **train** service into London is the high-speed, non-stop Heathrow Express to Paddington station (daily 5am–midnight; journey 15min); tickets cost £21 one way or £34 return. Heathrow Connect trains stop at intermediate stations (Mon–Sat 5am–midnight, Sun 6am–11pm; every 30min; journey 30–40min) but tickets cost around £10 single and £20 return. A cheaper alternative is to take the Piccadilly **Underground** line, which connects the airport to numerous tube stations across central London (Mon–Sat 5am–11.45pm, Sun 6am–11.30pm; every 5min; journey 50min); tickets cost around £6 single, or £8.50 for a Day Off-Peak Travelcard, zones 1–6 (see p.186). A **taxi** from Heathrow will cost in the region of £50–80, depending on traffic and the time of day.

GATWICK

Gatwick Airport (☎ 0844 892 0322, ⓦ www.gatwickairport.com) is around thirty miles south of London, and has a train station at its South Terminal. Non-stop Gatwick Express **trains** run between the airport and London Victoria (daily 4.30am–1.30am; every 15min; journey 30min); tickets cost around £20 single, £35 return (less online). It's cheaper, however, to take a Southern train to Victoria (every 15min; journey 35min), or a First Capital Connect train to various stations within London (every 15–30min; journey 30–45min), including London Bridge and St Pancras; online tickets for either cost from £10 single. easyBus (ⓦ www.easybus.co.uk) runs **buses** to West Brompton tube (4.30am–midnight; every 20min; 1hr 10min), with online tickets going for as little as £2 single (£10 if you buy on board). National Express buses run from Gatwick direct to central London (daily 5am–9.30pm; hourly; 1hr 30min); tickets cost around £7 single, £12.50 return. A **taxi** will set you back a ludicrous £100 or more, and take an hour or more.

STANSTED

Stansted Airport (☎ 0844 335 1803, ⓦ www.stanstedairport.com) is roughly 35 miles northeast of the capital. Stansted Express **trains** run non-stop to Liverpool Street (5.30am–12.30am; every 15–30min; journey 45min), and cost £24 single, £33 return. easyBus (ⓦ www.easybus .co.uk) runs buses to Baker Street tube (daily 7am–1am; every 20min; 1hr 15min), with online tickets going for as little as £2 single (£10 if you buy on board). National Express runs buses 24 hours a day calling at various places in London en route to Victoria Coach Station (every

10–30min; journey 1hr 30min), with tickets for around £10 single. Terravision (☎ 01279 662931, Ⓦ www.terravision.eu) also runs coaches to Liverpool Street (daily 7am–1am; every 30min; journey time 1hr 15min), with tickets £9 single, £15 return. A **taxi** will set you back £100 or more, and take at least an hour.

LUTON

London Luton Airport (☎ 01582 405100, Ⓦ www.london-luton.co.uk) is roughly thirty miles north of London and mainly handles low-cost flights. A free shuttle bus takes five minutes to reach Luton Airport Parkway station, which is connected by **train** to King's Cross St Pancras (every 15–30min; journey 25–35min) and other stations in central London; single tickets cost around £15. All year round, 24 hours a day, Green Line (Ⓦ www.greenline.co.uk) and easyBus (Ⓦ www.easybus.co.uk) run up to three buses an hour from Luton to Victoria Station (every 20–30min; journey 1hr 20min), stopping at several locations en route, including Baker Street; tickets cost as little as £2 if you book in advance online (or £10 single, £15 return if you don't). A **taxi** will cost in the region of £70–80 and take at least an hour to central London.

CITY

London City Airport (☎ 020 7646 0088, Ⓦ www.londoncityairport.com), the capital's smallest and used primarily by business folk, is situated in the Royal Albert Docks, ten miles east of central London, and handles almost exclusively European flights. The **Docklands Light Railway** (DLR) takes you straight to Bank in the City (Mon–Sat 5.30am–12.15am,

Sun 7am–11.15pm; every 8–15min; journey 20min), where you can change to the tube; single tickets cost around £5. A **taxi** from the airport to the City's financial sector will cost around £20, and take half an hour or so.

By train and coach

Eurostar (☎ 0843 2186 186, Ⓦ www.eurostar.com) trains arrive at the beautifully refurbished St Pancras International train station, next door to King's Cross, which is served by several Underground lines. Arriving by **train** from elsewhere in Britain (☎ 0845 748 4950, Ⓦ www .nationalrail.co.uk), you'll come into one of London's numerous mainline stations, all of which have nearby Underground stations linking into the city centre's tube network. Trains from the Channel ports arrive at Charing Cross or Victoria, while boat trains from Harwich, on the North Sea coast, arrive at Liverpool Street. Coming into London by **coach** (☎ 0871 7818 178, Ⓦ www.national express.com), you're most likely to arrive at Victoria Coach Station, a couple of hundred yards south down Buckingham Palace Road from Victoria train station and tube.

A better kind of travel

At Rough Guides we are passionately committed to travel. We believe it helps us understand the world we live in and the people we share it with. But the scale of modern tourism has also damaged some places irreparably, and climate change is accelerated by most forms of transport, especially flying. Rough Guides' flights are carbon-offset, and every year we donate money to a variety of environmental charities.

Getting around

London's transport system has vastly improved over the past decade. The congestion charge has reduced traffic by thirty percent within central London, and much of the money has been ploughed into improving the buses. That said, London still has one of the most expensive transport systems in the world.

Transport for London (TfL) provides excellent free maps and information on bus and tube services from its six **Travel Information Centres**: the most central one is at Piccadilly Circus tube station (Mon–Fri 7.45am–7pm, Sat 9.15am–7pm, Sun 9.15am–6pm), with other desks at Heathrow arrivals (terminals 1, 2 and 3), Victoria, King's Cross and Liverpool Street train stations. There's also a **24-hour helpline** and an excellent website (☎0843 222 1234, ⓦwww.tfl.gov.uk).

For transport purposes, London is divided into six concentric **zones** (plus a few extra in the northwest), with fares calculated depending on which zones you travel through: the majority of the city's accommodation and sights lie in zones 1 and 2. If you cannot produce a valid ticket for your journey, or travel further than your ticket allows, you will be liable to a **Penalty Fare** of £80, reduced to £40 if you pay within 21 days. Try and avoid travelling during the **rush hour** (Mon–Fri 8–9.30am and 5–7pm) if possible, when tubes can become unbearably crowded and hot, and some buses get so full they literally won't let you on.

Oyster cards and tickets

The cheapest, easiest way to get about London is to use an **Oyster card**, London's transport smartcard, available from all tube stations and TfL Travel Information Centres, and valid on the bus, tube, Docklands Light Railway (DLR), Tramlink, Overground and almost all suburban rail services. The simplest way to use an Oyster card is as a pay-as-you-go card – you can top-up your card with credit at all tube stations and most newsagents. As you enter the tube or bus, simply touch in your card at the card reader and the fare will be taken off. If you're using the tube or train, you need to touch out again or up to £8.60 will be deducted. Oyster operates daily price-capping at £8.40 for peak travel times and £7 at off-peak times (zones 1 and 2). The system will stop taking money off your card, though you still need to touch in (and out). To obtain an Oyster card you must hand over a £5 refundable deposit or you can purchase a patterned, non-refundable Visitor Oyster Card for £3, which can only be used for pay-as-you go travel.

If you don't have an Oyster card, you can still buy a paper **Travelcard** from machines and booths at all tube and train stations (and at many newsagents too – look for the sign). Anytime Day Travelcards start from £9 (zones 1 and 2); Off-Peak Travelcards are valid after 9.30am on weekdays and all day at the weekend, and cost £8.90 for zones 1–6. If you need to travel before 9.30am, it's worth considering a 7-Day Travelcard, which costs around £32 (zones 1 and 2).

Children under 11 travel for free; children aged 11–15 travel free on all buses and trams and at child-rate on the tube; children aged 16 or 17 can travel at child-rate on all forms of transport. However, all children over 10 must have an Oyster photocard to be eligible for free travel – these should be applied for in advance online. Without a photocard, you can buy an Off-Peak Day Travelcard (zones 1–6 after 10am) for children aged

11–15 for around £4, providing they're travelling with an adult.

The tube
Except for very short journeys, the **Underground** – or tube, as it's known to Londoners – is by far the quickest way to get about. Eleven different lines cross the metropolis, each with its own colour and name – all you need to know is which direction you're travelling in: northbound, eastbound, southbound or westbound (this gets tricky when taking the Circle Line). As a precaution, it's also worth checking the final destination displayed on the front of the train, as some lines, such as the District and Northern lines, have several different branches.

Services are frequent (Mon–Sat 5.30am–12.30am, Sun 7.30am–11.30pm), and you rarely have to wait more than five minutes for a train between central stations. **Tickets** must be bought in advance from automatic machines or from a ticket booth in the station entrance hall. Single fares are outrageously expensive – a journey in zone 1 costs an unbelievable £4.70 – so if you're intending to make more than one journey, an Oyster card (£2.20 per journey) or a Travelcard is by far your best option.

Buses
London's famous double-decker **buses** are fun to ride on, with most running at a frequency of five to ten minutes during the day. Some stops have live departure information and there are several apps that will do the same for you, like Bus London and Next London. Cash is no longer accepted on-board buses; instead you must pay with an Oyster card, Travelcard or contactless payment card. A single fare costs £1.45.

A lot of bus stops are **request stops** (easily recognizable by their red sign) – stick your arm out to hail the bus or it will pass you by, and when on board ring the bell to request it to stop. Some buses run a 24-hour service, but most run between 5am and midnight. **Night-buses** (prefixed with the letter "N"), operating outside this period, depart at twenty- to thirty-minute intervals, more frequently on some routes and on Friday and Saturday nights.

Suburban train lines
To reach some of London's far-flung sights, you may need to use the suburban **train** network, sections of which are now run by TFL and known as the London Overground. For enquiries, call ☎0845 748 4950 or visit ⓦwww.nationalrail.co.uk. In East London, the **Docklands Light Railway** (DLR) runs driverless trains to Docklands, Greenwich and beyond. Oyster and Travelcards are valid on all suburban, Overground and DLR trains.

Cycling
Cycling is increasingly popular in London because – in the centre at least – it's the fastest way to get around. Only folding bikes can be taken on public transport, although conventional bikes can go on certain tube and railway lines at off-peak times – check ⓦwww.tfl.gov.uk for details. **Cycle Hire** is London's public bicycle sharing scheme, perfect for short journeys, with over 700 docking stations. It's £2 for access, after which the first 30 minutes are free, the first hour's £1, increasing rapidly after that to £15 for three hours. Bikes can be **rented** from the London Bicycle Tour Company, 1a Gabriel Wharf on the South Bank (☎020 7923 6838, ⓦwww.londonbi-cycle.com), costing around £20 a day or £50 a week.

The London Pass

If you're thinking of visiting a lot of fee-paying attractions in a short space of time, it's worth considering buying a **London Pass** (ⓦ www .londonpass.com), which gives you free entry to a whole host of attractions including Hampton Court Palace, Kensington Palace, Kew Gardens, London Zoo, Westminster Abbey and the Tower of London. The pass costs around £49 for one day (£29 for kids), rising to £100 for six days (£70 for kids). The London Pass can be bought online or in person from tourist offices and from London's mainline train and principal underground stations.

Taxis

Compared to most capital cities, London's metered **black cabs** are an expensive option unless there are three or more of you. The minimum fare is £2.40, and a ride from Euston to Victoria, for example, costs around £12–15 (Mon–Fri 6am–8pm). After 8pm on weekdays and all day during the weekend, a higher tariff applies, and after 10pm, it's higher still. Tipping is customary. An illuminated yellow light tells you if the cab is available – just stick your arm out to hail it. London's cabbies are the best trained in Europe; every one of them knows the shortest route between any two points in the capital, and they won't rip you off by taking another route. They are, however, a blunt and forthright breed, renowned for their generally reactionary opinions. To order a black cab in advance, phone ⓣ 0871 871 8710, and be prepared to pay an extra £2.

Minicabs look just like regular cars and are considerably cheaper than black cabs, but they cannot be hailed from the street. All minicabs carry a private hire sticker and all drivers should have photo ID. There are hundreds of minicab firms, but the best way to pick is to take the advice of the place you're at, unless you want to be certain of a woman driver, in which case book a cab from Lady Mini Cabs (ⓣ 020 7272 3300),

or a gay/lesbian-friendly driver, in which case call London Cabs (ⓣ 020 7205 2677). Avoid illegal taxi touts, who hang around outside venues alongside licensed cabs, and always establish the fare beforehand as minicabs are not metered.

Last, and definitely least, there's currently a plague of pedicabs or **bicycle taxis** in the West End after nightfall. The oldest and biggest of the bunch are Bugbugs (ⓣ 020 7353 4028, ⓦ www.bugbugs.com). The rickshaws take up to three passengers and fares are negotiable, so you should always agree a price beforehand, based on a fare of around £3–5 per person.

Boats

Unfortunately, **boat services** on the Thames are not fully integrated into the public transport system. Timetables and services are complex – for a full list pick up a booklet from a TfL information office (see p.186) or visit ⓦ www.tfl.gov.uk /river. You can pay for your fare using your Oyster card (and get 10 percent off single fares), but price-capping doesn't apply. One of the largest companies is Thames Clippers (ⓦ www.thamesclippers.com), who run a regular **commuter service** (Mon–Fri 6am–11pm, Sat and Sun 9am–10.30pm; every 20–30min) between Waterloo and Greenwich (including the O2), with some boats going as far as Woolwich. Typical fares are £6.50 single, with an unlimited hop-on, hop-off River Roamer day ticket costing £15.

Other companies run boats upstream to Kew, Richmond and Hampton Court (see box, p.164). Look out, too, for the MV *Balmoral* and paddle-steamer *Waverley*, which make regular visits to Tower Pier in the summer and autumn (☎ 0845 130 4647, ⊛ www.waverleyexcursions.co.uk).

Sightseeing tours and guided walks

Standard **sightseeing tours** are run by several rival bus companies, their open-top double-deckers setting off every thirty minutes from Victoria station, Trafalgar Square, Piccadilly and other conspicuous tourist spots. You can hop on and off several different routes as often as you like with The Original Tour (☎ 020 8877 1722, ⊛ www.theoriginaltour.com; daily 8.30am–6pm; every 15–20min; £29). Alternatively, you can climb aboard one of the bright-yellow World War II D-Day amphibious vehicles used by London Duck Tours (☎ 020 7928 3132, ⊛ www.london ducktours.co.uk), which offers a combined bus and boat tour (daily 9.30am–6pm or dusk; £21). After departing from behind County Hall, near the London Eye, you spend 45 minutes driving round the usual sights, before plunging into the river for a half-hour cruise; advance booking is essential.

A much cheaper option is to hop on a modern **London double-decker** – the #11 bus from Victoria station, for example, will take you past Westminster Abbey, the Houses of Parliament, up Whitehall, round Trafalgar Square, along the Strand and on to St Paul's Cathedral. Alternatively, you can take an old double-decker **Routemaster**, with open rear platform and roving conductor, on a "heritage" route (daily every 15min 9.30am–7pm): #15 from Trafalgar Square to Tower Hill.

Walking tours are infinitely more appealing and informative, mixing solid historical facts with juicy anecdotes in the company of a local specialist. Walks on offer range from a literary pub crawl round Bloomsbury to a roam around the East End. You'll find most of them detailed on *Time Out*'s website (see p.193); as you'd imagine, there's more variety on offer in the summer months. Tours cost around £10 and take around two hours; normally you can simply show up at the starting point and join. If you want to plan – or book – walks in advance, contact the most reliable and well-established company, Original London Walks (☎ 020 7624 3978, ⊛ www.walks.com).

Congestion charge

All vehicles entering central London on weekdays between 7am and 6pm are liable to a congestion charge of £11.50 (£10.50 online) per vehicle. Drivers can pay the charge online, over the phone and at garages and shops, and must do so before midnight the same day or incur a £2 surcharge – 24 hours later, you'll be liable for a £130 **fine** (£65 if you pay within 14 days). Local residents, the disabled, motorcycles, minibuses and some alternative-fuel vehicles are exempt from the charge, but must register in order to qualify. For more details, visit ⊛ www.tfl.gov.uk.

Directory A–Z

Addresses

London addresses come with postcodes at the end. Each street name is followed by a letter or letters giving the geographical location of the street in relation to the City (E for "east", WC for "west central" and so on) and a number that specifies its location more precisely. Unfortunately, this number doesn't correspond to the district's distance from the centre. Full postal addresses end with a digit and two letters, which specify the individual block, but these are only used in correspondence.

Cricket

Most years three Test matches are played in London each summer: two at **Lord's** (☏ 020 7616 8500, ⓦ www.lords.org; ⊖ St John's Wood), the home of English cricket; the other at **The Oval** (☏ 0020 7820 5700, ⓦ www.kiaoval.com; ⊖ Oval). There are also numerous one-day internationals and Twenty20 matches, some of which are usually held in London.

Crime

Should you have anything stolen or be involved in an incident that requires reporting, go to the local **police station** (ⓦ www.met.police .uk) or phone ☏ 101; the ☏ 999 number should only be used in emergencies. Central 24hr police stations include: Charing Cross, Agar St ⊖ Charing Cross; Holborn, 10 Lambs Conduit St ⊖ Holborn; Marylebone, 1–9 Seymour St ⊖ Marble Arch; and West End Central, 27 Savile Row ⊖ Oxford Circus. The City of London Police (☏ 020 7601 2222, ⓦ www.cityof london.police.uk) are separate from the Metropolitan Police, and have a police station at 182 Bishopsgate ⊖ Liverpool Street. If there's an incident on public transport, call the British Transport Police on ☏ 0800 405040. For **Rape Crisis**, contact ☏ 0808 802 9999, ⓦ www .rapecrisis.org.uk.

Electricity

Electricity supply in London conforms to the EU standard of approximately 230V. Sockets are designed for British **three-pin plugs**, which are totally different from those in the mainland EU and North America.

Embassies and consulates

Australian High Commission Australia House, Strand ☏ 020 7379 4334, ⓦ www.uk.embassy.gov.au; ⊖ Temple tube. **Canadian High Commission** 1 Grosvenor Square ☏ 020 7528 6600, ⓦ www.united kingdom.gc.ca; ⊖ Bond Street. **Irish Embassy** 17 Grosvenor Place ☏ 020 7235 2171, ⓦ www.embassyof ireland.co.uk; ⊖ Hyde Park Corner. **New Zealand High Commission** New Zealand House, 80 Haymarket ☏ 020 7930 8422, ⓦ www.nzembassy .com; ⊖ Piccadilly Circus. **South African High Commission** South Africa House, Trafalgar Square ☏ 020 7451 7299, ⓦ www.southafrica houseuk.com; ⊖ Charing Cross. **US Embassy** 24 Grosvenor Square ☏ 020 7499 9000, ⓦ london .usembassy.gov; ⊖ Bond Street.

Football

Over the decades, London's most successful club by far has been **Arsenal** (☏ 020 7619 5000, ⓦ www.arsenal.com). However, since the arrival of Russian oil tycoon Roman Abramovich, fellow London club **Chelsea** (☏ 020 7835 6000, ⓦ www.chelseafc.com) have had a resurgence, winning the league three

Emergencies

For **police**, fire and ambulance services, call ☏ 999.

times in the last ten years. Chelsea's closest rivals (geographically) are **Fulham** (☏ 0843 208 1222, ⓦ www .fulhamfc.com), while Arsenal's are **Tottenham Hotspur** (☏ 0844 499 5000, ⓦ www.tottenhamhotspur .com). East London's premier club is **West Ham** (☏ 020 8548 2748, ⓦ www.whufc.com). Tickets for most Premier League games start at £40–50 and are virtually impossible to get hold of on a casual basis, though you may be able to see one of the Cup fixtures. A better bet is to head to one of London's numerous, less illustrious clubs such as **Crystal Palace** (ⓦ www.cpfc.co.uk), **Millwall** (ⓦ www.millwallfc.co.uk) or **Charlton Athletic** (ⓦ cafc.co.uk).

Gay and lesbian travellers

London Lesbian and Gay Switchboard (☏ 0300 330 0630, ⓦ www.llgs .org.uk) has a huge database of everything you might ever want to know, plus legal advice and counselling. Lines are open 24hr: keep trying if you can't get through.

Health

For minor complaints, pharmacists, known as **chemists** in England, can dispense a limited range of drugs without a doctor's prescription. Most pharmacies are open standard shop hours, though some stay open later: Zafash, 233–235 Old Brompton Rd, SW5 (☏ 020 7373 2798; ⊖ Earl's Court), is open 24 hours; while Bliss, at 5–6 Marble Arch, W1 ☏ 020 7723 6116 (⊖ Marble Arch), is open daily 9am till midnight. Every police station keeps a list of late-opening pharmacies.

If there's an emergency, you can turn up at the **Accident and Emergency** (A&E) department of your local hospital, or phone for an ambulance (☏ 999). A&E services are free to all. You can also go to a **Minor Injuries Clinic** such as the one at St Bartholomew's Hospital, West Smithfield (Mon–Fri 8am–4pm; ☏ 020 3465 5869; ⊖ Farringdon). For emergency **dental treatment**, make for Guy's Hospital, St Thomas St SE1 (Mon–Fri 8am–3.45pm; ☏ 020 7188 1234; ⊖ London Bridge).

Internet

Many hotels and hostels in London have internet access. After that, your best bet is a café with **wi-fi**; try the one in Foyles bookshop at 113–119 Charing Cross Rd (⊖ Tottenham Court Road). Alternatively, the Southbank Centre, the British Library and St Pancras station all have free wi-fi and, most **public libraries** offer free access.

Left luggage

Airports Gatwick ☏ 01293 734 888 or ☏ 01293 734 887: North Terminal (daily 5am–9pm); South Terminal (24hr). Heathrow ☏ 020 8759 3344: Terminal 1 (daily 6am–11pm); Terminal 3 (daily 5.30am–11pm); Terminal 4 and 5 (daily 5.30am–11pm). London City ☏ 020 7646 0000 (Mon–Fri 5am–10pm, Sat 5am–11pm, Sun 11am–10.20pm). Luton ☏ 01582 405100 (24hr). Stansted ☏ 0844 824 3109 (24hr). **Train stations** All are open daily 7am–11pm except where noted: Charing Cross ☏ 020 7930 5444; Euston ☏ 020 7387 1499; King's Cross ☏ 020 7837 4334; Liverpool Street ☏ 020 7247 4297; Paddington ☏ 020 7262 0344; St Pancras ☏ 020 7837 4334 (Mon–Sat 6am–10pm, Sun 7am–10pm); Victoria ☏ 020 7963 0957 (daily 7am–midnight); Waterloo ☏ 020 7401 8444.

Lost property

Airports Gatwick ☎ 01293 503162 (daily 10am–4pm); Heathrow ☎ 0844 824 3115 (daily 7am–7pm); London City ☎ 020 7646 0000 (daily 6am–10pm); Luton ☎ 01582 395219 (daily 7am–11pm); Stansted ☎ 0844 824 3109 (daily 1–5pm). **Eurostar** ☎ 0844 822 4411 (Mon–Fri 10am–5pm). **Train stations**: Euston ☎ 020 7387 8699 (Mon–Fri 9am–5.30pm); King's Cross ☎ 020 7278 3310 (Mon–Sat 9am–5pm); Liverpool St ☎ 020 7247 4297 (Mon–Fri 9am–5pm); Paddington ☎ 020 7262 0344 (Mon–Fri 9am–5pm); St Pancras ☎ 020 7837 4334 (Mon–Fri 9am–5pm); Victoria ☎ 020 7963 0957 (Mon–Fri 9am–5pm); Waterloo ☎ 020 7401 7861 (Mon–Fri 7.30am–7pm). **Transport for London** Lost Property Office, 200 Baker St NW1 ☎ 0343 222 1234, ⓦ www.tfl.gov.uk (Mon–Fri 8.30am–4pm).

Money

The basic unit of **currency** is the pound sterling (£), divided into 100 pence (p). Coins come in denominations of 1p, 2p, 5p, 10p, 20p, 50p, £1 and £2; notes come in denominations of £5, £10, £20 and £50. Many shopkeepers may not accept £50 notes – the best advice is to avoid having to use them. The exchange rate can fluctuate considerably, but at the time of writing, £1 was worth $1.60, €1.20, C$1.80, A$1.70, NZ$2 and ZAR18. For the most up-to-date exchange rates, visit ⓦ www.xe.com.

Credit/debit cards are by far the most convenient way to carry your money, and most hotels, shops and restaurants in London accept the major brand cards. There are ATMs all over the city and every area has a branch of at least one of the big-four high-street **banks** (NatWest,

Barclays, Lloyds and HSBC); opening hours are generally Mon–Fri 9.30am–4.30pm. Outside banking hours go to a **bureau de change**; these can be found at train stations and airports and in most areas of the city centre.

The high **cost** of accommodation, food and drink make London a very expensive place to visit. Staying in a budget hotel and eating takeaways, you'll still need in the region of £50 per person per day. Add in a restaurant meal and tourist attraction or two, and you are looking at £75–100.

Opening hours

Generally speaking, opening hours are Monday to Saturday 9am or 10am to around 6pm and Sundays noon to 6pm. Some places in central London stay open until 7pm, and later on Thursdays and Fridays (around 9pm).

Phones

Public **payphones** in London are iconic, ubiquitous and little-used. Most take coins from 10p upwards – the minimum charge of 60p will get you thirty minutes. Paying by credit card is expensive (20p a minute). Discount phonecards with a PIN number, available from newsagents, are the cheapest way to make international calls.

If you're taking your **mobile/cell phone** with you, check with your service provider whether your phone will work abroad and what the call charges will be. Unless you have a tri-or quad-band phone, it's unlikely that a mobile bought for use in the US will work in London. Mobiles in Australia and New Zealand generally use the same system as the UK so should work fine.

Post

The only (vaguely) late-opening post office is at 24–28 William IV St,

WC2N 4DL, near Trafalgar Square (☎ 0845 722 3344; Mon–Fri 8.30am–6.30pm, Tues opens 9.15am, Sat 9am–5.30pm); it's also the city's poste restante collection point. For general postal enquiries phone ☎ 0845 774 0740 (Mon–Fri 8am–6pm, Sat 8am–1pm), or visit ⓦ www.royalmail.com.

Smoking
Smoking is banned in all indoor public spaces including all cafés, pubs, restaurants, clubs and public transport.

Time
Greenwich Mean Time (GMT) is used from the end of October to the end of March; for the rest of the year the country switches to **British Summer Time** (BST), one hour ahead of GMT. GMT is two hours behind South Africa, five hours ahead of the US East Coast; eight ahead of the US West Coast; and nine behind Australia's East Coast.

Tipping
There are no fixed rules for tipping. However, there's a certain expectation in restaurants or cafés that you should leave a tip of ten percent of the total bill – check first, though, that service has not already been included. Taxi drivers also expect tips – add about ten percent of the fare – as do traditional barbers. The other occasion when you'll be expected to tip is in upmarket hotels where porters and table waiters rely on being tipped to bump up their often dismal wages.

Toilets
There are surprisingly few public toilets in London. All mainline train and major tube stations have toilets. Department stores and free museums and galleries are another good option.

Tourist information
There is no proper, central tourist office in London, as there is in just about every other major city in Europe. However, many of the 32 London boroughs have information offices, the most central one being the **City of London Tourist Information Centre**, on the south side of St Paul's Cathedral (Mon–Sat 9.30am–5.30pm, Sun 10am–4pm; ☎ 020 7332 1456, ⓦ www.visit thecity.co.uk; ⊖ St Paul's). Another useful borough tourist office is in **Greenwich** at the old Royal Naval College (daily 10am–5pm; ☎ 0870 608 2000; Cutty Sark DLR).

The weekly **listings magazine** *Time Out* is free and and comes out on a Tuesday, but for full listings, you need to visit their website (ⓦ www.timeout.com). Other useful **listings websites** include ⓦ www.londonist.com and ⓦ www .londonnet.co.uk and the website of the free weekday *Evening Standard* (ⓦ www.standard.co.uk).

Travellers with disabilities
London is an old city, not well equipped for travellers with disabilities, though all public venues are obliged to make some effort towards accessibility. Public transport is slowly improving, with most buses now wheelchair-accessible, and up to a quarter of all tube stations – they're marked with a blue symbol on the tube map.

Travelling with children
London is a great place for children and needn't overly strain the parental pocket. The city boasts lots of excellent parks and gardens, public transport is free for under 11s and many of the major museums can be visited free of charge. For the most part kids are tolerated in cafés and restaurants, less so in pubs.

Festivals and events

LONDON PARADE

January 1

ⓦ www.londonparade.co.uk.

At noon, a procession of floats, marching bands, cheerleaders and clowns wends its way from Parliament Square to Green Park. Admission charge for grandstand seats in Piccadilly, otherwise free.

CHINESE NEW YEAR

late January/early to mid February

ⓦ www.chinatownlondon.org.

Soho's Chinatown, Leicester Square and even Trafalgar Square all erupt in a riot of dancing dragons and firecrackers – expect serious human congestion. Free.

OXFORD AND CAMBRIDGE BOAT RACE

late March/early April

ⓦ www.theboatrace.org.

Since 1845 rowers from Oxford and Cambridge universities have battled it out over four miles from Putney to Mortlake. The pubs at prime vantage points pack out early. Free.

LONDON MARATHON

Third or fourth Sunday in April

ⓦ www.virginlondonmarathon.com.

The world's most popular marathon, with around 40,000 masochists sweating the 26.2-mile route. Most of the competitors are running for charity, often in some ludicrous costume. Free.

IWA CANALWAY CAVALCADE

May Bank Holiday weekend

ⓦ www.waterways.org.uk.

Lively three-day celebration of the city's inland waterways, held at Little Venice, with scores of decorated narrow boats, Morris dancers and lots of children's activities. Free.

STATE OPENING OF PARLIAMENT

early May

ⓦ www.parliament.uk.

The Queen arrives by coach at the Houses of Parliament at 11am accompanied by the Household Cavalry and gun salutes. The ceremony itself takes place inside the House of Lords and is televised; it also takes place whenever a new government is sworn in. Free.

BEATING RETREAT

early June

ⓦ www.army.mod.uk.

Annual military display on Horse Guards' Parade over two consecutive evenings, marking the old custom of drumming and piping the troops back to base at dusk. Tickets must be booked in advance.

TROOPING THE COLOUR

second Saturday in June

ⓦ www.army.mod.uk.

Ticket-only celebration of the Queen's official birthday featuring massed bands, gun salutes and fly-pasts. The royal procession along the Mall allows you a glimpse for free, and there are rehearsals (minus Her Majesty) on the two preceding Saturdays.

WIMBLEDON LAWN TENNIS CHAMPIONSHIPS

last week of June and first week of July

ⓦ www.wimbledon.com.

This Grand Slam tournament (played on grass) is one of the highlights of the sporting and social calendar.

PRIDE LONDON

late June or early July
Ⓦ www.prideinlondon.org.
Colourful, whistle-blowing lesbian and gay march through the city streets followed by a rally in Trafalgar Square.

HENRY WOOD PROMENADE CONCERTS

mid-July to mid-September.
Ⓦ www.bbc.co.uk/proms.
Commonly known as the Proms, this series of nightly classical concerts at the Royal Albert Hall (and elsewhere) is a well-loved British institution.

NOTTING HILL CARNIVAL

last bank holiday weekend in August
Ⓦ www.thenottinghillcarnival.com.
World famous two-day street festival established nearly fifty years ago, Carnival is a tumult of imaginatively decorated floats, eye-catching costumes, thumping sound systems, live bands, irresistible food and huge crowds. Free.

OPEN HOUSE

third weekend in September
Ⓦ www.londonopenhouse.org.
A once-a-year opportunity to peek inside over 750 buildings around London, many of which don't normally open their doors to the public. You'll need to book in advance for some of the more popular places. Free.

LONDON FILM FESTIVAL

Late October Ⓦ www.bfi.org.uk/lff.
A two-week cinematic season with scores of new international films screened at the BFI Southbank and some West End venues.

BONFIRE NIGHT

November 5
In memory of Guy Fawkes – who tried to blow up King James I and the Houses of Parliament in 1605 – effigies are burned on bonfires all over London, and numerous council-run fires and fireworks displays are staged. Free.

LORD MAYOR'S SHOW

second Saturday in November
Ⓦ www.lordmayorsshow.org.
Big ceremonial procession from the Law Courts on the Strand to the Guildhall of some 140 floats, military bands and even the odd piece of military hardware, followed by the new Mayor in his gilded coach and a whole train of liverymen in carriages. After dark, there's a fireworks display on the Thames. Free.

NEW YEAR

New Year's Eve Ⓦ www.london.gov.uk.
New Year is welcomed by thousands of revellers who get to enjoy a spectacular firework display centred on the London Eye. TfL runs free public transport all night, sponsored by various public-spirited breweries. Free.

Public holidays

You'll find all banks and offices closed on the following days, while everything else pretty much runs to a Sunday schedule (except on Christmas Day when everything shuts down): New Year's Day (January 1); Good Friday (late March/April); Easter Monday (late March/April); Spring Bank Holiday (first Monday in May); May Bank Holiday (last Monday in May); August Bank Holiday (last Monday in August); Christmas Day (December 25); Boxing Day (December 26). Note that if January 1, December 25 or December 26 falls on a Saturday or Sunday, the holiday falls on the following weekday.

Chronology

43 AD > Romans invade and establish a permanent military camp by the Thames called Londinium.

c.61 > Queen Boudica, leader of the Iceni tribe, burns Londinium to the ground.

c.100 > Londinium becomes the capital of the Roman province of Britannia, eventually boasting a vast basilica, a forum, an amphitheatre and several baths.

410 > The Romans abandon Londinium and leave the place at the mercy of marauding Saxon pirates.

871–1066 > The Danes and Norwegians fight it out with the kings of Wessex over who should control London.

1066 > Following the defeat of the English King Harold at the Battle of Hastings, William the Conqueror, Duke of Normandy, is crowned king in Westminster Abbey.

1290 > King Edward I expels London's Jewish population.

1348 > The Black Death wipes out a third of London's population of 75,000.

1381 > During the Peasants' Revolt, London is overrun by the rebels who lynch the archbishop, plus countless rich merchants and clerics.

1532–39 > The Reformation: King Henry VIII breaks with the Roman Catholic church, establishes the Church of England, dissolves the monasteries and executes religious dissenters.

1553–58 > The religious pendulum swings the other way as Elizabeth's fervently Catholic sister, forever known as "Bloody Mary", takes to the throne and it's the Protestants' turn to be martyred.

1558–1603 > During the reign of Elizabeth I, London enjoys an economic boom and witnesses the English Renaissance, epitomized by the theatre of William Shakespeare.

1603 > James VI of Scotland becomes James I of England, thereby uniting the two crowns and marking the beginning of the Stuart dynasty in England.

1605 > The Gunpowder Plot to blow up the Houses of Parliament (and King James I along with it) is foiled and Guy Fawkes and his Catholic conspirators executed.

1642–49 > English Civil War between the Parliamentarians and Royalists ends with the victory of the former under the leadership of Oliver Cromwell. King Charles I (1625–49) is tried and beheaded in Westminster.

1660 > The Restoration: Charles I's son, Charles II (1660–1685), returns from exile to restore the monarchy and as the "Merry Monarch" actively encourages the development of the arts and sciences.

1665 > The Great Plague kills some 100,000 Londoners, around a fifth of the population.

1666 > The Great Fire rages for four days, kills just seven people but destroys four-fifths of the City.

1714–1830 > The Georgian period: from the reign of George I to George IV, London's population doubles to one million, making it Europe's largest city. The period is one of boom and bust, gin drinking, rioting and hanging.

1750 > Westminster Bridge opens, the first rival river crossing to London Bridge in over seven centuries.

1836 > London gets its first railway line from London Bridge to Greenwich.

1837–1901 > During the reign of Queen Victoria, London becomes the capital of an empire that stretches across the globe. Its population increases to nearly seven million, making it the largest city in the world. Industrialization brings pollution, overcrowding and extreme poverty.

1851 > The Great Exhibition is held in a giant glasshouse known as the "Crystal Palace", erected in Hyde Park.

1855 > The Metropolitan Board of Works is established to organize the rapidly expanding city's infrastructure.

1914–18 > During World War I, London experiences its first aerial attacks, with Zeppelin raids leaving some 650 dead – a minor skirmish in the context of a war that takes the lives of millions.

1939–45 > During the course of World War II, London suffers a lot of bomb damage, with 60,000 killed and many thousands more made homeless.

1948 > The SS *Windrush* brings the first postwar immigrants to London from the West Indies; over the next two decades, thousands more follow suit from former colonies all over the world.

1951 > The Festival of Britain is held on the south bank of the Thames in an attempt to dispel the postwar gloom. The Royal Festival Hall is its one lasting legacy.

1960s > Pop music and fashion helps turn London into the centre of the "Swinging Sixties", with King's Road and Carnaby Street the hippest places to be seen.

1980s > Under the Conservative Thatcher government, the gap between rich and poor grows. Homelessness returns to London in a big way and London's governing body, the GLC, is abolished, leaving London as the only European city without a directly elected body.

2000 > London gets to vote for its own Mayor (Ken Livingstone) and its elected assembly. London's national museums introduce free entry, the London Eye enhances the city's skyline and the Millennium Dome opens for one year, and proves a critical and financial flop.

2005 > A day after London is awarded the 2012 Olympics, on July 7, the city is hit by four suicide bombers who kill themselves and over fifty commuters in four separate explosions.

2008 > Conservative candidate Boris Johnson defeats Ken Livingstone and becomes Mayor.

2012 > London hosts the Olympic games.

PUBLISHING INFORMATION

This third edition published February 2015 by **Rough Guides Ltd**

80 Strand, London WC2R 0RL

11, Community Centre, Panchsheel Park, New Delhi 110017, India

Distributed by Penguin Random House

Penguin Books Ltd, 80 Strand, London WC2R 0RL

Penguin Group (USA) 345 Hudson Street, NY 10014, USA

Penguin Group (Australia) 250 Camberwell Road, Camberwell, Victoria 3124, Australia

Penguin Group (NZ) 67 Apollo Drive, Mairangi Bay, Auckland 1310, New Zealand

Penguin Group (South Africa) Block D, Rosebank Office Park, 181 Jan Smuts Avenue,
Parktown North, Gauteng, South Africa 2193

Rough Guides is represented in Canada by

Tourmaline Editions Inc., 662 King Street West, Suite 304, Toronto, Ontario, M5V 1M7

Typeset in Minion and Din to an original design by Henry Iles and Dan May.

Printed and bound in China

© Samantha Cook and Rob Humphreys 2015

Maps © Rough Guides

Contains Ordnance Survey data © Crown copyright and database rights 2015

No part of this book may be reproduced in any form without permission from the publisher except for
the quotation of brief passages in reviews.

208pp includes index

A catalogue record for this book is available from the British Library

ISBN 978-1-40935-712-4

The publishers and authors have done their best to ensure the accuracy and currency of all the
information in **Pocket Rough Guide London**, however, they can accept no responsibility for
any loss, injury, or inconvenience sustained by any traveller as a result of information or advice
contained in the guide.

1 3 5 7 9 8 6 4 2

ROUGH GUIDES CREDITS

Text editors: Alison Roberts, Edward Aves and Alice Park

Layout: Nikhil Agarwal, Pradeep Thapliyal and Umesh Aggarwal

Photography: Roger Norum, Natascha Sturny, Mark Thomas

Cartography: Katie Bennett and Ed Wright

Picture editor: Michelle Bhatia, Mark Thomas

Proofreader: Stewart Wild

Production: Emma Sparks

Cover design: Nicole Newman, Emily Taylor and Nikhil Agarwal

THE AUTHOR

Samantha Cook was born in London and has lived in the city, give or take a few spells wandering
the globe, all her life. She is co-author of the Rough Guides to London and Vintage London.

Rob Humphreys has lived in London for over twenty-five years. He recently qualified as a London
Blue Badge Guide and spends the rest of his time directing shows on the Puppet Theatre Barge.

HELP US UPDATE

We've gone to a lot of effort to ensure that the second edition of **The Pocket Rough Guide to London** is accurate and up-to-date. However, things change – places get "discovered", opening hours are notoriously fickle, restaurants and rooms raise prices or lower standards. If you feel we've got it wrong or left something out, we'd like to know, and if you can remember the address, the price, the hours, the phone number, so much the better.

Please send your comments with the subject line "**Pocket Rough Guide London Update**" to ✉ mail@roughguides.com. We'll credit all contributions and send a copy of the next edition (or any other Rough Guide if you prefer) for the very best emails.

Find more travel information, connect with fellow travellers and book your trip on Ⓦ www.roughguides.com

PHOTO CREDITS

Index

Maps are marked in **bold**.

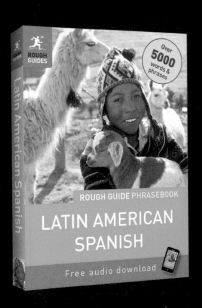

SO NOW WE'VE TOLD YOU
ABOUT THE THINGS NOT TO
MISS, THE BEST PLACES TO
STAY, THE TOP RESTAURANTS,
THE LIVELIEST BARS AND THE
MOST SPECTACULAR SIGHTS,
IT ONLY SEEMS FAIR TO
TELL YOU ABOUT THE BEST
TRAVEL INSURANCE AROUND

 WorldNomads.com
keep travelling safely

RECOMMENDED BY ROUGH GUIDES